Pelican Books

Letters to Thinkers

Edward de Bono was born in Malta and after his initial education at St Edward's College, Malta, and the Royal University of Malta, where he obtained a degree in medicine, he proceeded as a Rhodes Scholar to Christ Church, Oxford, where he gained an honours degree in psychology and physiology and then a D.Phil. in medicine. He also holds a Ph.D. from Cambridge. He has had faculty appointments at the universities of Oxford, London, Cambridge and Harvard.

Dr de Bono is the founder and director of the Cognitive Research Trust in Cambridge (founded 1969) and the Centre for the Study of Thinking and he is the founder of SITO (Supranational Independent Thinking Organization). He runs what is now the largest curriculum programme in the world for the direct teaching of thinking in schools. Dr de Bono's instruction in thinking has been sought by many of the leading corporations such as IBM, Shell, Unilever, ICI, Du Pont, Monsanto, United Technologies and many others. He has been invited to lecture extensively throughout the world.

He has written twenty-five books which have been translated into twenty languages. He has also completed two TV series, *The Greatest Thinkers* for WDR, West Germany, and *De Bono's Course in Thinking* for the BBC. Dr de Bono is the originator of the term 'lateral thinking' and also the inventor of the classic L game, which is said to be the simplest real game ever invented. He is the author of *Letter to Thinkers*, which is published ten times a year.

His books include *The Five-Day Course in Thinking* (1968), *The Mechanism of Mind* (1969), *Lateral Thinking* (1970), *The Dog-Exercising Machine* (1970), *Technology Today* (1971), *Practical Thinking* (1971), *Lateral Thinking for Management* (1971), *Po: Beyond Yes and No* (1972), *Children Solve Problems* (1972), *Eureka!: An Illustrated History of Inventions from the Wheel to the Computer* (1974), *Teaching Thinking* (1976), *The Greatest Thinkers* (1976), *Wordpower* (1977), *The Happiness Purpose* (1977), *Future Positive* (1979), *Atlas of Management Thinking* (1981), *De Bono's Course in Thinking* (1982), *Tactics: The Art and Science of Success* (1985), *Conflicts: A Better Way to Resolve Them* (1985), *Six Thinking Hats* (1985), and *Masterthinker's Handbook* (1985). Many of these have been published in Penguin. Dr de Bono has also contributed to many journals, including the *Lancet* and *Clinical Science*. He is married and has two sons.

Letters to Thinkers

Edward de Bono

Further Thoughts on Lateral Thinking

PENGUIN BOOKS

PENGUIN BOOKS

Published by the Penguin Group
27 Wrights Lane, London W8 5TZ, England
Viking Penguin Inc., 40 West 23rd Street, New York, New York 10010, USA
Penguin Books Australia Ltd, Ringwood, Victoria, Australia
Penguin Books Canada Ltd, 2801 John Street, Markham, Ontario, Canada L3R 1B4
Penguin Books (NZ) Ltd, 182–190 Wairau Road, Auckland 10, New Zealand

Penguin Books Ltd, Registered Offices: Harmondsworth, Middlesex, England

First published in Great Britain by Harrap 1987
Published in Penguin Books 1988

Printed and bound in Great Britain by
Cox & Wyman Ltd, Reading

Contents

Preface

This book is based on material taken from a series of *Letters to Thinkers* which were published periodically between 1982 and 1984. These letters were written for people interested in the practical aspects of thinking and creative thinking in particular. They were not intended to be philosophical letters but to be practical in nature. I suppose the majority of readers came from the business area because this has always been, in my experience, the sector of society that is more interested in thinking that produces results. Elsewhere the defensive type of thinking (I shall prove that I am right and you are wrong) is sufficient.

Not all the material from the *Letters* is reproduced here. Those who subscribed to the *Letters* have also had the advantage of having the material some years before their publication here.

It may be possible to re-start the *Letters*. Those who might be interested should write to me, care of the publishers.

Edward de Bono

Introduction

The horror of the simple

Over the years I have found that for mediocre minds there is horror in the simple. I do not mean a mild unease, distress or discomfort when faced with something simple but an absolute horror.

I am not sure why this should be. It may be that the mediocre mind finds threatening the inability to distinguish between something that is simple because there is nothing behind it, and something that is simple because there is a great deal behind it. This can be a distressing situation. Since the mediocre mind cannot see beyond the limits of its vision, such a mind must insist, vehemently, that there can be nothing behind the simple appearance: if I cannot see anything then there cannot be anything there. The uneasy feeling that there might be something lurking there, but invisible, is a standard component of horror.

A sudden request to write a five-page essay on a dried snail shell will often induce terror in the mind of a youngster. He or she would much rather write an easier essay on the rich events of the last holiday.

Mediocre minds are reactive rather than pro-active. They much prefer to react to what is put before them. They are describers and there must be something to describe. The richer the picture placed before them the richer their reaction and the greater the sense of achievement. Such minds are most comforted by complex and turgid prose full of multiple references to pundits both obvious and obscure. There must be qualifications sitting upon qualifications and nuances shading into further nuances. This then is serious stuff because this is the traditional idiom of seriousness. If something can be understood by most people how can it be serious? If you have not much to say then say it in the most complex and impressive way you can. You will easily find those who are more impressed by form than substance.

There is the almost expressed plea by the mediocre mind: 'Please make it so complex that I shall be impressed but unable to understand it.' Being unable fully to understand something is the greatest security for the mediocre mind. Being faced with something that seems too simple is the greatest insecurity.

I shall now provide a rather striking example of what I mean by the horror of simplicity. I shall contrast two reactions to an apparently simple idea.

The theme of my book *Six Thinking Hats* is simple. There is the white hat for neutral facts, figures and information. There is the red hat to allow a person to put forward feelings, hunches and intuitions – without any need to justify them. The black hat is for the logical negative and the yellow hat is for the logical positive. For creativity there is the green hat. The blue hat is the control hat and looks at the thinking itself rather than at the subject – like an orchestra conductor controlling the orchestra. The purpose is to provide a means for rapidly switching thinkers from one mode to another – without causing offence. You might say: 'That is great black hat thinking, now let's have some yellow hat thinking.' At the beginning of a meeting the organiser might say: 'Let us all put on our red hats for a few moments and say what we really feel about this project.' As with most worthwhile books the theme is so simple that it could be summarized on a postcard.

In Tokyo in December 1986 I was asked to talk at a very senior breakfast meeting to which had come the heads of many of those large Japanese corporations with names that are well known in the West. I had been invited there to talk about the recent Japanese edition of *Six Thinking Hats*. The talk lasted thirty minutes and the guests sat there politely (two seemed asleep) and asked a few questions at the end.

Three months later I was again in Tokyo and I had a meeting with Mr Hisashi Shinto who had just been chosen by his colleagues as Japanese Manager of the Year. Mr Shinto runs NTT (Nippon Telephone and Telegraph) which at that time had 350,000 employees – making it bigger than any corporation in Europe with the possible exception of Siemens. For ninety years NTT had been a government corporation and Mr Shinto had been given the task of taking NTT into the private sector. He was so successful that the price earnings multiple on the Tokyo exchange was an unbelievable 250 (average in Tokyo is 50, and in New York is 17).

Mr Shinto told me how he had been at the breakfast meeting in December and how he had like the idea of the six hats. He had listened and then gone away and bought several hundred copies of the book which he had given to all senior executives. He told me that the effect had been remarkable. Executives who had hitherto sat silently through meetings for fear of making a mistake or giving offence, were now using the ritual of the six hats to make comments, to criticise and to put forward creative ideas. He told me he felt the book had helped him in his most difficult task of making government employees think like private sector executives.

There are many other parallel examples of the use of the concept in Canada and the USA. The essential point is that Mr Shinto and the other users were attracted by the very simplicity of the concept for this meant that it could be put to use effectively. I now want to show the opposite reaction in which the simplicity of the concept appeared to cause acute distress.

Just two weeks before Mr Shinto attended that breakfast meeting in Tokyo, Mr Adam Mars-Jones reviewed the book for the *Independent* newspaper. Here we have a describer rather than a doer and a describer so horrified by the simplicity of the concept that he is reduced to almost puerile fury (directed at me as much as at the book).

'The whole enterprise stinks of the worst sort of American self-improvement.'

'There are valuable scraps here if anyone can be bothered to find them. But so infuriating is the constant repetition that it is tempting to regard *Six Thinking Hats* as a children's book in disguise. A sort of Dr Seuss approach to management.' (I almost regard this as a compliment since I do a lot of work with children and admire their thinking and also Dr Seuss.)

'With its glossy presentation and its generally inane contents, it reveals itself as the most tragic casualty of present-day book production: a magazine article trapped in a book's body.'

There is much more of the same. The interesting thing is that there is virtually no criticism of the actual concept of the book on the grounds that it would not work or does not make sense. The whole splenetic effort is used to express the reviewer's dislike of the simplicity, the style and the author. The unfortunate fact for Mr Mars-Jones is that the concept does work and work very well. I am rather more inclined to accept the opinion of Mr Shinto, who runs what is now by far the largest corporation in the world (NTT is actually three and a half times as large in market value as the next largest, which is IBM and five times as large as Exxon), than the opinion of Mr Mars-Jones, whose business experience is likely to be more limited.

I ought to add that in the same review there is a pure jewel of misrepresentation which I prefer to treasure as such rather than regard as malicious dishonesty.

'He (de Bono) takes credit, in a modest sort of way, for the financial success of the 1984 Olympics, on the basis that their organiser attended a lecture he gave in 1975.'

This suggests a preposterous claim on my part that since Peter

Ueberroth had attended a lecture of mine in the past that some credit for his success was due to me. Would I then make such a claim about anyone who had at any time attended a lecture of mine? Truly preposterous.

The truth is remarkably different. In an interview in the *Washington Post*, on 30 September 1984, Peter Ueberroth was asked how he had solved the problems and developed the new concepts that had made the games such a success. He replied quite specifically that he had used 'lateral thinking'. The title of the interview and the whole text is about lateral thinking – in some detail. Someone sent me this cutting so I wrote to Mr Ueberroth who reminded me that he had been my faculty host at talks I had given to the Young Presidents' Organisation in Florida in 1975. Indeed, after the first talk he had asked me to consider doing some lateral thinking for the travel company he then ran.

So it was Mr Ueberroth, himself, who said (in print) that he had used the lateral thinking techniques. This was indicated very clearly in the foreword to the book. That Mr Mars-Jones chose to distort it into a preposterous claim is a flagrant abuse of the licence of a critic.

In itself Peter Ueberroth's deliberate use of lateral thinking, and with such success, illustrates how simple techniques can have powerful results.

This brings me to a serious problem from which Britain seems to suffer more than many other countries. There are doers and there are describers. The doers like simplicity because simplicity means effectiveness. A complex description may be fine as description but falls apart in action. The describers are horrified by simplicity and can only exercise their egos by being negative and pseudo-clever – because to be positive about simplicity requires a great deal more talent. The doers are too busy doing to spend time writing, and may not even be talented in this direction. So communication is dominated by the describers with their dangerous limitations. This is not true in Japan, Germany or the USA. The result in Britain is a sort of 'literary' domination with a negative and deadening effect and a diversion of attention to very peripheral matters (yet further attention to the Bloomsbury set). The vigour of a nation is measured by those who do things not those who describe them.

It is a curious fact that the simpler a concept I put forward the more fury it seems to arouse. I could be inclined to ascribe this to pure envy: 'Why didn't I think of that?' 'Why should he get away with something so obvious?' It is likely that envy plays a part but I do believe that it is the horror of the simple that so disturbs the mediocre mind.

There are three things that can be remembered about the simple. The first is that simple things can be very effective in action (yet are difficult to teach precisely because of the simplicity). The second thing is that anything worth saying can usually be said in a simple manner: like summarising a book on a postcard. The third thing is that something that becomes obvious once it has been said may not have been so obvious beforehand.

I have chosen to write about this subject as an introduction to this book because the material in this book was deliberately designed to be simple and usable. The material was written for doers not describers.

I do not know if any of the reviewers of my books have bothered to understand what lies behind them. In 1969 I wrote a book called *The Mechanism of Mind* (Jonathan Cape). In that book I discuss how the nerve networks in the brain form a special kind of information surface. This surface allows incoming information to organise itself into patterns and sequences. This type of self-organising surface is very different from the usual passive system in which information is stored passively until some logical operator acts upon the information (as in a normal computer). The model I put forward has been simulated on computer (by M.H. Lee) and shown to behave as predicted. These concepts of self-organising systems were later to be described for thermo-dynamic systems by Ilya Prigogine (who won a Nobel prize) and to be called 'dissipative systems' by Eric Jantsch. There is a huge new direction opening up and only the first few steps have been taken.

Within the last three years (1984-87) the concepts I put forward in 1969 have surfaced as the basis of what are now called neurocomputers, neural net machines, Boltzmann machines, etc. The whole area is what is loosely called 'connectionism'. I am not claiming a linear connection between my book in 1969 and these ideas because other people have been working in the field and on the related perceptions. Nevertheless John Hopfield (at the California Institute of Technology and one of the pioneers in this field) is well aware of my work as is the Nobel Prize physicist Murray Gell-Mann (also at Caltech).

Unlike the others I have not been interested in building 'thinking machines' but in understanding the logic and behaviour of such self-organising patterning systems. The purpose of such understanding is to devise thinking tools that we can use effectively. For example the concept of PO which is a central part of the provocation aspect of lateral thinking arises directly from an understanding of the system (as also does the random word technique). In fact the mathematical necessity for provocation in such systems was discovered by IBM researchers with much fanfare in 1983 – more than ten years after I invented PO.

The logic of self-organising systems is the logic of perception. Our language (and symbolic) logic is the logic of passive systems – not of perception. Many of our problems arise from the application of this inappropriate logic to perception.

There are many interesting aspects of the logic of perception. For example the law of contradiction does not apply. Also, every valuable creative idea must always be logical in hindsight. Yet we make the mistake we have been making for two thousand years if we believe that such ideas must therefore be attainable by ordinary logic. In patterning systems there is also the powerful effect of context. It is precisely this context effect which underlies the value of the six hats concept.

We may soon reach the difficult point when in order to be a philosopher one may need to understand the information behaviour of self-organising systems. The ordinary language idiom may not be enough. Indeed language is an encyclopaedia of ignorance since concepts that emerge at a relative stage of ignorance are frozen into permanence and thereafter limit our thinking.

I do not go into these matters in all my books because the concepts and tools I put forward must stand on their own. They must make sense because they work. That is the ultimate test of reality. Yet behind the surface simplicity there may be much else – including years of experience in the field of thinking.

Only the simple-minded are upset by the simple.

A new concept for Democracy

We often feel that a concept which has withstood the test of time or has evolved over the ages must be beyond improvement. We often forget that a concept that was designed for one set of circumstances may not fit other circumstances so well.

One of the main operating advantages of the democratic system is the simple and finite way of making decisions. Instead of the force of arms there is the force of a head count. There can be no error in counting and the majority will prevail.

There are times, however, when this somewhat crude concept of head count can lead to unfairness and resentment. A single-seat majority in a legislature can give absolute power to the governing party for the life of the assembly (in Malta the Labour party had a one-seat majority and ruled with absolute power). The normal to and fro of elections can even out this apparent unfairness in most cases. But where there is a significant permanent minority (often determined on an ethnic basis) then the minority has no chance of power and is permanently dictated to by the majority, no matter how small the margin may be. Fiji is a classic example of this problem inasmuch as 49 per cent of the population are descended from Indians brought to Fiji by the British to work the sugar cane and 47 per cent are Melanesians. Where a minority is permanently frustrated there arises sectarian violence and a demand for a separate state in which the minority can govern. Sri Lanka, Cyprus and Northern Ireland may be seen as examples of this problem. In the United Kingdom the Conservatives obtained in the 1987 elections about 43 per cent of the votes but a large majority of seats because of the divided opposition. This may be a different sort of problem.

Without making any change to the one person one vote basis of democracy and without changing electoral systems (even though this may sometimes be a good idea), it is possible to introduce a new concept that would make the operation of legislatures more fair and more constructive where there is a permanent minority.

Every elected member of the legislature would be issued each year with a notional 'concern capital' of legislative units ('legu's'). Such units must be used up within the year and next year there is a fresh issue.

Both the government and the opposition (or any party) can introduce new legislation. Every introduction has a cost in legu's. This would be determined by the size of the assembly and also the number of matters covered in the legislation. This introduction cost would constitute the opening bid in an 'auction of concern' that would now follow.

The opposition to the legislation would now put in their bid (in legu's). The bidding would continue back and forth. If a final bid by the opposition equalled the final bid by the proposers the legislation is blocked. If the final bid by the opposition exceeds the final bid by the proposers then the opposition version is put into law. If the proposers' final bid remains the highest then the legislation is put into law. In all cases the units making up the final bids on both sides are consumed or lost.

Each new bid would have to exceed the existing bid by 50 per cent (possibly by 100 per cent).

To prevent tactical legislation there would be a need to ensure that once passed legislation could not be countered or repealed for three years. Similarly a bill that failed could not be re-introduced for three years.

With such a system the majority would only have absolute power up to a point. There would be an initial advantage in legu's but this advantage would be used up as more legislation was introduced. At this point the opposition could start introducing legislation.

In contrast to the usual absolute and permanent majority (even on the basis of one seat), majority power is consumed the more it is used.

In addition there is the advantage that if there is a piece of legislation that the opposition very strongly opposes, it could become very expensive for the governing party to push through such legislation (high cost in legu's). There would be a tendency to want to agree or negotiate legislation.

Ideally there would be three phases. The first or 'design' phase would be handled by a bi-partisan committee (not unlike the committees of the US Congress). This committee would look at the purpose of the proposed legislation and attempt to design it for the widest acceptability.

The second phase would be the 'negotiating' phase in which both sides would negotiate as in any other situation involving conflicting interests. Finally there would be the 'cut-off' phase which would involve the auction of concern. The finite nature of this cut-off phase would encourage more serious negotiation (a time limit might be set).

With this concept the absolute and permanent power of a majority now becomes finite and consumable. Yet at each point decisions are still made on the simple and finite basis of counting. But the counting is now of legislative units (legu's) not of heads.

Theoretically there would be no need for government and opposition parties since legislation could be introduced by any party.

1

Thinking about thinking about thinking

I have often wondered whether man's ability to think might not have arisen from a retrogressive evolutionary step. Instead of the brilliant, incisive and locked-on brain of an animal, some faulty gene gave a muddled, fuzzy indecisive brain that was always making mistakes. The locked-on brain has instant and precise recognition followed by appropriate action. The bee, the hawk and the deer have built-in circuitry that recognises the situation and releases the appropriate action. A fuzzy and blurry brain takes much longer to recognise something. It has to learn from experience and to devise images and a sort of language in order to re-run experience at the moment of action. The fuzzy brain can also make mistakes that allow for inappropriate action and the crossing of lines that leads to creativity. The incapacity of the human baby as compared to the operational efficiency of the newborn fawn is remarkable.

Man's relative stupidity is probably his greatest resource. I believe that within the next 50 years more will happen to change this than has happened within the last 2,000 years. There are areas in which human thinking has achieved quite remarkable progress. Travelling one day by Concorde I reflected that the spoonful of mashed potato that I was about to put into my mouth was moving faster than a rifle bullet. It is said that a Sea-Wolf anti-missile missile is so accurate that it can meet and destroy a 4.5-inch shell in mid-flight. The moon landings were remarkable not only for the fact that astronauts got there and got back safely but also for the fact that millions of people on Earth could watch in detail the astronauts walking on the moon's surface at the precise time that they were doing it. We take for granted the simple telephone and its connecting wires; and yet it is marvellous that a person in London can pick up the telephone and, in a few seconds, can be speaking to one selected person out of the many millions living 12,000 miles away in Australia. As for nuclear power, this is possibly the most remarkable of all man's technical achievements.

Why then, when we seem to have such effective thinking in the technical area, do we seem to make so little progress in the more human area: we still have wars and crime and inhuman behaviour; we still have poverty and ignorance. Are these areas where thinking can make no difference? Are these areas where only a huge increase in human wealth can so satisfy everybody that all problems are solved? Or are these areas only susceptible to emotional solutions through religious ideology or value changes? Or is it simply that the type of thinking that is so very successful in the technical area is much less use in the human area? Space exploration is relatively easy to deal with because nothing changes. The gravitational pull of Mars can be calculated centuries in advance and will not have altered by the time a space probe gets there. It could be that human matters are so complicated by interactive change and feedback loops that our ordinary linear thinking is unable to cope.

Advertising is a creative profession because its business is new ideas. Each product is a creation. To some extent the same goes for television. Yet it has been my experience that some of the least creative people I have come across have been in advertising and television. This apparent paradox is easy to explain. In physics and in mechanical engineering there are physical laws. So a thinker is free so long as he keeps these laws in mind and juggles them to produce a solution or an explanation. But in the 'soft areas' of advertising and television there

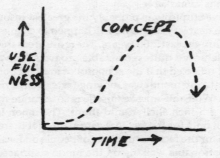

are no such laws. So the people in these areas have to *create* these laws. They create rigid orthodoxies in order to give them something to think with. Then they remain locked into those orthodoxies. When the television mogul said that what was needed were 'some new clichés', he was being both practical and perceptive. He wanted freshness within the accepted orthodoxy.

Now it may be that human thinking has evolved in a similar way. In order to make sense of a complex world, human thinking may have developed some habits and orthodoxies which had a certain usefulness at first but then prevented further progress. It is possible that such basic concepts as truth, meaning, identity and contradiction are examples. I have chosen these because they are at the base of so much of our thinking – not because I am ready to challenge all of them.

It is possible for evolution to evolve an anti-evolutionary process. Suppose genetic transformations took place in bacteria whose speed of multiplying is such that the chance of mutation is several million times what it would be in animals. Those genetic experiments would be transferred to the animal hosts by transference – we do know that transfer of genetic material can take place. Suppose now that, in the course of time, the host animals developed sophisticated immunity and protection systems that killed off the bacteria. At this point evolution would have brought evolution to a permanent halt.

We can see the same thing happening in society. Institutions evolve in order to serve a purpose, but then reach a point where they prevent further evolution. *Ideas and concepts are but organisations of experience.* They also evolve to the point where they so channel future thinking that further evolution is impossible.

In the diagram the two types of progress are illustrated. The first type illustrates technical progress. We go along and then an input of new knowledge leads to an acceleration of progress – and so on. The second type is to be found in the thinking involved in human affairs.

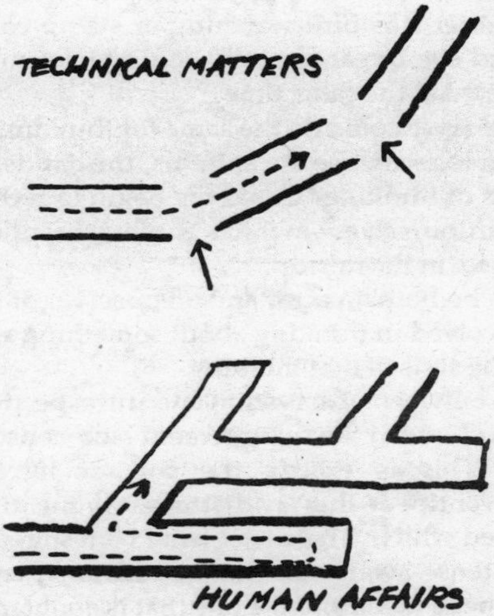

TECHNICAL MATTERS

HUMAN AFFAIRS

Patterns and tracks have to be formed at an early stage in order to give direction. Progress can only be made when we back track and escape from the established concept in order to find a new one. This has to happen again and again. That is why progress is so slow.

It is for these reasons that we need to think about our thinking. In this *Letter to Thinkers* I shall be thinking about the thinking about thinking that we need to do. Lateral thinking is only one of the aspects of thinking with which I am concerned. Among other things, I also run what is the largest programme in the world for the teaching of thinking as a full curriculum subject in schools. Several million children are involved. In Venezuela 100,000 teachers have been trained in the method.

(Note: Several other countries are now involved).

Bird-watching in a mirror

Bird-watching seems boring and incomprehensible to those who are not yet bird-watching. As with stamp-collecting, there comes a point when a critical mass of experience has been accumulated and suddenly it all becomes fascinating. Rare birds can be recognised and prized. Uninteresting random behaviour is suddenly recognised as mating display, protection, feeding patterns and so on. In short, patterns of recognition have been formed. Once this has occurred, then interest is guaranteed. Whether it is bird-watching or stamp-collecting or folk music, the trained eye or ear not only accumulates more experience but is also fascinated at the same time.

It would be nice if we could do the same for thinking.

Could we begin to recognise the patterns, the habits, the structures and the strategies of thinking? Could we begin to recognise these in others and also in ourselves – which is why the title of this piece includes the phrase 'in the mirror'.

It is not easy to be both an actor and an observer of the action. It is not easy to be involved in thinking about something and at the same time to observe the style of that thinking.

The borderline between observation and introspection is very fine. By introspection I mean an exaggerated self-consciousness that inhibits action. This is exactly the sort of introspection that immobilised the centipede that lay distracted in the ditch wondering which leg preceded which. That is *not* what I am suggesting. I am *not* suggesting an intense awareness that at each moment analyses the step that has just been taken and the one that is about to be taken. The watched bird is not influenced by the watcher, who is far away at the end of a pair of binoculars.

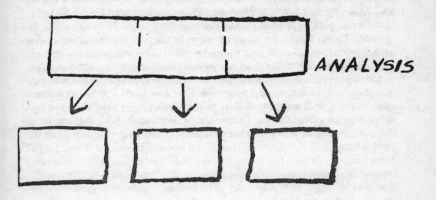

The model I am suggesting is almost as if a person could make a tape recording of observation. This method can be tried, but I do not particularly recommend it. The reason I do not recommend it is that at first there will not be enough recognition patterns available to the observer. In the absence of such patterns the observation will tend to become an analysis – and that is quite a different thing.

Pattern recognition and analysis are separate. You might analyse a mosaic into the component stones and completely fail to see the pattern. Or you may recognise the patterns and not bother with the individual stones. In the past much of our thinking has been concerned with analysis. This has been justified on two grounds. The first is that if the most basic elements are extracted then the larger patterns can be re-assembled from them. The second is that the elements that are analysed out are, in fact, the important 'patterns'. Both these grounds are fallacious when we are dealing with complex systems. This point is sufficiently made in the commonplace phrase 'cannot see the wood for the trees'.

So it is better not to tape record and analyse a piece of thinking. It is better not to try and extract all the patterns in a piece of thinking. Patterns cannot be recognised by diligence or analytical effort. They need to evolve through continued observation, prompted by a little outside help. It is best to notice just one or two salient points – and not bother with the rest.

Points and patterns

I am not going to be comprehensive about the sort of features that can be observed in thinking. I shall be coming back to this matter again and again in this *Letter to Thinkers*. So for the moment I shall just use some examples by way of illustration.

Value-laden works are easy to spot once they have been spotted. At other times they glide by and therefore seem to be accepted. I once had a discussion with a Californian psychiatrist about the tendency of modern psychology to 'dig deeper' in order to find the true self and the real meaning of action and neurosis. This has been a growing idiom ever since Freud suggested that surface behaviour was directed by sub-conscious frustrations. I was putting forward the idea that perhaps the surface self or mask was the real person and that 'digging deeper' only uncovered the garbage that could always be found if one looks hard enough. It was fascinating to see that the words which he could use were all positive value words like 'truth', 'real nature', 'deep self', 'natural feelings' and 'draw out'. The words which I was permitted to use had already been assigned negative values: 'mask', 'surface', 'artificial', 'superficial' and 'defensive'. It is somewhat frightening to think of those areas which cannot ever be discussed objectively because the words that have to be used have already been assigned a negative value by the idiom of society. For example the phrase 'cosmetic politics' immediately has a bad meaning of deceit and making things appear different from what they really are. Yet it could be argued that one of the main purposes of politics is to be 'cosmetic' and so lead the perceptions of listeners in ways that could be good as well as bad.

A style that is interesting to observe is what I call 'small circle rightness'. The thinker stands on some small patch of firm ground which cannot be challenged. From that he forays out in all directions using the initial base as justification. If successfully challenged, he retreats. Very often this style of thinking makes use of 'incontrovertible principles' which are universally accepted simply because chaos would result (or is said to result) if such principles were not held. Sometimes the use of this principle is overt. Othertimes it is hidden – even from the thinker who is using the principle. It can be a fascinating exercise for both parties to try to delineate the hidden principle. Value-laden words and principles may be combined for example in the principle that 'agression is a bad thing and cannot be allowed'. It is not a matter of disagreeing with such a principle but of *observing* its effect.

Example, instance and anecdote require a whole letter, series of

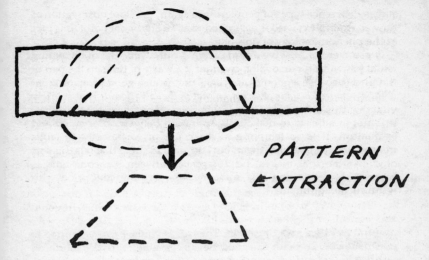

letters or a book, to themselves – so fundamental an aspect of thinking are they. I shall mention them here, but I will return to them much more fully in later letters. The most valuable use of an example is to carry a plausible function or process just as a mathematical formula might carry a process. *Once a process or idea is shown to be possible, then it cannot be unthought.* In searching for an explanation, the suggestion 'that it could have happened this way' introduces a new idea. An example may be used to show that an absolute generalisation is not absolute ('I have seen a black swan and therefore all swans are not white'). This harks back to the absolutism of medieval scholastic philosophy, and in practical terms it has relatively little value. In practical terms we can use the term 'by and large', which means that exceptions do not invalidate what has been said. For example, I could say: 'by and large, in England, swans are white.' The observation of a black swan no longer contradicts what has been said. Then there is the use of examples to back-up a point. Here one runs into statistical difficulties. Any number of examples cannot add up to statistical relevance unless the universe of possibilities is very small indeed. The fact that everyone you have talked to happens to dislike a certain politician is probably less significant than if only two-thirds of the people you had talked to disliked that politician. This is because the first instance suggests that you are only talking to a certain type of person, whereas the second instance suggests that the view cuts across difference types of people. Once again, the close observation of how an example is used is *not* intended as an argument point. It is part of the phenomenology of thinking.

If you were to observe a bird carrying out a very elaborate mating ritual you might, personally, consider it a waste of time on the part of the bird (because a good dancer does not mean a good provider). *But what is required is your observation, not you evaluation.* It is absolutely vital that this distinction is made when we set out to 'watch thinking'. It is not at all easy to make this separation betwen observation and evaluation. It is so tempting to make use of weaknesses or faults instead of just observing them. But I do want to stress that it is this sort of discipline that makes the difference between someone who is interested in thinking and someone who is only concerned with winning an argument.

The thinking place

This section is intended to fulfil the same function as a golf-course, a tennis court or a gymnasium. They are all formal places with formal rules for the carrying out of some enjoyable activity. As one carries out that activity there is enjoyment and practice and perhaps, with time, an improvement in skill. It is exactly that attitude that I want to convey with regard to this section of the Letter. We can also think about anything at any time and any place. Often we do. There is still a value in being asked (by me) to think about something in a particular way and at a particular time. That is exactly what this 'thinking place' is for.

I do not believe that thinking for a long time is better than thinking for a short time. In terms of practising thinking, then a short burst is more fun than a long burst. The cudgelling of brains for a prolonged period turns enjoyment into torture for many (but not all). What is important, however, is that a definite effort is made to direct one's thinking in a certain way and for a certain time. In other words, the deliberate application of thinking is important if there is to be pride in it as a usable skill.

The exercise suggested here is in two parts.

Part one
The task is to find a source of thinking. This is not as easy as it sounds. There are practical constraints. You could read traditional volumes on traditional philosophers. But that is a long task and the thinking used

is often neither practical nor interesting. Much of the thinking around us is purely descriptive with perhaps a small element of interpretation.

The task is to find examples of thinking that are brief and purposive. Two such examples might be readers letters in a newspaper or the leader article in a newspaper – though this is often too bland.

Part two
The second part of the task is to carry out the observation exercise discussed in another part of this letter (under the 'bird-watching' title). The observation should be carried out on the material turned up by the first part of the exercise. The observation should be carried out in a formal way. As mentioned before, there should *not* be an attempt fully to analyse the thinking that is being observed. Nor should there be an attempt to categorise the material in terms of the features it shows.

The observation should consist of two levels. The first level is to pick out in a deliberate way the patterns mentioned in the 'bird-watching' section in this Letter. Stick to these three areas: value-laden words; small circle rightness or hidden principle; the use of examples. The second level is to make any other observations that come into the observer's mind. Don't try too hard. Don't analyse. Just observe and see what patterns emerge. There may be none, in which case you just try again on another occasion.

Remember that the observation is directed at finding *patterns* not at finding fault with the argument.

2

Thinking and information

I once scandalised a roomful of school principals in the Republic of Eire by suggesting that God cannot think. We accept that thinking is a good thing, and to deny God this beneficial activity sounds like an insult to the perfection of God's being. But that perfection of being implies complete knowledge. Thinking is our way of moving from one arrangement of knowledge to a better one – a being with perfect knowledge is there already. There would be no difference between the starting position and the final one. So we must conclude that though thinking is beneficial to us it would be an insult to God.

If we had complete information in a situation then we would not need to think. Every piece of information we acquire takes us towards that state of complete information, and therefore it follows that every piece of information is valuable. Obviously, in any situation, the more information we get the better must it be for our decisions and our actions. I have always maintained that the size of a decision is proportional to the inadequacies of the reason for making it. If the information is more or less complete (circumstances, priorities, consequences, resources etc.) then it flows through to decision or action without there being that interruption for human decision. The bigger the load placed on human decision the bigger the information gap. Any system designer strives to remove the need for human decision and at the same time worries about doing so.

If it is so obvious that the more information we can get the better, then the matter is hardly worth writing about. Unfortunately it is not as clear-cut as that, and there are several dangers in following this 'obvious' precept that the more information we get the better it must be.

Clive Sinclair – the brilliant electronics genius and entrepreneur who sells more computers than anyone else – once told me that, when he wants to develop some ideas in a field, he reads just enough to become familiar with the idiom and the basic ground rules but then stops reading. This is something I have always done myself, and I suspect that many people concerned with innovation do the same –

either consciously or through impatience and the urge to get on with things. If we put aside such impatience, there is a logical reason for this behaviour. In a patterning system we feel that our perceptions would be contaminated by the established perceptions in the field. If a pattern is established – much as a river in a landscape – then we cannot lay down a pattern which cuts across it. Our perceptions are, as it

CROSS CHANNEL

were, drained by the existing flow system. At other times in these letters I shall be writing about the mind as a self-organising, patterning system. Readers who want to explore the background to this could read my book *The Mechanism of Mind* which was published in 1969 (available as a Penguin book).

If in our reading of the literature we come across an established idea or way of doing things then we are likely to adopt that method – even without thinking about it. Or, we are likely to rebel against it and take a distinctly different approach. What is almost impossible to do is to take an approach which is only slightly different. I remember an investigation I once did on kidney function. The results were positive and suggested an important principle. Whenever I talked about the results I was always asked how I had come to do the investigation in that way, because a well-known physiologist had carried out a somewhat similar investigation and had obtained negative results. The truth of the story was that I had not known about that investigation, and ignorance allowed me to do mine just slightly differently.

The situation can be even worse than I have suggested above. It is not just a matter of being contaminated by the existing framework and theory in its entirety. If we accept just one basic concept, this might determine the way we are forced to look at the field thereafter.

The dilemma is clear. On the one hand we cannot get started if we do not learn the basic idiom and knowledge in the field. We would spend a great deal of effort re-discovering what was already well known. We should not be able to stand on the 'shoulders of others' as we reached further. We should risk time, expense and motivation in

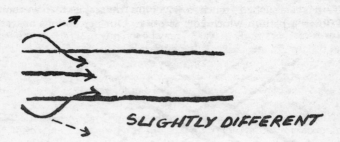

SLIGHTLY DIFFERENT

finding out things which were already well known. On the other hand, if we achieved the freshness and innocence of a child in that field we might look at things differently. We might create some new basic concept which cut right across existing concepts. We might try and experiment in a slightly different way. We might look at the results through a different viewing hypothesis.

Culturally we have long ago made up our minds. We venerate scholarship and review. The worker in a field is supposed to be familiar with the established work in the field and to keep up with what is being done. In industrial research laboratories there is the same need to know what is being done in order to build from it. Without such knowledge any work must seem to be of the hit or miss variety with all the expense that entails. Many Research and Development departments in the chemical industry spend much of their time finding a way around the patents of others in what is clearly a sensible effort to profit from the work of others.

The risks of abandoning the notion that the more information we can get the better it must be, are too great. *Yet if we really acknowledge the behaviour of patterning systems in perception, we are making much less than the best use of the available information in the field by knowing about it.* This sounds like an extraordinary paradox: we might make better use of the information by not knowing about it. The explanation is simple. If we can first develop some ideas and concepts then we become able to look at the existing information in a new way. If we first look at the information then we are inevitably looking at it through the old concepts within which the information is organised.

Information overload

As electronic technology makes data more easily accessible the phrase 'information overload' is going to become ever more fashionable. It is already bandied about in technology conferences. Like the devastating word 'patronising', there is no defence against it. Even if a piece of information is simple in itself it may be too much. It may be the straw that breaks the camel's back. It may be your small piece of litter, which is tiny in itself until accompanied by everyone else's tiny piece. There is great value in such 'conscience words' because they do guide our designs and behaviour. There is also a danger in their facile application at inappropriate moments.

When I was at Harvard the medical library was so fantastic that it was possible to find any reference one might want. This was a great joy after the frustrating search efforts in British university libraries (one set of journals would be in one department, another set in another department and so on). Reading through the directly relevant articles in the subject area took so long that, by the time it was done, there had been enough new material published to provide further reading. Instead of reading being the prelude to research activity the reading became a full-time occupation in itself – with no end in sight. I believe there are 33,000 medical journals published world-wide. Poor distribution has previously protected researchers from this exposure, but improvements in data storage and transmission (via satellite and facsimile machines) are removing this protection. It was always grossly unfair that the work of a French or Polish scientist would go unnoticed because it was written in an untranslated journal.

In system terms the phrase 'information overload' has a particular meaning. Too much input may mean that the system breaks down and becomes paralysed or reverts to some simpler and inappropriate behaviour. There are those who feel that this may be happening to society and may account for violence, stereotypes and gang-type behaviour. A gang is a way of simplifying the environment and the decisions it requires. In this piece I am not actually referring to this type of overload but simply to the amount of time needed to cope with the information that is available and relevant.

Traditionally we have relied on classifiers, reviewers and osmosis. The classifier or skilled librarian is supposed to tag the information in such a way as to indicate its relevance. By definition this is an impossible task, even if the author of the material helps as much as possible with tag words. Relevance is a matter of perception, and perception is dependent on individual need. Too many innovations and discoveries have come from cutting across classifications to make this any more than a very broad tool (but valuable nevertheless). The next method is by learned review, and particularly reviews by those wiser and older heads who see this as their continuing contribution to

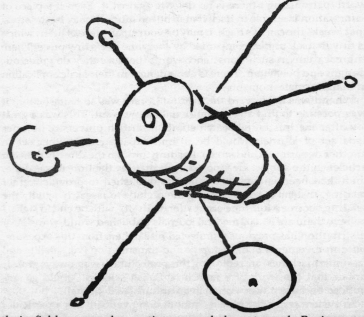

their field, even when active research has stopped. Reviews are valuable for what they include but very dangerous for what they leave out, for – like something misfiled – that may be lost for ever. Reviews are also dangerous because of the framework that is used, since this is more often based on a need for neatness than on the nature of the material. Osmosis simply means that if an idea or piece of work is significant enough it will gradually emerge and reach those who need it. It can be a very slow process, even though the talking (not the papers) at international conferences does accelerate it.

There are already many information intermediaries: librarians, researchers, journalists, consultants and writers of newsletters. In the past such people have often been the only channel through which information became available. For example a magazine was a physical way of distributing information, and the editor's role as information intermediary could not be dispensed with. Today electronic opportunity will allow us to go direct to the information source on microfilms or data discs. Will we then choose to bring back the editor in order to simplify life for ourselves? I foresee two new professions emerging. The first is that of 'information broker'. Such a broker would function at any level: collector, sorter, explorer, synthesiser or reviewer. The second profession would be that of information designer. Here the task might be to design information so that it is self-organising or so that it can be absorbed at a glance. Possibly the best example of an information design that we have is the graph, for it allows us to perceive at a glance what might be complex relationships. Histograms and pie charts are useful if primitive steps in this direction. I also envisage the design of higher order languages, and this is something I am working on. From the beginning these will need to be designed to be easy to learn; to cut across existing language barriers; to allow information to organise itself.

Until we reach this stage, we must continue with some direct reading; we must choose an intermediary whose perceptions we value and also engage in occasional random reading. To some people the idea of random reading seems contradictory when there is not even enough time to cover the field at a review level. It makes sense both in its stimulating aspect and also as a check on information intermediaries.

The thinking place

A friend of mine keeps a variety of exotic ducks in their wild state. Photographing a duck on its nest at close range is something of a problem because the duck waddles away at the first sign of intrusion. The construction of a hide is not very effective since the duck seems to sense that the hide is there for some unpleasant purpose. Apparently there is simple solution to the problem. The photographer strolls up to the nest with a companion. The duck waddles away. After a while the companion leaves, whereupon the duck comes back and sits on the nest, even though the photographer is in full view a few feet away.

The implications of this story are extensive. After all this could be said to be the way stock markets work: never mind the intrinsic value – just react to changes. There are many other implications.

I mention this story to illustrate one type of reading. We may come across something which causes us to pause and ponder and tease out the implications. It is probably best to do so at the time rather than to store the item away as an item for future consideration. If we can at least glimpse some of the implications, then we are more likely to remember the item. It may be that we come across such striking pieces of information in the course of reading, or it may be that we *set* our minds to find fascinating or interesting things whatever we may be reading – instead of waiting for items to catch our attention. This is one type of 'dense' reading. We read in order to tease out the full implications of what we read. We do not hurry along. We do not want to find out what happens next. We do not want to reach the conclusion. As if we were picking wild flowers by the wayside, we treat every potential source of interest with full attention and pause to consider it. This sort of reading is not easy becaue we have to have rather a lot of 'interest hooks' in our minds in order to find quite ordinary matters interesting. The sort of questions we might be asking include: what does this imply?, what does this link up with?, what does this illustrate?, what sort of thing is going on?, is this what I would have expected or different?. This first sort of 'dense reading' is for interest. The second sort of dense reading is for information.

I was once asked to talk to a big meeting of language teachers in Barcelona. At one point I put forward the sentence 'there seem to be a lot of shoe shops in Barcelona'. I invited the audience to tell me all the information they might get from that simple statement. There is a great deal that can be inferred with respect to me, to Barcelona, to the price of leather, to the structure of the town, to the structure of the retail trade etc. It is an interesting exercise to take this sentence and work out all the possible inferences. In most cases the inferences will be no more than suppositions (for example: shops may be run by families, and hence the staff overheads are low or, shoes are of poor quality and therefore wear out quickly). At some points a number of different possibilities may have to be put forward alongside each other, for example: margins are high enough to cover overheads or, people buy a lot of shoes or, property taxes are low.

There are many different levels of reading – quite apart from the physical speed of our reading. There is 'defensive' reading in which we skim through just to check that everything is as we assume it to be, and with the hope that we shall find nothing in what we read that might change our views. We just have to read through the material in case there is something of significance in it. Then there is what we might call 'gist' reading in which we try to work out the general thrust of what we are reading. We appreciate that this may have to be expressed in detail but we are only interested in the broad picture or the final conclusion. Then there is 'atmosphere' reading in which we read through a piece to get the general feel or mood of the piece, even though we are neither interested in detail or even in the broad gist of what is said. For example we may read through the comments of a financial journalist in order to get the mood of the market.

Finally there is 'information' reading where what we read has been designed to bring to us information that we want. Here it may be a matter of sorting our the linking material and the tone-setting material from the actual information. It is perfectly legitimate for facts to be framed in certain perspectives. After all a set of sales figures may have to be put in a number of frames: against a background of recession; in spite of re-organisation in the department; as compared with the sales of competitors; as compared to target sales. It would be somewhat easier if the communicator were to indicate in a formal manner the appropriate frame rather than indicate it in a roundabout way – which always sounds like an excuse. A communicator could state: 'these are the facts' and 'these are the frames'.

Because of the huge amount of information available and the considerable amounts that need to be read it helps to be clear about the appropriate reading mode: dense for implications; dense for inferences; defensive; overall picture; for atmosphere; for information.

There is a big difference between moment-to-moment interest and over-all interest. There are after-dinner speakers who are very funny from moment to moment and the audience is wide awake and enjoying itself. At the end of the speech a member of the audience may turn to his neighbour and say, 'that was great fun – but what did he say?'. The same thing happens with television programmes which may hold the viewers' attention from moment to moment, but at the end there is nothing implanted in the mind. There is the equivalent danger in reading. We may read something that is interesting, but at the end we only have the notion that it was interesting. We do not always need to pause at the end of our reading to spell out what we have learned but it can be a useful habit. As an exercise take any journal article and read through it. At the end try to crystallise what has been learned. This is not a memorising exercise and there should be no attempt to remember as many points as possible. Nor is it an exercise in summarising the piece. It is simply a conscious effort to pick out three or four significant points. The writer of the piece may have had quite different intentions as to what the main points were. But it is the reader who chooses the points to remember. Some of these points may have been tucked away in the text as minor points – yet they have the significance.

3

Is problem solving enough?

There are certain themes which I shall be coming back to again and again in these *Letters to Thinkers*. That is the purpose of this informal style of communication. Because a particular theme has been dealt with in one letter does not mean that it is finished and done with and that all that needs to be written about it has been written. The theme I am writing about here is one of those basic themes that needs a lot of attention. It is also a theme that is especially close to my own interests in thinking.

The idiom and style of many business schools was set in the 1950s and 1960s, even if a particular school was founded earlier or later. The idiom established in those days has remained a dominant idiom to this day. Unfortunately the idiom is a dangerous one. It is particularly dangerous because the idiom remains as valid today as it was in the

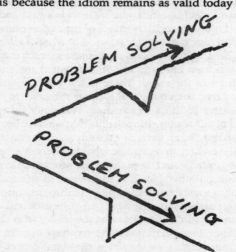

1950s and 1960s. I am referring to the idiom of 'problem solving'. Thinking is seen as an exercise in problem solving. You define the problem and then you set about solving it.

In the 1950s and 1960s the problem-solving idiom was indeed a sufficient thinking idiom. In a growing economy problem solving is sufficient. The path is clear and the market is growing. Provided you manage your resources efficiently (the definition of management) then all you need to do is to be a problem solver. When a problem arises you define it and solve it and you are back on track. If you have difficulty in solving it yourself you might call in outside consultants who have developed skills at problem solving. The combination of efficiency and problem solving meant a healthy growing business. So it was perfectly reasonable for business schools to turn out problem solvers and for corporations to snap them up. Many of those trained in this way are still in place in their organisations. In any case the idiom has not changed, and management training is still producing problem solvers.

Problem solving is still as vital as it ever was and no organisation could survive unless it employed some efficient problem solvers at all levels. Because problem solving is as necessary as it ever was there is no way I, or anyone else, could attack the validity of that idiom. Unfortunately problem solving is no longer sufficient. It *was* sufficient in the 1950s and 1960s because there was a growing economic baseline. That is no longer the case today in most industries.

Exactly the same problem-solving skills that kept an organisation on track when there was a growing baseline – will also keep it on track when there is a declining baseline. And so the decline continues.

In a very loose sense problem solving can be made to apply to 'anything we want to achieve' or, 'anything we need to think about'. As with so many other aspects of thinking, there is both a lack of adequate terms and a great deal of difficulty in introducing new ones (because they sound gimmicky and artificial). We talk about 'closed' problems when we know what we want to achieve. For example we might want to work out a mathematical equation or solve an industrial relations dispute or arrive at the correct pricing for a product. If we can define the end-point there is a closed problem. It is not unlike a journey to an agreed destination. Coping with deviations from the smooth running of an organisation provides problems of this sort. By definition, getting back to that smooth running signals the solution of the problem.

We then talk about 'open-ended' problems when we only vaguely know what we want to achieve. This may be a better product or a new product or an opportunity as yet unseen. Having acknowledged this totally different type of problem we then proceed to tackle it with the same methods and skills as for the closed problems. Of course this does not work. 'Open-ended' problems should never be called problems because if they are they will be treated as closed problems. This is why the problem-solving idiom has been – and continues to be – so dangerous. *Open-ended problems require thinking that is conceptual, creative and constructive.* Training in problem solving has usually not included this. That is why the idiom of the 1950s and 1960s has become so dangerous.

CONCEPTUAL

PROBLEM SOLVING

CATCH – 24

In my book *Future Positive* (Penguin Books) I introduce something I call Catch-24. This states that in order for a person to reach the most senior position in an organisation he (or she) should have kept hidden – or be without – exactly those talents that will be needed when he (or she) gets there. On the way up problem solving is valued, noticed and prized. Without successful problem solving there is failure – both on the part of the individual and eventually for the organisation. Problem solving is an action idiom. A problem presents itself. Action is demanded. The problem is tackled and solved. There is a result. There is achievement. Then there is the next problem and the next challenge.

When a person has reached the senior position then problem solving of this sort can be delegated: to existing staff, to new staff or to consultants. Now the need is for conceptual and strategic thinking. But the chief executive has not been selected for that. He has had no opportunity to demonstrate or practise it. Could he not delegate this sort of thinking just as he delegated the problem solving? Problem solving can be delegated to all those subordinates who have been busy showing their skill at it. But to whom would the conceptual thinking be delegated? A certain amount of help can be obtained from outsiders who may have made a speciality of this sort of thinking, but in the end it is the chief executive who is going to have to judge and use the concepts.

Is there a solution to this difficulty? I believe there is. I believe that, in future, organisations will came to realise that concepts are just as important as technical developments and legal procedures. I have suggested in various places that there is a need for a concept department to be set up in as formal a manner as we now have R & D departments. I shall be dealing with this in a future *Letter*.

The i.s.a.

Problems make themselves only too obvious. They land on your desk. Something has to be done about them. A bush fire is an obvious bush fire and needs to be extinguished.

Problem solving is a great deal easier than problem finding. If there is a problem you can define it and get your teeth into it. You can look around for a standard solution or assemble known elements into a new solution, or even be creative. With problem finding you set out to find a problem. It is not obvious and it does not signal its presence in the way a bush fire does.

In conjunction with the Perstorp Company of Sweden I once ran an inventions competition. There were over 5,000 entries. The standard of problem solving was high. The standard of problem finding was very low. Most of the technical ingenuity had been directed towards things that did not need doing. I suspect this must be the experience of anyone who has run similar events.

What does problem finding mean? It means defining an area in which the application of thinking could make a significant difference. It is defining an improvement area or a change area. As in so many other cases the word 'problem' is inappropriate. I apologise for using it. I did so in order to make the distinction between problem solving and problem finding.

In the teaching of lateral thinking to a great number of people over the years I have found that the most difficult aspect to teach is the i.s.a. Asking a person to define an i.s.a. means asking that person to isolate an area which he or she feels would benefit significantly from the application of lateral thinking. The term 'i.s.a.' stands for idea sensitive area. In this regard the word 'sensitive' is used in the same way as it might be used of the steering of a car: sensitive steering means that a slight turn on the steering wheel will result in a significant change in direction. It is also the same use of 'sensitive' as in the expression 'a sensitive person' or 'a sensitive photographic film'. In summary, an idea sensitive area is a defined area in which the thinker believes that a new idea could make a significant difference.

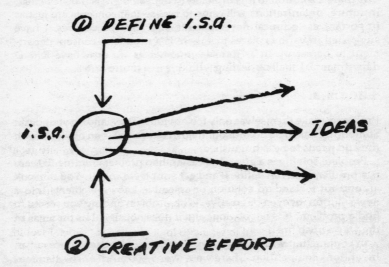

Whenever, in the course of a seminar, I ask people to define some i.s.a.'s in their own business area the result is always rather feeble. Part of that may be due to the novelty of the concept. Part of it may be due to the more usual problem-solving mode in which problems do not have to be found but present themselves. Part of it is due to the fact that the exercise is very much more difficult than it seems.

When we are thinking in the 'review' mode there is a very good case to be made for focusing attention on any part of an operation and seeking to do that particular thing more effectively, more simply of more cheaply. In this case everything can legitimately become an area for creative attention. An i.s.a. is somewhat different. An i.s.a. is an area where we feel that a new idea would make a significant difference. We have to feel that before we can define the area as an i.s.a. In effect we are saying:

'This area badly needs a new idea'.

'This area would benefit from a new idea'.

'In this area the pay-off from a new idea would be large'.

Bottlenecks, areas of high cost, areas with high failure rate and time consuming areas might all benefit from a new idea if the already applied methods of analysis and problem solving had not yet come up with an adequate solution. In such cases genuine problems and i.s.a.'s overlap. It can be worth listing such areas as i.s.a.'s so long as doing this does not exclude more conventional problem-solving approaches. I am, however, more concerned with the less obvious areas – with the ones we have to seek out and define.

In my experience i.s.a.'s are usually defined in too general a manner: 'to survive'; 'to make more profits'; 'to compete with the Japanese' etc. These are worthy thinking areas, but too general to be i.s.a.'s. Within each of these areas a number of tighter i.s.a.'s could be defined.

In the course of my seminars I sometimes give the following task. I ask participants to define some i.s.a.'s in the following situation: 'A resort hotel with 85 per cent occupancy year round. The intention is to stay in the hotel business and to increase profitability.' I usually get a lot of sensible suggestions which involve analysis of available information and appropriate action – but do not require any new idea. I also get a lot of specific ideas (like 'put in a casino'). But a specific idea is not an i.s.a. Many suggestions are very general, such as 'cut costs'. It seems difficult to put across the idea that I am looking for areas in which it would be useful to *set out* to look for new concepts. I would regard the following as good examples of i.s.a.'s.

'Ways of getting people who are staying in the hotel to spend more of their money in the hotel (instead of at outside restaurants, bars etc.).'

'Ways of getting some return from the rooms that are empty at 6 p.m. because of cancellations and no-shows. The possibility of some "stand-by system".'

'Ways of getting additional revenue from a room, quite apart from the room rate.'

'Ways of reducing the guests' expectancy of service.'

'Ways of getting satisfied guests to recommend the hotel to others.'

'Ways of moving up market without losing revenue in the transition period.'

'Ways of getting people who are not staying in the hotel to add to the revenue.'

'Ways of using rooms that are occupied but empty during the day.'

It can be seen that these range from the routine and sensible (ways of getting more revenue from people not staying in the hotel) to the rather unlikely (ways of using occupied rooms that are empty during the day). An i.s.a. can certainly be an area in which it is rather unlikely that you will come up with an acceptable idea. It can be seen that in general the i.s.a. defines what the new idea is supposed to do. At other times the i.s.a. may simply define a starting point. For example: 'Ways of deriving benefit from group bookings'.

It is difficult to define an i.s.a. very exactly as it lies along spectrums from problem to opportunity, from general to particular, from likely to unlikely.

Why is it important to define i.s.a.'s? One reason is that if we define a need for creativity then we are much more likely to use creativity. Another is that it focuses attention on potential opportunity areas which may never have presented themselves as problem areas.

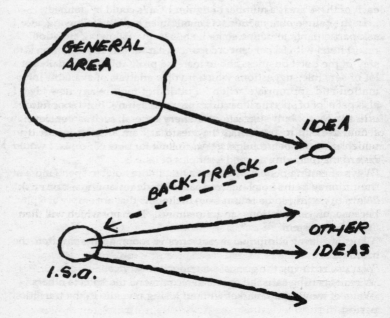

Back-track
In the hotel example someone might have said 'put in a casino'. Although this may be a sensible idea it is an idea rather than an i.s.a. It can be a useful exercise to back-track from a specific idea such as this in order to define the possible i.s.a.'s from which it might have come – had it been done that way round. For example we might back-track to the following i.s.a.'s. 'Ways of getting revenue from outsiders.'
'Specific attractions for people to stay at this hotel.'
'Ways of getting revenue from basic human interests.'
'Using the premises and management structure for other ventures.'

From these i.s.a.'s we could then develop further ideas. The move from a specific idea to a general category and then on to further specific ideas is a basic operation in thinking.

Stock-pile
An individual, or an organisation, should have a stock-pile of defined i.s.a.'s. From time to time creative attention should be paid to an item on this list. This could be done by an individual in his own time – for example whilst flying. There might also be specially convened creative sessions. The stock-pile can be an ever-growing one. Individuals can submit new suggestions. Bear in mind that an i.s.a. is not itself an idea but an area in which ideas are to be sought.

The thinking place

What is a concept? I shall be focusing on this more directly in future *Letters to Thinkers*. What I want to do here is to explore different levels of definition. For example, if I were to ask for a definition of the concept of 'insurance' I might get the following levels:
'Risk management.'
'The spread of risk.'
'A number of people paying in advance a fraction of the cost of a risk that might befall only one (or a few) of them.'
'The payment of premiums to an insurance company which will then settle the claims of those who are insured.'

The first level is pretty general since risk management may also include the avoidance of risk. The spreading of risk seems to be the most useful level. The more detailed levels explain a particular mechanism by which this is done. If we focus on the 'spreading of risk' level we might devise other methods of spreading the risk. If we move to the next level down we are already restricting our thinking to those who are at risk. For example the concept of Lloyd's of London is precisely to spread the risk to those who are not likely to suffer the risk directly. A name at Lloyd's is theoretically at risk when a ship sinks, even though he in no way owns the ship.

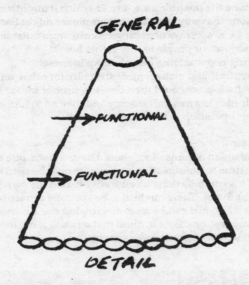

As I mentioned elsewhere in the *Letter*, the level of generality at which one works may make a big difference to the effectiveness of the thinking. Too detailed a level locks the thinker in. Too general a level does not give the thinker enough to work upon. There is no easy answer that I can give readers that will define the most appropriate level. The best I can do is to say that there is a spectrum that ranges from the very general to the detailed. The thinker should be half-way along that spectrum. In practice this means being aware of the situation and asking both questions:

'Is this too general a concept?'

'Is this too detailed a concept?'

Logically the most general concept includes all others. It is easy enough to move from particular concepts to the general one and to claim that they are all included there. It is much more difficult, however, to move back from the general concept to all the more particular ones. I have often been at creative sessions where the note-taker has included a wide variety of ideas under some broad headings. When these broad headings are read back the nature of the particular ideas and their flavour is often completely lost. On one occasion there was a suggestion that policemen should wear a different coloured hat depending on their activity of the moment: routine patrol, hot pursuit, investigating etc. This was put under the broad heading 'that policemen's activities be differentiated'. Anyone reading the report of that meeting would be very unlikely to go from the broad heading to the particular idea.

As an exercise, try to write out four levels of concept definition for each of the following:

package holidays
supermarkets (or hypermarkets)
hospitals.

4

A time to think

The 20 December 1982 issue of *Forbes* (USA) carried a feature about me and lateral thinking. Since I know that subject reasonably well, what was of more interest to me was the second part of the feature in which several leading businessmen were asked about their attitudes to thinking. Amongst other things they were asked when they did their thinking. George Ball (chief executive officer Prudential-Bache Securities) said that he set aside 10-15 minutes twice a day. Philip Knight (chairman Nike Inc.) tried to put in one hour a day three or four days a week. Robert O. Anderson (chairman Atlantic Richfield) did not set aside any regular time but found that travelling alone in his private aircraft provided a great deal of thinking time. There were several other comments, and it was interesting to see that many of these senior executives felt able to pin-point times that were specifically devoted to thinking. It would have been very easy to have said that no specific time was allocated to thinking since a great deal of thinking was taking place at every instant (while looking at a set of figures, whilst listening to someone, whilst communicating and so on).

It may be that the interviewer had framed the question in such a way that those replying knew that they were being asked about specific 'thinking only' time. Or, it may be that there was a natural distinction between the thinking that was called for by events and which occurred as a reaction to the surroundings, and that which required either a deliberate effort of will or the maintenance of a habit. Since all habits require an effort of will in the initial stages and further efforts of will along the way, the distinction may not be that important.

We have a curiously ambivalent attitute towards thinking. 'Thinking' is a good thing. To be able to think is a good thing. Yet the actual employment of thinking seems sometimes to be a sign of weakness. To have to think about something implies a lack of decisiveness. A teacher would rather a pupil came straight out with the answer instead of pausing to think about it. A politician who made an obvious pause to think about something would be accused of not knowing his own policy on the matter. *There are times when we have less regard for a man* who thinks than for a man who appears to know all the answers. After all, if he thinks he might get it wrong. There are other times when a man who does not think can (or should) terrify us.

The statement 'I need to think about that' is too often regarded as a sign of weakness or prevarication. Perhaps we should alter it to: 'I do not need to think about that – but I want to, and I am going to'. This leads on to the notion of thinking that is continued even after the 'solution' has been found.

We could probably identify three sorts of thinking (in very general terms).

1. PURPOSE

2. IMPROVEMENT

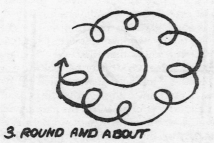

3. ROUND AND ABOUT

1. Thinking to achieve a purpose. Classically this is problem solving, whether of the open or closed variety. There is an end point. The thinker is trying to reach some destination.
2. Thinking for improvement. A solution has already been reached. An answer is available. Things are going well. The thinker simply wants to do better.

3. Thinking around and about. This is musing, freewheeling, preparing the field, setting the context, exploring the situation. Just as an intending purchaser might prowl around a house he is to buy so the thinker prowls around the situation. There is no definite point of focus.

It is not normal practice to go on thinking after an adequate solution has been found. There are many very practical reasons for this. The problem that has just been solved may be only one of a whole string of problems. The thinker is anxious to move on to the next problem. If we do not accept the first solution as being adequate why should we accept the second? This could mean that we go on thinking with no point of satisfaction. Sir Robert Watson-Watt of radar fame had a saying: 'You get one idea today, a better idea tomorrow and the best idea . . . never'. Clearly there has to be a cut-off: there has to be a freezing of the design so that the action people (production etc.) can get to work. If we suspect that there may be a better solution then how can we have full confidence in the one we have just found? If we do not have the full confidence how can we inspire such confidence in those people we are encouraging to carry out the solution? We also suspect that a great deal of thinking effort may produce another solution but one that is only slightly better than the first one. Finally, we may genuinely believe that there can be no better solution.

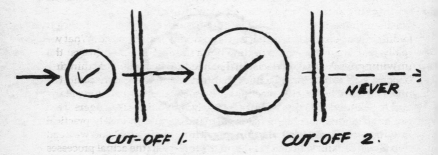

All these reasons for not thinking beyond the first solution are practical and realistic. Nevertheless there is no reason whatsoever for supposing that the first solution we come to must be the best. Thinking to solve a problem (the first type mentioned earlier in this piece) does not require a special effort of will since the problem is there as an ache, pain or need and we are naturally inclined to do something about it.

Thinking beyond the first adequate solution does require an effort of will, for it is no longer natural behaviour. The simplest way to make that effort of will is to have established a habit of some specific thinking time. Once such a 'thinking time' has been established as a habit then the agenda for that thinking time follows. It is on this agenda that thinking beyond an apparently satisfactory solution can find its place. After all, the thinking time is there to be used.

The other major use of specified thinking time is the third type of thinking: thinking around and about a situation or subject. In fact this is what most people would understand by 'thinking time' because problem solving of the ordinary type would be regarded as an ongoing part of normal work. Time for musing is when the thinker stands back from what is taking place in order to view it from different angles or in a broader perspective. Time spent in this fashion is regarded as an investment. From this time there may arise an important new insight or a specific idea. Or, there may be no more than a general preparation of the background, which may not seem significant at the time but which will pay dividends later when more focused thinking is being applied to the matter. Even at the least productive level, the time is still an investment. Nothing useful at all may have happened on this occasion – except for the maintenance of the thinking habit. But the maintenance of that habit and the exercise of thinking may give a valuable yield on future occasions.

Do we really ever waste time in thinking? We may pride ourselves on thinking quickly, and therefore slow thinking must seem to be a waste of time. But slow thinking is often much more valuable since it avoids the obvious clichés that can accompany fast thinking. What we really fear is not the waste of time but a number of other things: the unwillingness to make a decision that needs to be made; that thinking becomes an excuse for inaction; that further thinking may cloud the nice certainty of our first reactions. There is validity in all these fears, and to acknowledge this validity is largely to avoid these dangers. I am not at all against our being harsh, demanding and intensely practical in what we require from our thinking. Thinking is a tool and we need two levels of skill: skill that resides in the tool itself (the actual processes and techniques of thinking) and skill that is concerned with how and where we use the tool. It is this last type of skill that I am writing about in this piece. To set aside a definite time for thinking is part of this skill.

The edge effect

Imagine the outrage at a bank robbery in which three policemen were killed. On 5 January 1983 at Blackpool two policemen and a police-woman are believed to have died – all because of a dog. The man who owned the dog and the dog itself are also believed to have been drowned. It seemed that the dog got swept into the sea. The owner tried to rescue it and got into difficulty. The first policeman tried to rescue the owner and also got into difficulty – and so on.

The pressure on the dog owner to jump in to rescue his dog that was floundering a few feet from the shore must have been unbearable. So he jumped in. This is what we might call the 'edge effect', a term I first used in my book *Future Positive*. The edge effect arises from the precise circumstances of that moment – never mind long-term or even other broader considerations. A lump of ice melts at the edge – no matter how cold the centre may be kept. Actions that are seen to be quite unreasonable may take place because at each moment the action at that moment seems reasonable.

The edge effect can of course work both ways. It can work to cause an action to happen or to prevent an action from happening. For the moment we might consider how it works to make things happen. Consider a heavy steel ball placed on a foam rubber mat as shown in

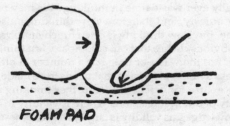

FOAM PAD

the drawing. If a finger is used to depress the rubber ahead of the ball then the ball will move across the mat. At each moment the ball rolls 'downhill' into the hole. There is no overall reason for the ball to roll across the mat, but at each moment there is a reason for the ball to roll a little bit forward into the dip that has been created just in front of it. Salesmen and negotiators are well aware of the power of the edge effect. A person who starts off with no intention whatever of buying an expensive life insurance policy ends up by buying one. Moment to moment the skilled salesman has edged the client forward by creating ahead of the client an attractive position. In exactly the same way as the steel ball was edged across the foam mat so the client is edged forward to complete the final purchase. In any negotiation the search is on to find 'local' attractions that will lead the other party forward to a new position.

In negotiating there is something of a dilemma. In the end what matters is the overall value of the package. This is especially so if the negotiator has to present the final result to others (a union leader to his men; a chairman to his shareholders). Yet during the actual negotiations the emphasis is on moment to moment activity of the edge effect type. An unskilled negotiator can find himself edged along and may have the impression that he is doing rather well. At the end, however, the unskilled negotiator is left with a package that does not look at all good when all the moment to moment attractions have been forgotten. Such a negotiator needs to keep reminding himself 'what is this going to look like in the final package?'.

In general, the edge effect means that the logic of the next step may not be the logic of the situation but the logic of the immediately preceding step that has been taken. In any conflict once the initial step has been taken the logic of the conflict takes over from the logic of the situation. Once the Falklands conflict had started then it was no longer the logic of the Falklands crisis (or of the awkward position of the islands) but simply the logic of a difficult operation. In a later letter I shall be writing about 'self-organising' information systems, but it is worth noting that the organisation or coherence of the situation may change sharply. History is full of instances where major events have come to be influenced by the local logic of the dislike of two negotiators for each other at a particular time and place. The coherence (or logic) of that animosity has created a special local situation and the main situation (which is what the negotiations were all about) takes second place.

A journey to a wonderful utopia may be completely inhibited by a deep ditch that prevents the very first step. This is a negative exercise of the edge effect. A union leader may agree in principle to a particular course of action but cannot see himself taking the very first step of explaining that course of action to his executive. A wife may really want to leave her husband but cannot see herself taking the very first step of telling him or the children that she wants to leave.

The negative effect of the edge effect may be considered in two ways. The first way is in the sense of a local barrier. That barrier, or ditch, has to be crossed, and if there is difficulty in crossing it then nothing can happen no matter how powerful the more distant attraction might be. The second way is to consider it in terms of the logic of the situation – as discussed earlier in this piece. A person acts according to the logic of the immediate situation. If, however, he succeeds in breaking out of that then he can enter the logic of a different situation.

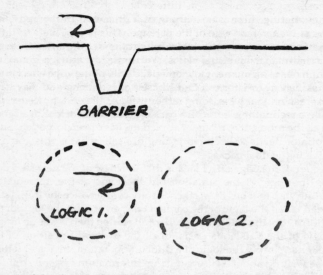

BARRIER

LOGIC 1.

LOGIC 2.

But until he breaks out he is always drawn back to the existing situation. For example a production-oriented company might have considerable difficulty turning itself into a marketing-oriented company because the people, culture and bases for decisions are all based on the previous logic.

It is always difficult for a person to believe that, if he escapes from the present logic of a situation, he will snap into the logic of another situation. It must always appear that to escape from the present logic will leave the thinker nowhere and floundering in a chaos. That belief is a barrier that creates a powerful negative edge effect.

Of what practical value is an awareness of the 'edge effect'?

1. Where you want to get something done and somehow it does not get done, even though everyone is agreed upon it. It is well worth looking for the negative edge effects: those moment-to-moment barriers and difficulties which may be providing the block. In designing options it is well worth giving some design attention to edge effects.

2. In trying to get done something which is initially unattractive or at best neutral, then a series of careful positive edge effects may achieve the result. Attention to these edge effects may be a better investment than trying to improve the total attraction.
3. A constant awareness of the difference between the local logic of the moment and the logic of the overall situation. The moment will pass but the overall situation will remain.
4. An awareness that taking a certain step may change the whole logic of the situation and may create a different logic (as with moving from a negotiating to a conflict logic). Note that this point appears contradictory to the previous point, but it is not really so. There are times when a step has only transient value. There are other times when a step takes the thinker to a totally different situation.

Far too often we assume that if something is good it is desirable, and if it is bad then it is undesirable. We forget that moment-to-moment logic (in the form of the edge effect) can completely reverse the basic values.

At this moment I am not writing about the moral considerations of whether the end justifies the means. That is a whole story in itself, and the general conclusion seems to be that one of the bases of civilisation is that the end does not justify the means. There are many who have argued otherwise, and such operations as the Spanish Inquisition no doubt had a local logic that excused behaviour that otherwise seemed inhuman. What I am writing about is the edge of action, the edge effect. What happens next when 'next' means the very next moment.

The thinking place

'I do not need a fur coat and have never really wanted one, but to see a fur coat reduced from £1,500 to £400 is irresistible'. No woman would be as honest as that during the January sales but that is the logic of such sales and the logic of bargain hunting. It is a classic example of the edge effect. The immediate logic overcomes the overall logic. Four hundred pounds is still four hundred pounds and, if you do not need a fur coat, then it is a wasted four hundred pounds. The logic of the moment is considerably enhanced by the knowledge that if you do not take the bargain immediately someone else will, with the result that you will be without the bargain and with the feeling that you let slip a wonderful opportunity.

Convenience is one of the most powerful edge effects. Some item of lesser value may exceed in sales another item because the first item is more convenient to use or to buy. Convenience is the most saleable of values. Only a very few people are prepared to put up with hassle and inconvenience. Inertia selling takes into full account that the bother of sending something back may be so great that the person keeps and pays for something he or she would never have set out to purchase. This is another classic example of the edge effect. Getting around to packing it up and posting it is too much trouble – at any moment in time.

Government regulations may be resented not because they are harsh or unjust but because they are inconvenient. Conversely deliberate inconvenience may be an effective way of deterring action.

In many Eastern bloc countries you queue to pay for an item you want and then you queue to get the item. Before that you may have had to queue to get a note of the price of the item with which to join the paying queue.

As an exercise it is worth looking around for examples of the operation of the edge effect. An easier version of this would be to look around (in the course of a day) for examples of inconvenience. What would be the effect if petrol could only be bought one gallon at a time? What would be the effect if petrol could only be bought five gallons at a time?

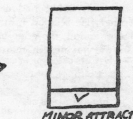

MINOR ATTRACTION

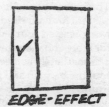

EDGE-EFFECT

Newspaper placard headlines and the feature titles on the cover of some women's magazines are good examples of the edge effect. They always sound more interesting than they really are. Yet the reader does not get disappointed; he or she has enjoyed the moments of hope. Packaging is another classic example but not a pure one. Packaging offers status, credibility and value that can last right through the use of the item. The image of a cigarette, perfume or confectionery is just as much part of its value as the actual ingredients. Inasmuch as packaging is the first indication of value then it partakes of the edge effect; inasmuch as the value is sustained it is not.

Mothers persuading younger children to do something the children do not want to do often use the edge effect in a most blatant way: 'Come here, I have something for you' (when the child is running away).

Airlines operate in a highly competitive market and their advertising is always focusing on some small item to distinguish them from the competition; a better steak, a little more leg room, prettier stewardesses and so on. This is not a use of the edge effect even if such items may tip a purchaser into choosing that airline. If, however, an airline offered to compensate you for every moment you had to wait at the ticket or check-in counter or guaranteed more people to answer telephones than any rival, then there would be genuine edge effects (i.e., they operate at the moment of making the purchase). An airline could offer an advantage (like ample overhead luggage space) which is really an edge effect that operates when a passenger comes to stow his luggage in the usually inadequate space.

Self-correction typewriters offer an example of a great convenience and an edge effect; what happens at the next moment after you have made an error?

Look around for further examples of the edge effect.

5

Think slowly

In this *Letter to Thinkers* I want to take further two points which I mentioned briefly in the preceding *Letter:* thinking slowly and point of satisfaction. There are few prizes for slowness. In fact I cannot think of any at all. Were I to claim that there were *no* prizes for slowness I am sure some reader would write to point out that I had overlooked some special situation in which there was indeed a prize for slowness (such as a slow bicycle race). There are many prizes for speed. Getting somewhere faster is important for horses, athletes, Grand Prix drivers and computer designers. In a way speed is almost synonymous with productivity: if the same thing is done in less time it seems obvious that there is a gain in productivity. In practice this is not always so, for example driving at a high speed may consume a greater amount of fuel over the same distance.

In general, 'fast' is a good word and 'slow' is a bad word. This is especially so when it comes to activities of the mind. We have the 'slow-witted' and we have the 'slow learner'. Someone who is slow in his or her thinking is deemed to be ponderous and dim. Fast and slow are classic examples of value-laden words. There are occasions when we do appreciate slowness over speed. We would be happy if the Parthenon were to deteriorate at a slower rate; we would prefer a slower increase in street crime; we might choose a slow puncture rather than a blowout. These examples only reinforce the negative value of the word 'slow'. We only appreciate it when we use it in a double negative situation: the slowing down of a negative process.

To advocate thinking slowly seems perverse and bizarre. The brighter people are always supposed to think quickly. The expression 'quick-witted' is a clear contrast of 'slow-witted'. There are emergencies when we suppose that only quick thinking will save our lives. There are negotiating traps which only the fast thinkers might be able to avoid. Quick thinking followed by a quick reply can turn the tables in the course of a confrontation. A problem may be turned into an opportunity by quick thinking.

We could list many situations in which quick thinking seems to be an obvious advantage. Some of these are not so clear cut. It is estimated that in hotel fires more people are killed as a result of panic reactions than by the fire. Is that an example of quick thinking?

Perhaps we should distinguish between a thinker who can only think slowly and a thinker who can think fast but chooses, at times, to think more slowly. Perhaps there should be a different word for the two sorts of slowness. There are the words 'careful' and 'deliberate', and perhaps I ought to use these words rather than the word 'slow'. But careful implies thinking that is cautious and risk free, and that is not what I mean. Deliberate thinking implies firm and definite steps, and that is not what I mean either. I mean thinking 'slowly'.

We might suppose that there are occasions when we have a limited amount of time and have to carry out a required amount of thinking. If we do not think fast then we feel we will never get it done. This is not a problem, for even slow thinking can take place at a very fast pace. It is well known that certain dreams that seem to take a long time may actually take no more than a few seconds. Under hypnosis a person may experience in a few seconds a series of events that can take up to half an hour just to recount.

Thinking slowly does not refer to external time. It is an attitude as much as anything else. The first part of the attitude is to get rid of the idea that thinking fast or being rushed is any sort of advantage. When a youngster is learning to catch a ball he will move his hand towards the catch very soon after the ball has left the hand of the thrower. The catcher may then have to correct the position of his hands when the ball gets nearer. Much later the catcher makes no move at all until the ball gets very close and then makes the minimal effort necessary. The good batsman seems to have a lot of time. The poor batsman is always rushed.

It is this sort of slowness that I am advocating. Imagine you see a shape in the distance. At once you may jump to some recognition. Alternatively you could list the features you see, almost leisurely, and then acknowledge the different possibilities. The young medical student wants to rush to a diagnosis and the sense of achievement it brings. The more experienced physician lists the signs and symptoms and then works more slowly towards the diagnosis.

Is the admonition to think slowly any more than a caution against jumping to conclusions? I believe it is. Thinking slowly means pausing to look backwards at what has been covered instead of just looking forward towards the destination. Thinking slowly means extracting the maximum from one's own thinking and the thinking of others. It is not unlike the dense reading I mentioned in a previous *Letter*.

Thinking slowly means pausing at many points to look around and see what options are available. If you drive fast you cannot read the different signposts. When driving you want to read the signposts to be aware of the directions you are not taking. Getting to a destination is important, but getting to a destination and having a good map of the terrain is even better.

Can slow thinking be crisp, clear and decisive, or is it just drift and waffle? Observe a surgeon in action. The good surgeon appears to be slow but actually take no more time that the surgeon who is always rushed. There are restaurants where a few waiters seem to be forever scrurrying around to cope with the number of tables. There are other restaurants where a single waiter seems to cope quite calmly with the same number of tables.

Consider one of my favourite problems. It is the one I used in the first programme in the BBC series ('de Bono's Thinking Course').

In a tank of water there is floating a tin tray. On the tray is a glass bottle filled up with water. Someone comes along and upsets the whole arrangement. The glass bottle and the tray are both completely submerged under the water. Does this upsetting of the tray and bottle cause the level of water in the tank, taken at the side of the tank, to go up or to go down – or does the level remain unchanged?

Fast Thinker Since this is obviously a trick question and de Bono is putting it to me, I imagine he wants me to look stupid by saying that the level goes up. I shall say it stays the same. In any case this seems reasonable since the bottle and tray floating on the water must have pushed it up at the edge.

Slow Thinker After the upset the bottle, its contained water, and the tray are displacing water – so the level might be expected to rise. But what was happening when they were floating? They must have been displacing water too. Was this the same amount of water? When they were floating it could only have been the 'weight' of the bottle, contained water, and tray that displaced the water. After the upset it is the volume of the bottle, contained water and tray that displace water. Since the bottle and tin tray sink they must be heavier than water. So their weight displaces more water than their volume. So the water level goes down at the side of the tank. The water contained in the bottle is irrelevant since its weight displacement and volume displacement are exactly the same.

Had there been only two options the fast thinker would have been right. As there is a third option the fast thinkers tend to get it wrong. That is very often the trouble with thinking fast. It is much more difficult to see the options.

Point of satisfaction

Why does a thinker stop thinking? Occasionally this is obvious. If a schoolchild is asked to solve a mathematical problem and succeeds in doing so then there is an obvious point of satisfaction. But this 'obviousness' is not always as obvious as it seems. If you are asked to figure out a way of getting from A to B, do you stop thinking as soon as you have figured out that way?

I once had to get to St Tropez for a meeting. All the flights to Nice were full. Clever people thought of clever routings such as going via Paris, Amsterdam, Zurich and even Rome. Somehow the flights were still full. The solution was simple: fly from London to Marseilles. The flight was only half full and the drive not much longer. The trouble was that Nice and St Tropez were both regarded as Riviera destinations. Marseilles is regarded as a port and nothing to do with the Riviera. In this case perception and geography were not aligned.

Unfortunately life does not consist of mathematical problems laid out as in a school textbook. There may be a well defined problem, but this does not mean that the first solution that turns up is the best one. Logically there is no reason at all to suppose that the first solution must be the best. In practice we are inclined to take this first solution for a variety of practical reasons.

- There is a list of other problems that await our attention.
- There is a time pressure to find any solution at all.
- We suspect that other possible solutions might only be marginally better and yet require a lot of effort in their finding.
- In order to get others to work on the solution, we must have full confidence that it is the best one. To suppose that there might be a better one destroys that confidence and provides nothing in place if we do not find a better solution.
- Another solution might take a long time to find.
- If we are not happy with the first solution, why should we be happy with the next – we could go on for ever?

We need to acknowledge the practicality of these attitudes. There are times of urgency when an immediate solution is better than a delayed one. There are times when we have to 'freeze' the design in order to get on with implementing it.

Nevertheless we should not be too easily satisfied.

In problem solving we tend to think in terms of the major objective. We tend to imagine the solution we want to find. All else is a matter of factors, constraints and considerations. When we have found the solution we want, we do tend to try to square that solution with the other factors. Only too often this is a matter of forced fit. We have found as sales manager a man with the right experience and knowledge of the market. It is too bad that he is difficult to get on with and wants more salary than we had envisaged – but we can live with these drawbacks.

The drawing suggests two alternative approaches. In the first one we go for the main objective of our thinking, and then assess whether we can live with the rather poorer fit with the surrounding factors. In the second alternative all the factors have become objectives and our solution must achieve an all-round fit. Clearly this second version is likely to be too idealistic. Are we likely to find the sales manager with experience, a wonderful personality and at the price we had in mind? The next point is concerned with how hard we are prepared to look for this paragon – or do we settle for something less? There is another alternative and this is to redesign our requirements so that we reduce the number of factors we have to fit – and still go for a complete fit.

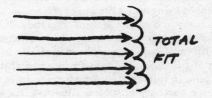

Trade-offs are an inevitable part of 'point of satisfaction'. Should we make trade-offs after we have found a more -or-less adequate solution? This is a way of adjusting our problem to the available solution. Or, should we make trade-offs in the solution requirements when our first set of requirements proves too idealistic? This second approach seems to me to make far more sense. The wonderful sales manager who is impossible to work with could well disrupt the whole sales department.

There is almost an aesthetic quality about 'point of satisfaction'. A scientist searches for the elegant explanation. A mathematician searches for the elegant method. There is a feeling that simplicity is a worthwhile objective. There is a feeling that processes are ultimately simple, and that as we approach the truth matters get more and more simple. Einstein's famous formula relating mass to energy has that feeling of ultimate simplicity.

It is easy to see the appeal of simplicity as far as science or mathematics goes, but does it apply to other areas – for example business matters? In business the underlying forces may be highly complex rather than simple. So on this point there is no direct equivalence to the science situation. Simplicity still implies robustness, ease of understanding, ease of implementation, fewer things to go wrong. All these are very attractive, especially if many people are going to have to work with the idea.

I suspect, however, that the intellectual appeal of simplicity may sometimes be misleading . It would be more aesthetically satisfying to have an all-electric car. But in practice this may never happen, unless we are prepared to go for a hybrid petrol-electric car first. This route may be more practical and, once the market has developed, then the research effort devoted to batteries and other aspects of the electric car may be sufficient to bring about the pure version.

No-one likes fussy or complex designs, and they are often examples of poor architecture or poor engineering. There is no reason, however, why the same idioms should apply to human affairs. In fact, there may be a fundamental difference. In engineering and architecture we have to solve a problem. In human affairs we have to solve the underlying problem – but we also have to solve a situation. The situation is the state of the parties considering the problem, and this may be a locked-in confrontation. So the solution has to serve both purposes. A solution which only solved the underlying problem may have no chance of acceptance. To solve the 'situation' aspect, concessions may have to be designed to save face or to show some gain – and this leads to complexity.

This failure to distinguish different types of situation may be why business executives, scientists and engineers have traditionally not made good politicians. In one idiom there is a search for the direct, simple and effective, whereas in the other the search is for the acceptable (in line with the old saying that politics is the art of the possible).

In practice there are a number of questions the thinker can bring to mind as appropriate:

What would I be satisfied with? (including the redesign of requirements)
Am I satisfied with this?
Why am I not satisfied with this?
At how many levels does the solution have to work?

The thinking place

We have carried out a pilot programme in San Francisco for the training of 5,000 teachers in the use of the Cognitive Research Trust Thinking lessons that now form the largest project in the world for the direct teaching of thinking in schools. In a future *Letter* I shall discuss what has been happening. In Venezuela, for example, 106,000 teachers have been trained and, by law, every schoolchild in the country has to have two hours a week of thinking skills. In San Francisco the pilot project involved an initial number of teachers. I was in San Francisco talking to the person who had been organising the training of the teachers and who had attended the training sessions. He told me how he had been listening to a radio talk about the problem of funding the US Social Security system. He had heard the talker say: 'There can only be two ways of setting about this . . .'. Immediately the listener had said to himself: 'Hold on! Are there really only two ways, or is it just that he can only think of two ways?'. The listener attributed this attitude to the effect of the exposure to the thinking lessons.

In Sydney, Australia, I was giving a two-day seminar on lateral thinking. There was someone there (from the DP world) who belonged to the group that believe that ideas do not really matter for, if you collect all the facts and process them with the right computer analysis, you can get all the decisions and designs you need. At the end of the second morning, after the coffee break, this person came to me with a totally changed attitude. The story he told was as follows:

'For 35 years I have been drinking coffee. I always put two packets of sugar in my coffee. This morning, without even thinking about it, I found myself placing one packet over the other and opening them both simultaneously with one tear. This is much more efficient than my previous habit of opening each packet in turn. If lateral thinking can make me do better something that I have been doing in the same way for 35 years (when I am not even focusing on that matter, and also resisting the ideal of lateral thinking) then there must be something in it.'

Both these are examples of what I call the background effect of interest in thinking as a process. *There are changes in attitude and changes in behaviour, even when the thinker is not consciously applying some technique and not consciously following some precept.*

Thinking is a set of skills, habits, attitudes, intentions, perceptions, techniques and so on. The big jump is to move away from regarding it as a natural part of one's own intelligence, towards regarding it as a matter of skill, habit, attitude etc. I shall be dealing in a later *Letter* with the problems of the 'Intelligence trap' which I regard as the single most dangerous and damaging fallacy in education.

What I am looking for is not a fierce condemnation of one's thinking abilities: 'Wasn't I stupid there', 'Why did I not look for an alternative?' etc. I would much rather a sort of quiet and affectionate look at one's own thinking: 'Curious that I should have jumped to that conclusion', 'Interesting that I found it so difficult to see his logic bubble', 'That is

61

obvious in hindsight; what was blocking me from seeing if before?'.

Quite recently I was waiting on the platform for an underground train on the Victoria Line in London. An announcement said that this line was not operating at the moment, and would passengers seek an alternative route to their destination. I went back to the upper level and then went down the escalator to the Jubilee Line. It was only when I got to the platform that I realised I could have moved directly from the Victoria to the Jubilee Line without having to go back all the way to the surface level. It just did not occur to me. Since I had to change my routing, it seemed natural to go back to the starting point in order to do so. I did not feel foolish – just a curious observer of the patterning nature of the mind. Had I followed my own precept of thinking 'slowly' I might have gone through the following process:

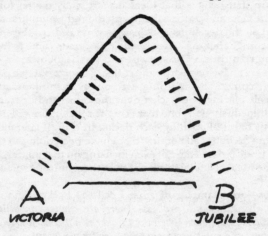

'I need another route. Can I get another route from this station? Yes. How do I get on to that other route? By going back to the surface level. How else might I get there? If people are changing from one line to another they do not always have to go back to the surface level. Let's see if there is connecting tunnel.'

I like to set tasks for thinkers in this section of the *Letter*. Try to observe your own thinking. Try also to notice whether there has been any background change in your thinking since you have begun to take a more direct interest in it.

6

Levels of alternative

If you ask someone who has had a little bit of training in creativity to improve an umbrella, you are likely to get the reply: 'Why do we need an umbrella at all – is there some other way of keeping the rain off?' This reply does make sense – but only on one level. If you are in the business of making umbrellas and want to continue in that business then you may want to make improvements within the general concept of umbrellas rather than moving clean away from them. You may even want to invest some of your thinking in finding a completely different approach to protection from the rain – but the rest of it in improving umbrellas more or less as we know them. Consider the following levels of alternative:

- a small improvement in the design of the pivot joints
- a way of reducing the number of ribs
- a system of raising the canopy without using ribs
- a totally different concept of umbrella
- rain protection without using umbrellas

Creativity can be applied at any of these levels. It is a mistake to assume that creativity can only be used at the most fundamental level.

Three basic levels
Imagine that we are considering the problem of traffic congestion in cities. One way to tackle this might be to attempt to reduce the number of cars in the city – which might be expected to reduce the congestion. In order to achieve that reduction we might choose to discourage drivers from entering the city. We now have our starting point (as the defined problem); we have our destination (reduction of cars in the city) and we even have our means of getting from one to the other. We now seek out alternative ways of implementing the chosen approach.

We might only allow in cars with an even licence number on one day and odd licence numbers the following day and so on alternately (as they do in Lagos). Another way might be to charge a special extra licence fee for entry into the city before a certain hour (as they do in

Singapore). A third way might be to do very little about providing parking facilities in the hope that motorists would get discouraged and stop driving into town (as they do in some US cities). There would be other alternatives as well.

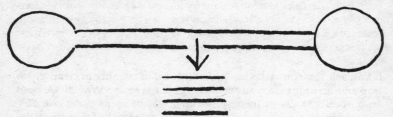

At the next level of alternative the starting point and the destination might be the same. But this time there is a choice of routes in getting there. We still want to reduce traffic. One way is to discourage drivers (the way we have seen). Another way might be to encourage car sharing. I once suggested that each driver might get as part of his registration package a 'day of the week disc'. On that day he would be a privileged driver in town. He might park at meters without paying,

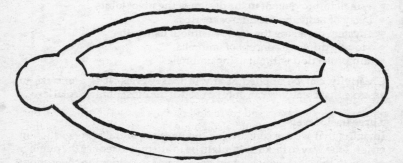

traffic fines would be reduced and there might even be special free parking places. The idea is that one commuter might get a Monday disc, his neighbour a Tuesday disc and another neighbour a Wednesday disc. There would be an incentive to share cars and so overall traffic might be reduced. Another alternative might be an education campaign to show how much quicker and more economical public transport really was. Another way might be to provide 'edge effect' incentives to get motorists at least to try public transport (on the basis that if they tried it they might find out how convenient it was).

These are all alternative ways of reducing traffic quite distinct from 'discouraging drivers'.

The third level of alternative is to alter the destination itself. In both previous instances the destination was the same: the reduction of traffic. At this third level we might try for some alternative destinations or objectives. We might say: how can we make congestion more tolerable. Or, we might say: how can we ensure that public transport and essential service vehicles are not caught up in the congestion –

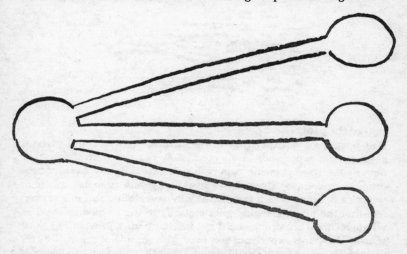

and then leave the motorists to sort themselves out. This could lead to the idea of special bus and service lanes. Immediately we would return to the first level and try to find practical ways of designing bus and service lanes. We could also go to the second level to try to find other ways (other than the special lanes) to protect buses and service vehicles from the general congestion. Elevated roads might be an answer.

It is the ability to realise at what level one is thinking that matters. And then the ability to flit between one level and another at will. The levels might be summarised as follows:

Level 3: choosing alternative destinations or objectives
Level 2: destination is fixed – choosing alternative routes to get there
Level 1: both destination and route are fixed – choosing alternative ways of using the route (alternative ways of implementing the chosen approach).

Design styles

Imagine that you are set the task of designing an advertising campaign for a new chewing gum. Let us assume that this chewing gum is new in some ways but not in any outstanding way which would form the basis for the advertising campaign. Your style of approach to this design task might take one of the basic forms outlined here.

Seat of the pants

You have a lot of experience in the advertising world and perhaps even special experience in the confectionery field. Even if you have never advertised chewing gum before you are certainly aware of how other people have advertised it in the past and probably aware of those campaigns which were unusually successful. You might even feel that the major chewing gum makers are still in business and so whatever they are doing could not be that bad. You would let your seat-of-the-pants experience take over. You would not consciously try to work things out, but would absorb yourself in the task and just wait for ideas to start emerging. Sometimes this seat-of-the-pants (derived from the notion of flying an aircraft by sensing the reactions of the plane through the seat of the pants) approach is called hunch or intuition. In all cases it means the bringing together of experience, feelings and judgements that may be too vague or too complex to be verbalised. When you recognise a friend at the airport you do not do so by measuring the distance between that person's eyes and adding in the length of the nose. Recognition is based on a general impression which takes all these features – and many more – into account in a sort of 'holistic' (fashionably called 'right brain') way. People pride themselves on this type of approach and often regard it as the equivalent of talent. It is probably true that the judgement aspect of this hunch or intuition is invaluable. There may be no other way of sensing whether something is going to work. There may be no other way of telling how people are going to respond to an advertisement. But this 'judgement' quality may not be the same as the 'design' quality. Hunch based designs may be fine or they may be disastrous.

Comparison
Here the designer looks around, consciously or unconsciously, for an advertising campaign for a product that is similar but not too similar. There is a search for a type of approach that could be applied to the chewing gum without any fear that it would be regarded as a direct copycat approach. Suppose that the 'Pedigree Chum' approach was used. Testimonials would be sought from well known people. It

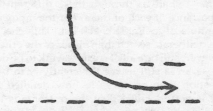

would have to be credible, however, that these people were gum chewers. It would also be difficult with the introduction of a new gum: unless the effect of a trial or tasting was used. This search for a related basic approach is the basis of most problem solving. That is how we consciously get to apply acquired experience to a new situation. Whether we like it of not, we are most of the time looking for comparisons. In the advertising world talent may lie in recognising an appropriate but somewhat remote comparison and effecting the transfer. In other fields the effective tackling of the design problem is what matters. In the advertising world there is the additional need to demonstrate originality and the creative ego. Whether this has any special selling power can be argued.

Attention areas
This could also be called the check-list method. The designer would have a simple check-list of matters towards which he or she needed to direct attention. In the design of more tangible objects such a check-list might include: suitability of materials; costs; production methods

etc. Although these are judgement criteria they need to be brought into mind at the design stage. One very broad principle of design is to look at the constraints and specifications and then to design something to fit. In the advertising world a few broad headings might suffice. Each individual has his or her own check-list. One possible check-list might include the following broad headings:

VISIBILITY: catching attention and being noticed.
DESIRABILITY: a good feeling and why anyone should want it.
CREDIBILITY: that what was claimed was true and not hype.

In a later *Letter* I shall go through these different headings and explore the importance of each of them. For the moment, I am using them as an example of a simple check-list. This check-list method involves a more deliberate search than either of the other approaches. There may, however, still be a lot of creative work to be done. Directing attention to these areas still leaves the creativity to be done in the areas. The question then arises as to how detailed the check-list should be. If it is very detailed then the outcome is likely to seem artificial and contrived in the same way as a camel is said to be a horse designed by a committee with a check-list of needs (actually a camel is a pretty good design – as was the dinosaur which lasted for 40 million years).

The check-list may, of course, be applied after any of the other approaches have produced a preliminary design. It is then used as a judgement or 'improving' strategy.

Single line
This could be call the 'inspiration' approach. It is also the way lateral thinking works. There is some single concept which is then used for its 'movement' value'. For example, with the chewing gum, the single concept might be that gum would stop people from talking. Clearly this cessation of talk would have to been seen to be either humorous or beneficial (to someone). The search would now be directed to the finding of such situations. It might be a husband about to complain

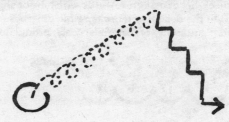

about his wife's cooking. It might be a highwayman about to demand money. It might be a cricket umpire about to give someone out as l.b.w. It might be a judge about to pronounce judgement in court. In all these cases the 'strength' of the chewing gum as 'gum' would be suggested – and with it connotations of being good stuff. The next problem would be the getting of the gum into the right mouths at the right time. This may lead on to a concept of a 'gum gun' which was a special magic device that would shoot the gum though an open mouth – with deadly aim.

In this way the basic theme would be extended out further and further. When it had reached a point that seemed interesting the task would now become one of bringing the idea back to reality so that it would serve as a useful advertisment.

It is perfectly possible to use combinations of these different styles. Indeed some people would claim to use all of them at once. It may also be that different situations demand a different approach. It is, however, useful to be aware of the four basic styles – and to note which particular style you use yourself.

The thinking place

Alternatives

As an exercise put down (on a piece of paper) alternatives for each of the words given in the list below:

CAKE	MONEY	SPIDER
RED	HOLIDAY	JOB
BICYCLE	SMOOTH	CLEAR
UMBRELLA	HAMMER	

It is suggested that you do not read further until you have at least made some attempt to put down alternatives to these given words. When you look back over your alternatives you will find that, although the instruction to find an alternative is clear enough, the result seems to cover many things. As an alternative to 'smooth' many people put 'rough'. In a sense this is an 'opposite' though it could be said to be an alternative 'type of surface'. The same can happen for clear (where we might get 'confused', 'foggy' and 'unclear'). For 'cake' we might get 'bread' as an alternative member of the carbohydrate group – and perhaps influenced by the famous Marie Antoinette story. For 'bicycle' we might get 'car' or 'motorcycle' as alternative forms of transport. If, however, the lack of a motor is seen to be important we might get 'walking'. It can go further. If a bicycle is seen as a transport device which uses simple mechanical means to increase man's power of movement then the alternative may be a pair of roller skates. Against 'money' we may find 'credit-cards' as a way of carrying out the money function without actually using money. The use of something else to

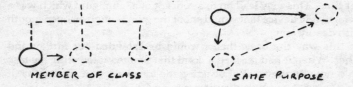

MEMBER OF CLASS   SAME PURPOSE

achieve the same purpose is one of the easiest ways to get an alternative. So against 'hammer' we may find a 'brick' or a 'stone' as a way of banging in nails. On the other hand someone may have put down 'screwdriver' as an alternative member of the class of 'carpenter's tools'. The same thing applies to the word 'red'. The most usual alternative is to give another primary colour such as 'blue'. A few people see 'red' as performing a warning function and so many suggest a buzzer or other alarm sound. 'Holiday' and 'job' are quite difficult. Most people usually take one aspect. For example, 'voluntary work' is seen as an alternative since it is work – but without pay. 'Business travel' is sometimes put as an alternative to 'holiday' because there is the element of travel but not the enjoyment. With 'spider' we may get another type of insect, or we may get another type of phobia such as 'snake'.

In this matter there is not really a 'right' or 'wrong' answer. It is all a matter of how you look at it. When we are asked for an alternative we set a simple framework in our minds. The frame might be: 'an alternative which carries out the same function' or, it might be 'an alternative member of this class of things'. It could be argued that the two are really the same since a member of the same class may be assumed to carry out the same function. This may be so but the mental route is different – since in the second case the function need not be defined (what is the function of a primary colour?). Opposites seem to be a special case, although we can construct a sentence in which an opposite is seen as an alternative quality.

7

Being negative

As readers of this *Letter* might suppose, this piece is likely to be negative about being negative. In many of my books I write against negativity. So I shall try to be fair here.

If we believe in a sort of Darwinian evolution of ideas, then being negative has a strong place. Negativity would then provide the hostile environment in which only the fittest of ideas would survive. It would follow that these ideas were best fitted to the environment just as surviving animals are best fitted to their environment. Here we come to an interesting point. To what environment are the surviving ideas best fitted? If it is the hostile environment of negativity then only the most bland of ideas are likely to survive. Being on the side of mother-hood and angels is a reasonable protection against criticism. If negativity is directed against change then the surviving ideas will best fit the existing framework. By definition such ideas will be unlikely to change frameworks.

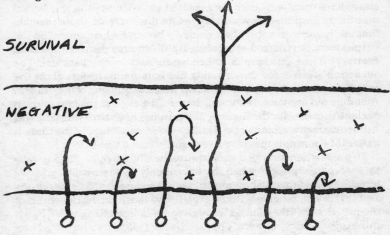

SURVIVAL

NEGATIVE

FERTILE

So the purpose of negativity could be to provide the hostile environment that might ensure the Darwinian evolution of the best ideas. There is another purpose for negativity. This is the positive purpose of seeking to improve the idea by removing its weaknesses, or at least focusing upon them so that the designer of the idea can improve these aspects. It is not often that negativity has this constructive intention. It does not, however, matter what the intention might be, provided the person receiving the negativity chooses to treat it as constructive. I have always felt that negativity of this sort is a vote of confidence in the thinker just as excessive wage demands are a vote of confidence in a management that is then expected to make enough money to pay those wages.

Then there is the Hegelian view. From a clash of thesis and antithesis a marvellous new idea is supposed to arise through a process of synthesis. It is not clear whether this synthesis combines the best elements of both ideas or whether, in the chaos that follows the clash, both ideas disintegrate into their separate elements, and from this soup of chaos a new idea forms itself. In practical terms a clash of this sort seems to freeze and crystallise the opposing ideas instead of loosening their coherence.

It has long been the aim of education to promote the critical intelligence. Debate and argument are much encouraged. Scoring points and claiming victory is the aim of debate. It is claimed that the triumphant view is the correct view. This is because it is logically more consistent with both feelings and knowledge. It is also hoped that the triumphing view will lay before the audience those insights that allow them to apply their ready-to-be-applied emotions. So the suspicion must remain that debating is a skill (rather than an intellectual exercise) if the outcome is to be determined by the listeners. The attraction we feel for the debating mode is partly historical. In the Middle Ages the thinkers of the world were the thinkers of the Church. All educated men were educated by the Church, and the best of them became thinkers for the Church. The purpose of Church thinking was – quite correctly – to preserve the doctrine and theology of the Church in the face of innovators who were usually called heretics.

To prove a heretic wrong was to prove the Church right. Theoretically this would only apply when there were only two mutually exclusive hypotheses, so that disproving one would ensure the other (assuming also that one or other was necessary). It says much for the cleverness of the heretics that they forced through some radical changes in Church thinking. St Augustine was opposed by the Donatists who forced him into one corner after another. Often he could only extract himself by inventing some new theological entity. It was in this manner that 'Divine Grace' and 'predestination' came about. It could also be said that in such cases the heretics forced an insight by focusing on areas that had not hitherto been subjected to focused thinking. As in so many other instances, we here see negativity in defence of the status quo. 'If you wish me to change, prove to me that what I am doing needs changing.'

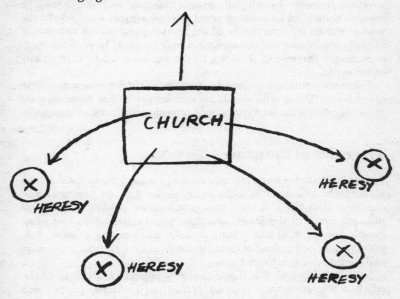

In practice these intellectual justifications for negativity tend to be less important than the emotional justifications. To prove someone wrong means that you are superior to that other person. To agree with another person makes your individuality superfluous. It also makes you a follower. Being negative gives an intellectual sense of achievement that cannot be equalled by more constructive attitudes. If you succeed in proving someone wrong there is an immediate and complete achievement. Contrast this with the putting forward of a constructive idea. With a constructive idea there are two possibilities. The first is that you must show that the offered idea does work. Instant proof is usually only possible in mathematics, occasionally, with insight. In other cases it may take weeks or years before the suggested idea can be shown to work. If the value of the idea cannot be demonstrated instantly then a person offering the idea has to hope that the listener will like it. It is rather like telling a joke: if the listener does not think it funny then no joke has been told. That is a weak position to find oneself in. *Just as a criminal does not want to be dependent on either market or investors for his success, so many brilliant minds do not enjoy the risks of being constructive.*

Outside the world of business, defence is the most consistent survival strategy. In religion, science, politics and art, it may be enough to defend an existing point of view against all attack. In the world of business the reality of the market place makes defence an inadequate intellectual strategy. That may be why I have found more exploratory interest in thinking in the business world than in any other world.

There are virtures in negativity, but most of them can be achieved in other ways. Those who should be encouraged to use negativity are those who find it the least appealing, both emotionally and intellectually.

The rules of the game

People learn dance steps and make a point of sticking to them. Chess players do not expect to make those moves that are permissible in checkers (draughts). A child may watch other children play a complicated game in the street, and then join in and follow the rules. People are not at all bad at learning rules and keeping to them. Role playing may be a matter of learning the rules for a particular situation and then sticking to those rules.

It is probably true that if you change a person's attitude he or she will be a better thinker. It is probably true that if you change a person's character that person will behave differently – in thinking as well as elsewhere. It is probably true that increasing a person's confidence and motivation will make that person less of a negative thinker. There are people and training courses that have set out to do this in the past ('T' groups and sensitivity training) and there are training approaches that today pursue the same line. They probably have some degree of success where the whole culture of an organisation can be changed – and less success where only a handful of people get changed (and revert back to their former selves when returned to their former environment).

There is another way to get a change. This is to create new rules for the game (or even new games) instead of trying to change the nature of the player. The rules can be quite mechanical and even arbitrary. An architecture student may be encouraged always to look first at the main door of a building – so that his eye can then move from a point of detail to the over-all shape. This rule may be accepted and practised as an arbitrary rule. In time it become a habit.

One of the fundamental idioms in lateral thinking is the idiom of 'movement'. I shall be dealing with this idiom on many occasions in future *Letters*. At the moment I just want to use it as an example of how a change of 'rule' can make a difference to a person's thinking. The 'movement' idiom is defined to contrast with the 'judgement' idiom. *Judgement is always the first stage in perception: can I identify the pattern; does this correspond with an existing pattern?* There are various approaches to creativity that talk about 'suspending judgement' or deferring judgement'. I find this approach must too weak. Telling someone not to do something is weak. It is much better to give the thinker something else to do instead of using judgement. This is where 'movement' comes in.

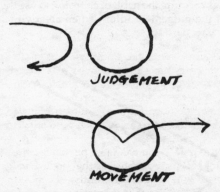

Judgement is used to decide whether an idea fits experience: whether the idea is right or wrong. If it is wrong we label it as such and then reject it or seek to alter it. With the movement idiom we operate outside the judgement system. We use an idea for its 'movement value': we use the idea to see where it takes us. It is not that we treat bad ideas as good ideas. We do not even bother to judge whether an idea is good or bad – we just use the movement value of the idea. If we cannot hold ourselves back from judgement, then we can label the idea as bad but still decide to use that idea for its movement value.

Someone may come to us with an idea that we do not like.

Nevertheless we can use that idea for its movement value. We can even treat a deliberately provocative idea for its movement value.

'Po planes should land upside down' is a deliberate provocation (the word 'po' indicates provocative operation). When offered this provocation someone immediately commented that 'the pilot would get a much better view'. This led to a consideration of the optimal positioning for a pilot. Had pilots remained in the same relative position to the plane ever since planes were very small (and the pilot naturally sat on top)? The same provocation also led to the notion of 'positive landing' by means of a retractable inverted wing which gave downward 'lift' toward the ground (perhaps achieving a more sensitive landing). Several other ideas came from this provocation.

It is not my intention here to go into the nature of either provocation or the movement idiom. What I do want to do is to illustrate that once the 'movement' idiom is provided as a 'rule' then a thinker may be asked to use an idea for its movement value. The personality of the thinker need not be changed in any way. Just as the architecture student may get into the habit of always looking first at the main door, so the thinker might acquire the habit of choosing to use the movement idiom instead of the judgement idiom when creativity seems to be required.

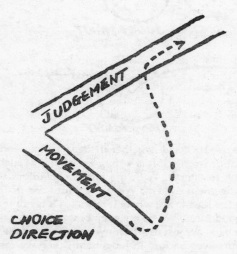

In driving a car we have a choice of gears (provided the car has manual rather than automatic gears). There are two learning stages. We have to know how to use the gears. We also need to know *when* to use them. The latter type of learning is the most similar to the learning of rules in a game. Rules involve an exercise of will – at least until they become a matter of routine. *Using an idea for its movement value is not natural behaviour until after it has become natural behaviour.* Judgement is natural behaviour. Just as a motorist knows that he has a choice of gears, so the thinker knows that he has a choice of idioms: judgement or movement. Sometimes the situation itself makes clear which idiom is to be used. When a provocation is as obviously a provocation as the notion of a plane landing upside down – then, clearly, movement rather than judgement is demanded. If, however, the suggested idea was: 'We should lower fares in order to encourage business travel by air' then the listener could well snap straight into the judgement mode. Alternatively, he might have trained himself to react in the movement mode first.

In the large schools programme that I run, the first lesson focuses on a tool that I shall introduce later in these *Letters*. The tool is the P.M.I. and it gets the children to look first at the 'Plus' points, then at the 'Minus' points and, finally, at the 'Interesting' points. Children learn the rules of this game – as they do with other games.

The thinking place

I was recently having lunch in Montecito (part of Santa Barbara, California) when I was told the following story by Bob Fitzgerald. He grows avocados and also keeps two dogs. One of the dogs became very fond of avocado pears and was in the habit of eating them when he was not supposed to. The other dog showed not the slightest interest in avocados. One day an avocado pear, liberally sprinkled with cayenne pepper, was placed so that the avocado-eating dog might notice it. The avocado-eating dog did indeed notice it and took a bite. He did not like the taste at all, so he left most of the pear behind. Along came the other dog and took a bite. He found it delicious and gobbled it all up. As a result Bob Fitzgerald now has two dogs that are addicted to avocados.

What are the morals that may be drawn from this story?

1. That obvious strategies may turn out to be counter-productive.
2. That dogs, like people, are unpredictable.
3. That if you make something spicy enough at first bite you might entrain a buyer (the edge-effect I have mentioned before in this *Letter to Thinkers*).

Stories and metaphors are most useful for carrying lessons and principles. There is much more appeal than with a simple statement of an abstract point. A story is much easier to remember. Metaphors are not meant to be extended or worked over in detail. Once the point has been made it floats free and must be challenged as such. The metaphor is only the 'carrying case'. Destroying the metaphor does not destroy the principle. Occasionally there is a delight when exactly the same story can be used to illustrate an opposite principle. See if this can be done with the avocado story.

A good story – no matter how amusing – never proves a point in an argument. Nevertheless a story can show a type of relationship or process which then becomes a possibility. Once it has been thought a 'thought' cannot be unthought.

Ordinary language is rather poor at describing complex processes and relationships. It is much better at describing things. We are beginning to inject into language 'function' words which do manage to convey functions. Such words as 'threshold effect', 'take-off point' and 'win-win situations' are a step in this direction. Some people are inclined to dismiss such words as jargon – which they may sometimes be – but there is a usefulness in a higher order language which allows us to deal with processes as well as things. As I wrote above, once the possibility of a certain type of interaction is raised then that possibility must be considered.

To say that 'this is a threshold type of investment' means that nothing might happen for quite a while; there is nothing to be seen; then – when the threshold has been exceeded – it all begins to happen. In other types of situation the same thought might be expressed with the term 'critical mass' (this suggests that nothing happens until there are enough interactions for an explosive effect to take place).

So there is a spectrum from words to 'function' words to metaphor and on to stories. What I like about stories is that the listener can see not only the obvious meaning but also other levels of meaning.

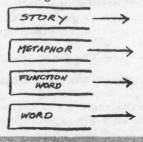

8

The PMI

I am going to describe what the PMI does before I explain what the letters stand for. The PMI is a deliberate thinking tool. I want to emphasise this point. Improvements in thinking skill can be brought about by changes in attitude: for example the habit of looking at every problem as an opportunity. Improvements can also follow through the avoidance of mistakes, once a type of mistake has been pointed out. For example, in one of my books (*Practical Thinking* – published in Penguin books) I describe the 'Village Venus' effect: the villagers in a remote village cannot conceive that there can exist a girl more beautiful than their Village Venus (concepts and alternatives are limited by our lack of imagination). With the PMI there is a tool that can be used deliberately. The thinker can set out 'to do a PMI'. The thinker can ask someone else to 'do a PMI'. The PMI is a defined task. Thus there can be the matter that is to be considered, and the thinking operation that is going to be performed. For example, the reader may set himself, or herself, the task of doing a PMI on the suggestion that there should be a flat tax rate with no exceptions and allowances.

Two-stage thinking
With something like the PMI thinking becomes a two-stage process.

The first stage is deciding to do the PMI. The second stage is carrying out the PMI procedure. It requires skill to choose an appropriate tool. It requires skill to use that tool effectively. Instead of the thinkers 'just thinking about the matter', the thinker has a task to perform.

When the thinking is taking place in a group, one thinker can ask another to 'do a PMI on this matter'. The thinker on the receiving end of this request is now going to be tested on how well he, or she, performs the required thinking task. It is no longer just a matter of 'tell me what you think', for it may now become a matter of 'let me see how well you can do a PMI on this'.

The 'intelligence trap'

I have referred to the 'intelligence trap' in previous *Letters*. A person with a high IQ is not necessarily a good thinker. Thinking is the 'skill' with which innate intelligence is used – not just the operation of an innate intelligence. The intelligence trap has many components. One of the most common components is the way a highly intelligent person will use his, or her, intelligence to defend a point of view. The more skilled the thinker is in defending that point of view the less does there seem to be any need actually to explore the subject. So a well defended prejudice becomes a substitute for a proper exploration followed by a judgement (or decision). Decisions that by-pass exploration are usually based on emotion: 'I do not like this . . . now let me tell you why'; 'this idea will not work . . . and I will prove to you why it won't work'; 'this is the obvious course of action to take . . . and this is why'.

Because of this natural tendency amongst thinkers at all levels, the PMI is put as the first of the thinking lessons that we teach in schools. I was once asked to run a demonstration class at a school in Sydney, Australia. The class consisted of 30 boys aged between 11 and 12 years old. I was to demonstrate the use of the PMI as a 'thinking tool'. I asked the boys how many of them liked the idea that 'every schoolboy should be given $5 a week for going to school': a sort of education wage. All 30 of the boys raised their arms in approval. They reckoned they would be able to buy sweets, chewing gum, comics and all the other items that mattered to boys of this age. As might have been expected there was an instant assessment of the suggestion. This triggered an emotion which then determined the point of view. I now explained the PMI – taking about three minutes to do so. The boys then sat together in groups of five and deliberately applied the PMI procedure. I want to make it very clear that I, myself, took no part at all in this thinking. I did not offer suggestions. Nor did I call their attention to the consequences of their decision. I had simply explained the 'tool' and now I stood back as the boys used it. At the end of four minutes, the boys reported their thinking back to me. There was a suggestion that the bigger boys might beat up the smaller boys in order to take the money. It was felt that the school might raise its charges for meals or other things. There was doubt as to whether parents would continue to give presents if the boys were on a wage. There was concern over where the money might come from ('there would be less money for teachers'; 'there would be no money to buy a school minibus'). At the end of this exercise I again asked the youngsters to indicate what they thought of the idea. Twenty-nine out of the class of 30 had now completely changed their minds and reversed their 'first reaction'. Twenty-nine out of the 30 now decided that $5 a week for going to school was not a good idea at all. We later found that the lad who held out and refused to change his view along with the others, received no pocket money at all – so the $5 was worthwhile no matter what complications it led to.

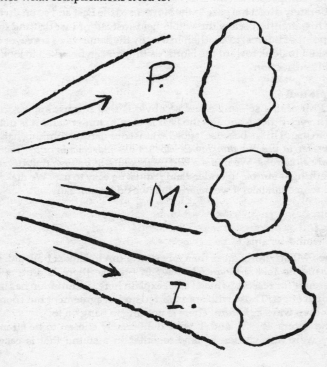

Scan

The PMI is a very simple scanning procedure. The 'P' stands for Plus. The thinker is asked to scan in the Plus direction even if he or she dislikes the suggestion intensely. What is there to see in the Plus direction? Are there any good points at all? At first a person who dislikes an idea claims that there are no good points at all to see. After a while, however, there is an ego shift to carrying out the PMI operation effectively, and now the thinker begins to admit that he or she can see some plus points – if asked to look in that direction. The next scan direction is towards the Minus direction ('M' is for Minus). What are the bad points? What are the negative aspects of the matter? The final scan is towards the Interesting point ('I' for Interesting). The Interesting points include those points which are neither good nor bad but are worth noting. The phrases: 'it would be interesting to see if . . .'; or, 'it would be interesting to see whether . . .', can be used to elicit such points. The 'P', 'M' and 'I' directions serve the thinker in the same way as the compass directions serve the surveyor. The surveyor can deliberately direct his gaze to the North or to the East and so on. In this way his attention scans the whole field instead of just drifting from one point of interest to another. In exactly the same way a surveyor can be asked to 'look toward the North', a thinker can be asked to look 'in the Plus direction'.

Simple tool

The PMI seems so simple and so obvious that it must appear to be worth very little. Although the PMI is easy to understand it is not so easy to use. This is because it goes against our natural thinking habits. *We prefer to use our thinking to back up our judgements rather than to explore situations.* We make a bad mistake if we believe that because something is simple to understand it must be easy to use. We make an even worse mistake if we believe that we do it habitually.

Tool

Is the PMI anything more than an exhortation to look at both sides of an issue, to take a balanced view? In practice there is quite a big difference for reasons which I shall explain here. Exhortation has little residual effect. Those who are exhorted nod in agreement but soon go their own ways as before. There is nothing to hang on to.

The letters 'P', 'M' and 'I' were deliberately chosen to be strange. They were also chosen to flow together in a sound that is easy to remember and easy to pronounce. Children, and adults, get used to saying 'PMI'. Although is sounds artificial and 'jargon' at the beginning it soon becomes a natural part of language. It is deliberately intended to seem strange at first: so that attention can focus on the tool. In this way the 'tool' can be practised directly and deliberately. In fact the teaching method involves the repeated practice of the same tool on a wide variety of 'thinking items'. Each item lasts for no more than four minutes (or less). In this way the only constant thing is the tool itself. Skill builds up in the deliberate use of the PMI. The PMI – and the attached skill – can now be transferred to new situations. In this way the main difficulty in training thinking – the difficulty of transfer – is overcome directly.

In one school two teachers started to teach the CoRT (Cognitive Research Trust) Thinking Lessons (obtainable from Pergamon Press, Headington Hill Hall, Oxford). One of the teachers used the term 'PMI' but the other teacher objected to the 'jargon' and just encouraged his pupils to think 'in a balanced way'. The teachers compared notes. Half-way through the first term the teacher who had refused to use 'PMI' switched over to using it. What the 'PMI' does is to create in the mind an 'operator concept'. Our minds are full of 'description concepts' such as 'chair', 'meeting', 'plan' and so on. But there is a shortage of succinct action concepts that cause us to operate in certain ways. PMI (and the other CoRT tools) are intended to provide such 'operator concepts'. Just as we recognise a 'chair' so we ought to be able to recognise a situation that calls for a PMI. Another way of looking at it would be to regard the PMI almost as a 'sub-routine' in data processing. In compiling a computer program the programmer might call for a certain type of data processing at a point. In the same way the thinker calls up a PMI.

Not judgement

The PMI is not a judgement process but a scan process. Some people ask it they cannot just list a number of points and then sort them into three boxes: P, M and I. This is a totally different process. The points have been produced and are now being classified. In the proper PMI procedure the thinker scans in the 'P' direction and sees what he sees. In the classic 'pros and cons' procedure the thinker lists the different points and is then supposed to make a decision according to whether the pro or con points dominate. In the 'scan' procedure of the PMI there may only be one 'P' point and as many as 10 'M' points, yet the thinker can still choose to go ahead. The purpose of a scan procedure is to direct attention all around in order to create a good map. The thinker then finds his or her way about the map – according to the desired destination and the value system in use. This process was described rather nicely by a thirteen-year-old girl who said that at first she felt the PMI process to be a waste of time 'since she knew very well what she thought about the matter'. She then said that after she had put down the 'P' points, then the 'M' points, and finally. the 'I' points, she found herself reacting to what she had put down. Once the map is there it cannot be 'unseen'. *The point about the perceptual part of thinking is that when a situation has been seen in a certain way, that view cannot be unthought.*

Subjective

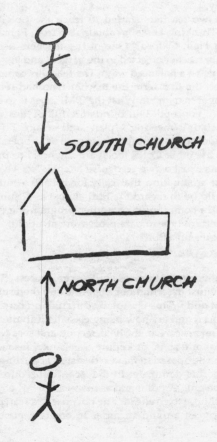

Just as a surveying scan is from the point of view of the surveyor, so the PMI is always from the point of view of the thinker doing the PMI. In one exercise children were asked to consider the suggestion that 'all cars should be coloured yellow'. One boy gave it as a positive point that cars would then be kept much cleaner. Another boy gave this same point as a 'Minus' point 'because he had to clean his Dad's car and would end up having to clean it more often'. Both were right. One person sees a church spire by looking North. Another person sees the same spire by looking South. Both are right: the spire is neither North nor South. In the PMI no point is of itself Plus or Minus. Those are just directions in which the thinker looks.

I have occasionally seen a PMI done by putting three headings across a flip chart (P, M, I) and inviting the participants to put items down under the different headings as the items arise. This is not a good method. To look for a finite amount of time in the 'P' direction is not the same as looking in all three directions at the same time. We even suspect that the brain chemistry may be slightly different when a thinker is looking in the 'P' direction from what it might be when he, or she, is looking in the 'M' direction. There are theoretical considerations arising from the behaviour of 'self-organising information systems' that suggest this might be the case.

Interest

With very young thinkers (under nine years) the 'I' direction is not very important. As the age and sophistication of the thinker increase so does the importance of the 'I' (Interesting) direction. In time the mind gets into the habit of going beyond the usual judgement aspects to open up aspects of interest. These interesting aspects considerably enrich the 'map' of the situation. Once the thinker knows that in the end a judgement is going to be made, then there is no need to adopt the judgement stance at every instance. Instead there is the 'exploratory stance' and that is where the 'I' direction comes into its own. Under the 'I' umbrella the thinker can speculate and can explore possibilities: 'it would be interesting to see what might happen . . .'; and, 'it would be interesting to see if this would happen . . .'. this type of exploration has much in common with the processes of creativity. There is the same speculative exploration – as a sort of scaffolding on which perceptions can then grow.

Attention directing

It must be obvious by now that the PMI is no more than a simple attention-directing tool. The thinker uses the tool in order to direct attention to those aspects of existing experience which might otherwise be ignored. One of the most difficult aspects of thinking is to direct our attention to areas that turn out to be important only after we have looked at them.

Using the PMI

I have had two purposes in describing the PMI here. The first is to give an example of a simple thinking 'tool' that can be learned, practised and used (to effect). The second purpose is to provide the reader with the formality of this simple tool. It may be that some readers will already know and be using the PMI. In such cases the notes given here should be regarded as both review and amplification of their existing skill. It would not be fair on other readers to refrain from important aspects of thinking because some readers have an acquaintance with such aspects.

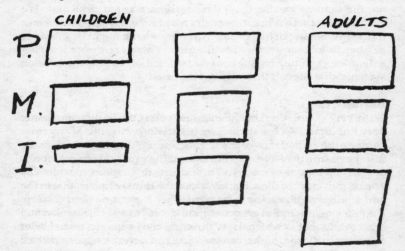

The PMI in use

The thinker may develop and practice the PMI for his or her own use. The reader may also wish to introduce others to the PMI so that it may be used thereafter as part of a normal 'thinking conversation'. The PMI is not difficult to explain. A practice example is more valuable than a philosophical explanation. It is always important when practising a thinking skill to use a mix of remote (and humorous) items and serious items. The skill is most clearly illustrated and practised on the remote items (for example: 'should everyone wear a badge showing his, or her, mood of the moment?'). The tool can then be applied to a serious matter. One executive told me how he introduced the PMI to a senior meeting of one of the major corporations in the USA and how the immediate use of it solved a problem around which there had been wrangling and bitterness for months. This effect is not surprising. People learn the rules of a game very quickly. Thereafter they pride themselves on how well they play the game.

The PMI is a fundamental thinking tool because *our natural reaction to ideas and suggestions is an emotional and reactive one*. The PMI serves as an effective by-pass: 'I know you do not like this idea, but do a PMI on it nevertheless'. It is easy to see how the PMI could become a fundamental tool of 'quality circles'. The PMI allows suggestions to be made and then explored. It protects suggestions from instant rejection because they do not fit in with someone's experience or notion of how things ought to be done. If the PMI does nothing else it does provide a common language or notation for thinking. The value of an in-house training seminar is that enough people in an organisation become acquainted with a common language and idiom – even if they are not very skilled at using the tools. There is a similar advantage when one reader of this *Letter* is having a discussion with another reader.

Decisiveness

I am sometimes asked whether the ability to see many sides of an issue does not impair decisiveness. The answer is that where decisiveness is based on blindness then anything which increases vision must interfere with that type of decisiveness. This would include information, market evidence, advice, the PMI or anything similar. The case is similar to that of the mythical character who is supposed to have said: 'I have made up my mind – don't confuse me with facts'. There are many instances where blind decisions have succeeded and have been valuable. There are many more cases where they have been disastrous. It is up to the thinker to decide: does he wish to make a blind decision (if so it would save time just to toss a coin); or a partially sighted one (looking at only the agreeable part of the data); or a fully sighted decision. Do you make the best choice in a restaurant when you cannot read the menu? My standard reply is that anyone who does not like making decisions should not be in management.

The thinking place

My definition of a skilled thinker is a thinker who can direct this thinking at will and use it to carry out tasks that the thinker sets for himself – or has set for him (by others or by the world around). There are brilliant thinkers who are inspirational and will, on occasions, come up with brilliant ideas. There are other thinkers who under the right circumstances and pressures will perform well. I am quite prepared to regard such thinkers as 'brilliant thinkers', but I am not sure I would be prepared to call them 'skilled thinkers'. My view of skill is that there is some element of control and direction. The skilled carpenter knows when and how to use his tools. Such knowledge does not stop him being a genius. It seems that the greatest painters were usually skilled craftsmen when it came to applying paint to canvas.

I am going to set some specific thinking tasks for the reader. I want the reader deliberately to apply the PMI process. The direct purpose of the exercise is for the reader to use the PMI in a forced manner. The thinker should also watch himelf, or herself, carrying out the task.

Exercise 1
Set a time limit of two minutes in each case, and list only the PLUS points for both of the suggestions given here.

(a) Human beings should have noses on their ankles (a child's suggestion for improving the human body)
(b) There should be an equal number of men and women politicians in legislative assemblies.

Exercise 2
Set a time limit of two minutes in each case, and list only the MINUS points for each of the suggestions given here.

(a) The retirement age should be lowered to 55 years for both men and women.
(b) Computers should be designed to be 'user friendly' so that ordinary people can use them without getting confused.

Exercise 3
Do a full PMI (P then M then I) on each of the following suggestions. Allow only one minute for each of the directions (i.e., one minute for 'P' etc.).

(a) Every patient should buy his or her own medical insurance before seeing the doctor or entering hospital. If anything went wrong then the patient would claim from the insurance company rather than sue the doctor or hospital.
(b) Hamburgers should have a square shape.

Variations
The above exercises can be carried out in a group situation (with family or colleagues). It is important to keep to the timing strictly. With a group the timings given for individual exercises can be doubled in each case (to allow for talking time).

Another variation is for individuals to do the exercises in parallel on their own and then to compare their output. This involves writing the points down. To provide time for this the time originally set can again be doubled.

9

What difference does it make?

In the USA the salary of a senior executive might be anything from $30,000 to over $1 million. What difference in performance or motivation would it make if an extra $100 a year were to be added to these salaries? After tax that would, in any case, be reduced to an extra $50 a year. At the lower levels this would amount to a salary rise of 0.166%.

What difference would it make if the extra $100 a year were in the form of a subscription to this *Letter*? This leads to the much larger question of whether paying attention to thinking as a skill can really make any difference to a reader's thinking skill in practice.

I think it would be extremely good value if, from each year's subscription, a reader took just one point and built this in to his or her thinking habits. It might be an awareness point or it might be an actual tool. Sometimes even the simplest point can have a dramatic effect.

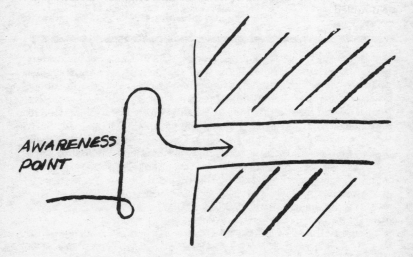

AWARENESS POINT

Ten days ago (from the time of writing this) I was speaking to the General Foods' Presidents' Council in White Plains, New York. To this meeting are invited the senior General Foods executives and also the presidents of the large supermarket chains from all over the USA. After I had finished speaking Bernie Paroly (president of the well-known Pathmark supermarket chain) told how he had come across the 'Course-book' published by my School of Thinking in New York and how he had read about the simple PMI tool. A short while later he was involved in some difficult union negotiations. He introduced the PMI tool to the negotiating table. Those taking part first scanned the Plus points, then the Minus points and finally the Interesting points. He told how the negotiations were speedily concluded to the satisfaction of all concerned. The use of this extremely simple tool (which is the first lesson in the school programme, and was included in my last *Letter*) had saved hours of negotiation and possibly hundreds of thousands of dollars in costs. There have been other instances of this sort.

Of course, it all depends not so much on what I write but on the attitude and motivation of the reader – and especially the reader's willingness to try something out. This brings up the matter of motivation. I can always assume that anyone who comes to my seminars or reads this newsletter is interested in thinking. This may, however, not be the case if the custom grows of taking out a subscription for all senior executives as some organisations have started to do.

To persuade someone to take an interest in thinking as a skill is a hard task and not one I am going to try in this *Letter*. All I will say is that in the matter of thinking the simplest things done consciously and done well can make a quite astonishing difference. Those readers who might claim that they know it all and do it all anyway may, just possibly, be deluding themselves. When I first started writing about creativity (as lateral thinking) I half suspected that really creative people would tell me that they knew all about it and did not need to read about it. In fact exactly the opposite thing happened. Such well-known creative people as Henry Dreyfus, Milton Glaser, Misha Black, Alex Moulton, Paul MacCready were among the first to see a value in writing and reading about these matters. The people who 'know it all' usually know so little that they cannot conceive there to be anything beyond what they know. Something like the man who declared that he had no need to buy a book because he already had 'a book' at home.

There are those who crave an elaborate structure for thinking: do this, then this and then this. . . . I sometimes offer such structures as in

91

the TEC-PISCO system. I may even offer such structures from time to time in this *Letter*.

But that is not the only approach to thinking. Many elaborate structures are imposing to read about and may also work quite well if rigidly adhered to. Too often, however, people pretend to think in that way but rarely do. The other approach is to offer individual tools, insights, considerations and perceptions in the hope that from time to time they will enter a person's thinking. Some of those things (like the PMI and the 'po' concept) are valuable both in themselves – at the time of use – and also for the general effect they have on a person's thinking. For example, the PMI encourages the discipline of 'scanning'. The 'po' concept encourages the attitude of treating ideas as provocations instead of judgement positions.

I suspect that from time to time I may repeat myself in these *Letters*. This is the readers' best assurance that the *Letters* are written directly evey month and are fresh. If I was simply ploughing through a large 'book' which had already been constructed, then there would never be any repetition. There are many points which bear repetition. There are other points which need 'walking around' and viewing from different perspectives.

The opposite of effective thinking strategies are those points of particular difficulty that seem not to yield to ordinary thinking: such matters as difficult decisions and dilemmas.

The 'random word' lateral thinking technique is well known to those who have read my books or attended a seminar of mine. I shall deal with it in a later issue of this *Letter*. It is an example of an extremely simple technique that can be learned in seconds and used immediately. Yet it seems so impossible that no-one ever believes that it will work. The theory underlying the 'random word' technique is quite complicated and has to do with a basic understanding of self-organising patterning systems. There is, however, no need to understand the theoretical basis in order to use the technique effectively. When I was talking at a Bank of America Far East meeting in 1983 someone told me how he had deliberately used the random word technique to design an investment instrument to fit the Hong Kong market conditions. That is another example of the deliberate use of a simple technique.

I would not like a reader to try to remember every point I make in the *Letter*. The last thing I would want is confusion. Some things can be read through lightly for their residual effect; other points can be focused upon and deliberately noted. I would also suggest browsing through previous *Letters* to pick up points not noted at the time.

So the answer to the title question: 'What difference does it make?' is that it can make a considerable difference.

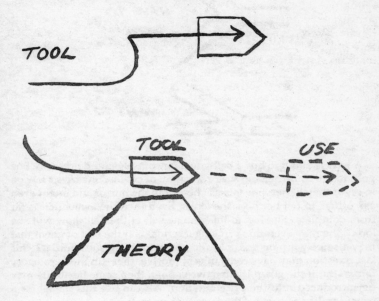

Evaluation

Evaluation is a vast subject which merits a whole book to itself. So I shall be coming back to the subject again and again. What I shall be dealing with here covers only some aspects of the field.

There are many methods for financial evaluation of a project or an investment and I do not propose to go into those here. As usual, I am more interested in the conceptual aspects.

You might be in a position where you have to choose someone for a job; or, you have to choose the theme of an advertising campaign. In such cases a decision has to be made. The decision to buy a personal computer may be different. You do not need to make the decision – you could probably get along with the computer. The second type can be converted into the first type simply by regarding the 'do nothing' alternative as a real chosen alternative. In practice – and emotionally – it never seems to be so even though logically it is so.

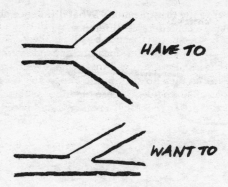

A lady is about to buy a ball-gown for some splendid occasion. She goes to the couturier and sees a selection of gowns. She tries a few on to see if they fit her. She looks at herself in the mirror and might even ask others to tell her how she looks. Even then the evaluation is far from complete. She has to imagine herself at the ball: how will she look? She may even think in longer terms: is it the sort of gown that may also be worn on less splendid occasions? Can she afford it? This last question may have come in very much earlier – in broad category terms. But if the gown is attractive enough then some flexibility may be introduced into the price criterion. We can use this model for a consideration of some of the aspects of evaluation.

Does it work?
Is it really an option? Does it do what it is supposed to do? Are the mechanics of it sound? Does the pilot plant scale up? These sort of questions refere to the nature of the option. Is the dress a dress? Is it wearable?

Will it sell?
This question may not be easy to separate from the previous one for performance in the market may be the only way something 'works'. You might imagine, however a new type of insurance policy. In this case 'does it work?' refers to the actuarial mathematical and legal technicalities. 'Will it sell?' refers to market performance when all the technical points are in order. You could also imagine a new game. Then does it work refers to the mechanics of play; the 'will it sell?' refers to the likely success of the game in the market place. It might seem that the 'will it sell?' phrase focuses a bit too much on the

marketing of a product to have a more general application. The word 'sell' can, however, be taken in its broadest application. If any other people at all are involved, can the idea be sold to them? There are only a few occasions when an option does not depend on other people. Criminality is one of them. Criminals might make good entrepreneurs (except for one thing: they do not want to depend on either investors or the market place). So the paraphrase of 'will it sell?' might be 'will those who are involved in making it a reality want to do just that?'.

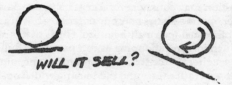

Can I afford it?

As with the price of the ball-gown there is some elasticity here. On one level there is a cut-off of those things that are simply out of the question. 'Afford' does not only mean money but also time, effort, hassle, image and all similar expenditures. Below this absolute cut-off there is usually a balance between 'appeal' and 'cost'. If the appeal is very high then sacrifices might be made or a large risk taken. Therein lies a danger: the danger of over-extending the cost flexibility to encompass an option that is very attracive.

There is another aspect of the 'afford it' question. Resources are seldom unlimited. Being able to afford one thing means that something else cannot be done with the same resources. Which immediately leads to the concept of opportunity cost. What else could be done with the resources? This can be taken too far. If we all made sound 'opportunity cost' judgements then most restaurants would be out of business. There are a lot of far more permanent and far more valuable things that can be done with the money than spend it on a meal which is consumed and forgotten. At this point it may be necessary to introduce the concept of a balanced value portfolio. This means that an option need not always be assessed against the best possible use of funds. For example, an expenditure on advertising may be more cost effective than spending money on R&D – in which case R&D would never be done.

Which is the better value?

Having gone through the absolute criteria, we now come to the relative ones. Assuming that something can be afforded and that it does work and does sell, we may still have to choose between options. There are a number of ways of doing this and I shall deal with only three of them here.

Priorities, criteria and profile

This is a well established method. You list your priorities and these become the criteria for evaluation. It sounds easy but it is not. This is because one option may satisfy several criteria in a mild sort of way whereas another option satisfies only one criterion – but in a spectacular way. For example, consider a truly beautiful house that is really too far from work and schools and shopping as compared to a dull house that satisfies all those criteria. Constructing a profile is very similar. It can mean setting up a style of choice and then seeing which option fits that style. Here the word 'style' covers needs, strategies and general mode of action. Would this option fit our (or my) style?

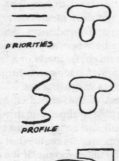

PRIORITIES

PROFILE

BEST HOME

The PMI

I dealt with the PMI in my last *Letter*, but I must mention it here as one approach to evaluation. The P stands for Plus points or what makes something attractive. M stands for Minus or what makes something unattractive. the I stands for interesting aspects. The PMI is a scanning procedure not a judgement one. There may be many more Minus points than Plus points and yet the option may be chosen. Similarly it is not possible to compare PMIs for different options. It is the general feeling that arises from the scanning of a PMI that is useful. The PMI simply forces the thinker to spell out the attractive and unattractive (and interesting) points so that now they are operating on a conscious rather than an unconscious level.

The best home

Here the emphasis shifts away from the options themselves and towards the 'best home' for each option.

If we return to the dress-buying analogy it is possible to image the lady looking at a particular creation and saying: 'that would look very well on a young lady of about 24', and looking at another gown and saying: 'that would suit a lady who was plain and rather fat'. For each option the ideal home is imagined. Then that ideal home is compared to the existing 'home' or set of circumstances. A product that might be suitable for a large organisation might be quite unsuitable for a smaller organisation. It takes about $30 million to launch a new cereal in the USA, so devising new cereals is not a suitable option for small corporations. As elsewhere there is a danger about being too rigid in this test of suitability. Who would have though that IBM would make a success of introducing a personal computer? On the other hand the reassurance provided by the esteemed IBM name may have made the pc an ideal product, since so many pc's were going to be bought by people who needed a lot of reassurance.

Risk

Things can go wrong. Things might not turn out as expected. There may be unfortunate interferences which could not be foreseen. De Lorean's attempt to build a new luxury car for the US market happened to meet a severe fall-off in auto sales just when the cash flow was critical. To hope that a present climate or trend continues is a very different sort of risk from hoping that a certain set of circumstances will come about. Anything to do with the future has risk elements. The trick is to spell out the risks and to know what they are. The other need is to design a concept or a course of action which will still work under a variety of circumstances, even if the ideal circumstances fail to appear (or continue). The worst form of risk is to have a number of 'if's' in series: if this technology works, if we get the price right, if the competition stands still, if the price of oil stays stable, and so on.

Fall-back position

There are a number of aspects of options that have nothing to do with their intrinsic merit, or even likelihood of success. For example, the ease of testing an option is an important part of its value. In education, for example, an innovation whose effect can be easily tested will be of more practical value than one which is more difficult to test. The design of a fall-back position is also part of the evaluation procedure. If things do not go according to plan, what will we be left with? Will we be left in an exposed position of vulnerability and danger? Will we have achieved 'half a loaf', which is valuable even though less satisfactory than a full loaf? Will we have achieved nothing but benefited from the learning experience? Will failure simply mean a 'write-off'? Will we have the courage to draw a line and accept failure? Unfortunately the history of business is full of instances when persistence and determination have paid off – but also full of instances where a refusal to accept failure has led to disaster. There is a useful saying: 'What is the worst that can happen?'. If the person can live with that 'worst', then the course of action has an acceptable position of failure.

Perception

The features and qualities I have discussed in this piece are rarely as obvious as the texture or colour of a dress. They usually depend on perception: the way we look at things; what we focus upon; the concepts that we use. A manufacturer with a very successful year may invest in new plant, R&D, marketing campaign, increased dividends and so on. A retailer might use the surplus to set lower prices on some items – regarding this as just as much of an investment as the manufacturer who buys new plant. Value lies in the eye of the beholder. Some people are willing to pay a lot for a 'learning experience'. We are quite good at picking values out of disasters but, when it come to evaluating options, we prefer to look at the negatives in our attempt to narrow the field. This does make sense inasmuch as no degree of positive value can make do-able what is not do-able. But once something has passed those preliminary tests (does work and is affordable) then it is possible to focus on the positive aspects.

The thinking place

Ideal snap

I once invented a word-game which I called EVOL which is simply short for EVOLUTION. The task is to take a four letter word and then evolve it into another four letter word which has been chosen beforehand. I published a series of EVOLs in the *Daily Telegraph* magazine. I received a lot of rather irate letters telling me that I had not invented the EVOL at all but that Lewis Carroll (who wrote *Alice in Wonderland*) had invented it in the last century. I accept that verdict and find that I had re-invented something that was already invented. In this instance the inventing matters far less than the product.

The rules are simple. Only one letter may be changed each time. At each stage the word formed by changing the single letter must be a real word in its own right. Consider the following examples:

Example 1. Change LONG to TALL
... LONG
... LONE
... DONE
... DOLE
... ROLE
... ROLL
... TOLL
... TALL

The challenge is, of course, to carry out the evolution in as few moves as possible. No doubt many readers will find shorter ways of working out my examples.

Example 2. Change NICE to SOFT
... NICE
... NINE
... LINE
... LONE
... LOSE
... LOST
... LOFT
... SOFT

The exercise is fun in its own right. It is also rather compulsive. There is always an urge to do it in a neater way. New avenues and new lines are always suggesting themselves. It will be obvious to readers that the conversion can be effected from either end – or from both ends at the same time.

In short, the EVOLs provide rather a nice model for watching the emotional side of thinking. There is frustration and block. Then there is hope as a new line suggests itself. The new line moves forward, perhaps for several steps. Then it might peter out.

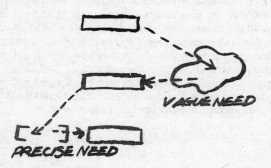

What is particularly fascinating is the feeling that accompanies 'snapping' into a line that is felt to lead directly on to the solution. It is as if the road is recognised even when it has not been travelled before. There is the traditional 'Eureka' feeling. The EVOL might indeed be the simplest model for experiencing the eureka feeling. That is why I am introducing it here. I want readers to watch their emotions as they work through the EVOLs. I am not introducing them simply as a 'games or puzzles' section.

With a little practice it becomes possible to make a jump and then to fill in the gap. It is possible to set a strategy and to define what is needed.

Try the following Pairs:

POOR to RICH
FOOL to WISE
WIFE to GOOD
HOPE to FAME
MORE to LESS
LOVE to HATE
COLD to HEAT

Strive for the minimum moves in each case.

10

The future of thinking

I believe that in 100 years time people will look back with incredulity at the primitive nature of our thinking systems today. They will regard it as astonishing that the idea of teaching thinking skills in schools should ever have been a pioneering idea. Problems like Northern Ireland and the Falklands and disarmament will have obvious solutions. Is this a science fiction utopia?

Is such a vision contrary to the nature of the human system with its old-style brain (as Koestler would have believed)? Could it happen only in a world that had become one large organisation with a centralisation of crucial thinking issues? Could it come about without such centralisation but with a better system design?

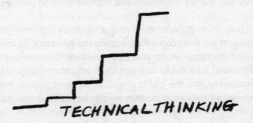

Computers are getting better and better. Our software idioms are also improving. We are beginning to create 'expert system' software which allows an expert to transfer his expertise into the machine and then use it for solving problems. Might the world leaders queue up at a super-computer and feed in their problems and then abide by the decisions as they might have done with the oracle at Delphi?

How about ordinary thinking? Can better thinking ever be democratic or must it be done by the experts? Will we become so good at understanding brain chemistry that we will be able to dole out 'positive attitude' pills and 'problem-solving pills'? Will there be new concepts and new ideologies that have a way of coping with conflict?

Is our thinking so bad if we can get to the moon and back; cross the

Atlantic faster than a rifle bullet; probe to the very nature of matter (in particle physics); and conquer many of man's diseases (a new vaccine against malaria is on the horizon)? Surely those things that have remained untouched by this power of human thinking (emotional, belief-based, and political issues) are untouched because that is the very nature of man? Why else is there this discrepancy between technological power and social failure in our thinking habits?

Have we perhaps taken the wrong logic turning in the development of thinking? Is the only way back through the application of technical logic to the design of hardware and software that will eventually rescue us from the limitations of that technical logic? Have our thinking systems evolved habits and institutions that effectively prevent further evolution of our thinking habits? Does language and the impossibility of changing it, lock us forever into antiquated concepts and perceptions? Is any effort at change going to be regarded as gimmicky at the point of presentation (like any efforts to reform spelling)?

Is there any point in speculating or should we just leave it to natural evolution and hope that man's attention to thinking will eventually give us better systems? Is thinking of any importance if we cannot change human emotions, values and beliefs?

Well, I have my views, as readers of this *Letter* and of my books may suppose.

I believe that a very great deal is going to happen in the next 50 years. We are just on the edge of an explosive advance in this area. The advances will not come from philosophers or the literary crowd or, indeed, our leaned institutions – not for a while anyway. They are too much the custodians of the past. *It will come from system explorers and those who probe the nature of system universes.* It will come from those

SOCIAL THINKING

who can take the findings and translate them into usable idioms. There is a great deal of design work to be done. It will not be a matter of revealing the truth and hoping that all else will follow. The truth (as in economics) will be too complex to be understood by everyone. It will be a matter of designing concepts and tools that can be seen to make sense in their own right and to be an advance over existing habits. There has to be a very great deal of thinking. Yet the end result must look simple and obvious and usable.

Focus on thinking

The first stage is that we should focus directly on thinking as a subject area worthy of attention in its own right. It does not come under philosophy, linguistics, semantics, systems behaviour or psychology, even though it enters into those fields. Such fields have their own idioms and cultures. I am leaving Cambridge University precisely because it is not longer possible to fit 'thinking' into the Department of Medicine. Curiously this has been a suitable home because thinking depends on the system behaviour of one part of the body, and I believe that the biological idiom is a more useful entry point than either mathematics or philosophy or computer science. It is not surprising, however, that a medical department should see its role as the practical care of patients rather than broader conceptual issues.

So we need a deliberate focus on thinking. There is also a need for a body of people with such an interest. There is a need for funding because many of the necessary activities will not have an immediate commercial value. It has always been of interest to me, however, how the business community has shown more interest in the development of thinking than most others. The reason is obvious. In most fields it is possible to survive by defence: by defending a point of view (academic, political, religious and cultural worlds – and scientific). In business a skilled defence is of no avail if the market thinks otherwise. For this body of interested people, and the institutions which may emerge, there will always be the very difficult problem of keeping a bridge between the deeper theoretical developments on the one hand and the practical application on the other. Can we get a better understanding of what happens in thinking and at the same time develop methods that can be used by nine-year-olds in the Venezuelan jungle? That is, more or less, what I have been trying to do.

Information universes

Consider three people holding similar blocks of wood. The first person releases the block which falls to the ground. The second person releases the block which then moves upwards. The third person releases the block which remains exactly where it is. The behaviour in the first case is easy to understand. The behaviour in the other two cases is very mysterious and strange. It is strange precisely because we assume that cases two and three are happening in exactly the same 'universe' as for case one. Actually, in case two the person is underwater – so the block of wood floats upwards (simple, natural and logical behaviour). In case three, the person is orbiting the earth in a space-craft, so there is zero gravity and the block stays where it is (again, simple, natural and logical behaviour). *The mystery is cleared up once we can specify the universe in which the action is taking place.*

In dealing with thinking we have always assumed that we are dealing with a passive information system. This can also be called a discrete system. You make marks on paper and they stay there. You make marks on a magnetic disc and they stay there. Our logic and thinking systems are based on this. The very notion of 'anaylsis' and 'truth' depends on such an information universe. *But perception and creativity cannot be understood in such a universe, so we regard them as mysterious.* That is why our thinking systems have been so good for technical matters but so poor for social matters.

There is another type of information universe. This is the active information surface. It is a surface on which information can organise itself into patterns. It is a self-organising system. I wrote about this in 1969 in my book *The Mechanism of Mind*. At the time not many people noticed the book. It is now suddenly becoming fashionable amongst those who deal with the frontiers of information handling. Since I wrote that book the notion of self-organising systems has become very fashionable (people like Prigogine and Jantsch have written about them extensively). Many of the things I laid out in that book have been re-discovered.

Once we can define an information universe then we can explore what happens in that universe. Such exploration can lead to a better understanding of such things as 'the belief system', 'creativity', 'insight', 'teaching methods' and so on. The exploration can also lead to the deliberate design of thinking tools. For example the random word technique of lateral thinking is nonsense in the ordinary world of passive information systems but perfectly logical in the patterning world of self-organising systems.

I do not expect everyone who uses the random word technique or such tools as the PMI to understand the theory behind their design. As I mentioned, the tools must stand in their own right and be usable and useful.

What I am saying is that once we have made a universe shift we can move ahead much faster. We are no longer restricted to empirical descriptions of what seems to happen. That is why I am optimistic of what can be done in this field.

SITO

One of the projects in which I am involved is the setting up of a Supra-national Independent Thinking Organisation. This would act outside and across boundaries of nations, politics, ideologies or religions. It would provide a reference system that the United Nations (being a representative political body) could never provide. I shall deal with SITO in a future *Letter*.

Race

The crucial question is whether our technological capability (in terms of nuclear weapons) will lead to a destruction of the human race before humanity has time to develop the thinking idioms that will save it. There had to come a point at which the technological idiom (essentially a much simpler one) would outrun the social idiom. Since we invest billions of dollars in technological development and virtually nothing in the direction of social 'thinking', we have reason to be worried. For the price of a single F-11 fighter it would be possible to change the world.

Intuition, hunch and instinct

When I give a seminar I am very often asked what I think about intuition. On such occasions there is rarely time to give a full answer and I usually distinguish two or three processes that come under that heading. Intuition is used to cover a very broad range of non-conscious mental processes including the following: hunch; instinct; seat-of-the-pants; composite judgements; holistic (right-brain); aesthetics; internalised processes; feeling and gut-feeling; style; self-image; 'sleep on it'; and insight. Some of these overlap and describe the same process in a slightly different way.

We have all heard about hunches that have led to brilliant investment decisions. We have heard about entrepreneurs who have built fortunes

INTERNALISED

on a hunch. We read about executives who put much store in their hunches when it comes to decision-making. As with so many other examples of success we do not hear about the disasters that have followed hunch thinking. The disasters are not around to be noticed.

We do know for sure that in certain areas human intuition can be disastrously wrong. If a run of eight reds comes up at the roulette table, then intuition tells us that the next play is likely to be black. Yet each play is independent of the previous one so the chances are still fifty-fifty. We know that people's estimation of their chances of winning in a lottery is far higher than reality.

We know that intuition is by no means infallible. It is yet another example of Lord Leverhulme's much quoted comment about advertising: 'I know that half the money we spend is wasted – but you tell me which half'. We know that intuition can be right and it can be wrong, but we do not know when it is going to be right or wrong.

Because intuition is unconscious it is out of our control and observation, so we cannot check what is going on. And so we mistrust it. This leads on to another famous anecdote. On his hands and knees the slightly drunk reveller is looking for something under the street lamp. A policeman enquires what the matter may be. 'I've lost my keys,' replies the reveller. 'Where did you lose them?' asks the policeman. 'Oh, back there by my car,' says the reveller. 'So why are you looking for them here?' 'Because the light is better here.'

That is a classic story that fits very well with a lot of scientific research. We like to look where the light is best. *We may ignore the really important areas because we have no measuring instruments for use in those areas*. There is the same relationship between conscious and unconscious thought.

Orthodox medicine has a highly sceptical attitude towards folk remedies. Many of these are seen to be examples of witch-doctoring and mumbo-jumbo (old wives' tales). Orthodox medical people are well aware that many famous drugs (such as aspirin and digitalis) were once folk remedies and are now accepted basic remedies. Such orthodox scientists also know that each year some other ancient folk remedy is found to have valuable properties. So why do they resist the idea of folk remedies? Because such remedies include both the valuable and the nonsense. Rauwolfia had been used in India for about 2,000 years. Because the plant looked like a snake it was said to be good for snake-bite. It was also used with mad people. Rauwolfia was investigated by Dr Nathan Kline and was found to be an effective drug for anxious people. It was also found to be valuable for treating high blood pressure (as reserpine and now superseded by safer drugs).

I have just finished writing a book about 'Success'.* This is based on a number of interviews with people who have achieved success in one form or another. Their comments about intuition and instinct are most interesting. For example, it might be supposed that the champion Grand Prix driver, Jackie Stewart, would react instinctively because there would be so little time for conscious decision. On the contrary it seems that he thinks in a cold, analytical almost syllogistic way even in the midst of a split-second crisis. Antonio Herrera, a top, world-class polo player, puts a similar emphasis on thinking, even in the midst of a hectic game. Then there is Jim Rogers, the money manager who turned $600 into $14 million. For his decisions there is 'instinct', but it is really a process of rational thought that has been used so often that it has become internalised and automatic. This is the way he gets a 'feel' for an investment. Norman Lear, the famous American TV producer, has a 'slide rule in his belly' and relies on gut-feeling to know if something is going to work.

We can now look at some of these unconscious thinking processes in order to try to distinguish what happens and their value.

Internalised processing

A step-by-step conscious process is used so often that, like a computer sub-routine, it can be called up and used in a totally unconscious way. A real estate developer has so often gone through the selection points for a deal that he can now do so automatically and therefore seems to react with 'intuition'. The same thing happens with a scientist who looks at data and feels that they are not right. Where there is indeed an

---

* The book is now published as *Tactics: the art and science of success* (Fontana).

internalised processing of this sort it is clearly both convenient and reliable. The only problem is that the routine cannot be varied or improved since it has become packaged as a whole.

COMPOSITE
JUDGEMENT

Composite judgement

Under this heading I shall also include the holistic (right-brain) type of reaction. If you see a friend at an airport you do not recognise him by analysing the distance apart of his eyes, the shape of his nose and the set of his ears. There is a composite or 'whole' judgement. When we judge something consciously we have to atomise it or break it down into analytical detail. Often the 'system qualities' which are only there when the thing is a whole are lost during this analytical process. So there is real value in composite judgement. An executive making a 'hunch decision' may be exercising such composite judgement on all the features of a situation.

Seat-of-the-pants

This is a special type of composite judgement that provides reactions and actions based on experience. Its obvious weakness is that it is a summary of the past. Where things have not changed at all then this type of judgement may be most useful. Where they have changed it can be disastrous. It can be like driving a newer and faster car with the reactions that are derived from a slower car. In practice we do not need to use past experience, so the trick may be to see if the new situation can be changed (perceptually) into a more familiar one so that experience can be applied.

Aesthetics

This is much more difficult. At its simple level 'taste' may be based on experience and the environment in which you grew up. At its artistic level, what is aesthetics? Is it composite judgement? Or is it more like an inborn animal instinct? To an artist, putting the wrong line into a drawing is a disagreeable thing. He or she is guided by a personal sense of what is right. The same holds for a designer. Cannot businessmen claim to have this 'feel' for their own special idiom? I suppose an artist has an internal image of what things should be and then compares what he sees to that image. I see no reason why a business executive should not act in the same way. There may be physical aspects of the perception of colour and line and sound that are distinct from conceptual aspects, so the artist may be different. One key point of difference is that the artist can react to his internal world whereas the businessman must react, and live in, the external world. And if an internal image does not fit reality he may go bankrupt (an artist will starve in his garret).

Feeling and gut-feeling

Some of this overlaps with aesthetics. The rest is directly related to emotions. Many of the decisions made in the Falklands conflict (on both sides) were based on a strong sense of feeling – a feeling for what was 'right'. If a situation excites certain feelings, then should we not let those feelings dictate our judgement and action in that situation? I have often said that feelings must be the final arbiter of action and that the purpose of thinking is to so arrange the world that we can apply our feelings usefully. The question is not easy. But here is a practical way out of the dilemma. If our feelings on the matter are going to remain constant, then thinking based on feeling has a validity (provided the feeling is applied after the perception stage and not before it). If our feelings are likely to alter (or simmer down) then the effect of the feelings on the thinking may be in error. *Feelings probably change the chemical basis of the brain, so that it is really a different brain that is doing the thinking.*

Style

Some people have a strong sense of style: their way of thinking and their way of doing things. This overlaps with the concept of 'self-image' – how people see themselves in the mirror of their mind. In any situation this feeling or style can act unconsciously to influence a decision. An entrepreneur may feel that risk-taking is in his style, so the risk-taking decision 'feels right' to him. The style of another entrepreneur is that of caution, so the deal 'feels wrong'. Does the style follow the type of decision the person would make anyway, or does it lead it? There is probably a bit of both. When someone is publicly known for a style then it is possible that the sense of style does affect decisions.

Sleep on it

Many are the examples of how a person slept on some problem and came up with the solution in the morning. At other times the person has gone to play golf or gone on holiday or just stopped thinking about the problem. There are many possible explanations for this observed phenomenon. One supposition is that the brain is doing unconscious processing and working things out. As a youngster going to my first dinner-jacket dance I learned to tie my bow-tie in a dream. Another supposition puts the emphasis not on unconscious brain workings but on the fact that conscious thinking has been interrupted. *If the brain has been following the same pattern round and round, then an interruption allows it to start again at a different point.* Similarly if emotional overtones have established a type of thinking, then a more relaxed atmosphere (holiday or golf) will allow a different type of thinking. Matters settle into a truer perspective. Finally, a preparedness of the brain in relation to the problem may allow a chance input or remark to trigger a solution. It is possible that there may be truth in all these suppositions. The practical point is that there is value in sleeping on it (or breaking off from thinking). But we cannot simply delegate our thinking to this process and just wait for results.

Insight

There is no mystery about this. It is the pattern-switching process that is at the heart of both humour and lateral thinking. If we enter a pattern at one point we go in a certain direction. If we enter at another point we go in a different direction. Insight involves this switching: suddenly we see something differently because we have crossed patterns (or entered at a different point). I described the process in my book *The Mechanism of Mind* and in several books since. The key point is that we suddenly see something differently and, since the switch-over is sudden and not the result of careful analysis, we sometimes call it intuition.

Hunch

This can cover any of the things I have mentioned here. It can be composite judgement or internalised processing. There is, however

INSIGHT

another aspect to it. A person who can imagine an alternative that others cannot see, may suddenly realise that the alternative fits. In a way this is insight. It is the provision, through perception, of an outcome and its reasonableness. The person having the hunch may be unable or unwilling to formulate the alternative – which may be rather hazy.

Sensitivity

Someone who is very sensitive to nuances and trends may feed these into a composite judgement that leads to the sort of intuition on which fashion is based. Sensitivity to 'climate' and 'atmosphere' is part of this. A negotiator who is sensitive to the mood and direction of the negotiations may feel – 'intuit' – what the next step should be. In such cases, heightened perception is showing a different world and the reactions in that world are quite logical and straightforward. If you sense that people want to reach agreement, then you offer an acceptable one at that point.

It is often claimed that women think intuitively. This is a claim made by men on behalf of women and by women for themselves (some women). It has to do with working backwards and with map-type thinking rather than syllogistic step-by-step forwards that is supposed to be the masculine mode. A consideration of this will take a full feature in its own right and I shall deal with it in a future issue of this *Letter*. I shall also deal with the practical use of intuition. For the moment I have wanted to clarify what we usually mean by intuition. That in itself has a practical value: should we use intuition here? How far can we rely on it? Is it a composite judgement? Is the emotional base going to remain constant?

The thinking place

Intuition exercises

In the exercises set out below the answer should be given as quickly as possible. After the answer has been given, the reader should try to see what led him (or her) to that answer. In each case there should be a definite answer. It is quite true that the reader may feel that under one set of circumstances the answer might go one way and under another set it might go the opposite way. In such cases intuition can still be

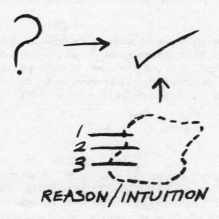

REASON/INTUITION

applied but this must also cover the circumstances. The outcome must be a definite yes or no (for the purpose of this exercise).

I do not wish to suggest that intuition is the same as superficial or 'top-of-the-head' answers. I just want readers to listen to their 'intuitive feelings' on the matter.

Go through the list first, giving an answer to each question. Then go back and, for each answer, try to see what lay behind this answer. In some cases there may well be an explicit rational answer or it may be something you have discussed so often that your opinion is grounded in argument. Be honest with yourself and try to spot the role played by your intuition.

- Is high-level unemployment here to stay?
- Will there be a major nuclear war this century?
- When will the next oil crisis happen?
- Will a major Third World country default on its loan?

- Will Japan come to dominate the computer field?
- Will inflation enter double figures again by 1992?
- Will government spending (as a proportion of GDP) continue to increase?
- What will happen to the power of the unions?
- Will jeans ever go out of fashion?
- How will the US be involved in Central America?
- Will the SDP be a real force at the next election?
- Is a new religious revival possible?
- Is increasing protectionism likely for European industry?
- Will TV programmes get better or worse?
- Will you be in the same job in two years time?
- Will there be a harsh winter this year?
- Will the quality of life improve?

In the Delphi technique it would be normal to record your answers and then feed them back to you so that the group tendency became an influencing factor. The purpose of this exercise is quite different. The right or better answer is not important. What is important is your observation of your intuition in action. If you wish to compare your answers with a friend or group of colleagues then do so. Try to get the others to examine what underlies their intuition.

11

Concepts of function

Many years ago I was doing research on the circulation and the blood and I had to use a specially designed pump that would force blood through blood vessels with a pressure profile that imitated the profile normally provided by the heart. The pump worked well, except that the table on which it was placed vibrated so badly that it practically 'walked' across the room. Various experts were called in to solve this problem of the vibrating pump. Sandbags were suggested and tried – without much success. Finally, it was recommended that the equipment be transferred to the basement floor where the feet of the table could be embedded in concrete. This was going to take some time and was going to cost some money. I thought I would try a different approach. I placed an ordinary rubber bathroom sponge on the top of the pump table and then put a two-kilogram weight on top of the sponge. The vibrations were immediately killed and there was no more trouble. The experiments continued. This approach might have been obvious to anyone usually concerned with vibrations (that is the reason why the tread of tyres is not quite uniform). To me it seemed worth a try since it would be so very easy to try. There was a concept switch from 'making the table so firm that it would not vibrate' to 'killing the vibrating frequency'.

If you are inflating balloons for a children's party there comes the moment when you need to tie the neck of each balloon. It is far simpler to tie a knot in the neck than to use string. The only trouble is that in most balloons there is not enough length of neck to make this knotting easy. One day, in frustration, I devised a knotting method that used the cap of a pen. The balloon neck was wound around the cap and then the loop was pulled off the cap over the end which had been tucked into the mouth of the cap. It worked well and simply. The concept change was suggested by the well-established medical technique of using Spencer-Wells forceps for making knots in sutures. We tend to think of a knot as involving only the material in which the knot is tied so the concept change involves introducing an intermediate object which acts as a sort of scaffolding for the knot.

I was driving along a motorway at about 70 m.p.h. when I attempted to switch on the headlights. The whole switch came away in my hand and all the lights seemed to go out. I brought to mind the vague notion of a function 'that would perform what the switch had been performing'. There had to be an object that would 'somehow fit where the switch had been and would depress whatever needed depressing'. I remembered noticing the stick from an ice-lollipop on the floor of the car. I reached down and found the stick. I jammed the stick into the switch socket and it performed the switch function so well that it was some days before I got the switch properly repaired. As in the previous examples there was a vague notion of 'function' and then a simple trial.

In the days before most cars had reversing lights I had to drive down a dark country lane in order to park near my Cambridge cottage. It was a matter of driving in and then backing out in the dark or backing in and then driving out using the headlights. Leaving the lights on in the cottage did not help much. The solution was to use the flashing indicator lights as reversing lights.

In an invention of mine to test lung function there is the use of a whistle. When the patient cannot make the whistle sound, then the Peak Expiratory Flow rate (related to bronchial narrowing) is determined. The general function concept here was that of 'finding a way to tell what the lungs could not do' and also the vague idea of using 'noise' as an indicator.

I once asked some children to draw a vehicle for 'going over rough ground'. One child drew a vehicle which had a nozzle in front and another nozzle behind. The nozzle in front was for putting down 'smooth stuff' and the nozzle behind for sucking it up again for re-use. I used this drawing in one of my books and several people – including the late Sir Misha Black – commented upon it as an excellent example of a broadly defined function concept. 'Smooth stuff' does not, of course, exist but as a function concept it can exist.

All the examples I have used here have been very simple and have required no special knowledge. I have used them to illustrate concepts of function. Our thinking is usually based on things rather than on functions. There is the famous experiment in which students were asked to solve a problem which involved completing an electrical circuit. In one version of the experiment only a few of the pupils thought of using the metal of the screwdriver itself as an extra bit of 'wire'. In another version only a few students thought of using the picture-hanging wire from a picture in the room. We tend to feel that we need certain objects when all the time what we need is a certain function. *Thinking in terms of function is difficult and children tend to be better at it than adults.* A ladder is not a ladder but a way of getting up to places. At the same time it can also be a bridge.

SMOOTH STUFF

. . . I need a piece of string here.
. . . I need anything that will tie these two things together.
. . . I need some way of keeping these two things together.

In this example we see an apparent need for a piece of string ending up as a much broader function concept.

The trick is to define a need in broad terms: 'I need something to do this and this . . . .' If the definition is too narrow then it's little better than defining one particular object to provide that function. If, on the other hand, it is too broad then it can become useless: 'I need whatever is needed to solve this problem'. Imagine that you are dropping an egg from a height of six feet on to a mat, which cannot be more than half-an-inch in depth and which must serve to stop the egg-shell from breaking. How might you define that function? If you defined it as 'something to absorb the impact of the egg' the definition would be rather broad. If you defined it as 'something which would crumple slowly' then you might think of layers of wrinkled aluminium foil – which does the job rather well. Strawberry jam on a piece of bread is also rather good. So is a wet sponge – but not a dry one (I once set this problem in a competition). Obviously these three solutions do not all come from the same function 'need'. In fact the wet sponge probably arises in two stages. The first idea is to use a sponge, but when tried this collapses too quickly and the egg shatters. So there is a need for 'something to slow up the compression of the sponge' or to create a 'soggy sponge', and the addition of wetness follows. The strawberry jam and bread (suggested by a vicar) probably arose from a concept of 'something rubbery but not too rubbery'. I am not sure if the strawberry jam is strictly necessary, although it does serve to stop the egg bouncing off and shattering elsewhere.

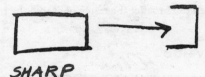

SHARP

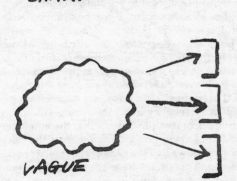

VAGUE

It is often said that defining the problem is the first step towards solving it. Unfortunately, we can usually only define a problem correctly after we have solved it. Defining the needed function is very similar. *The better we define the function the more likely are we to find something to fit that function.* Nor should we be content with a single definition. We can try several definitions ranging from the narrow to the broad. It is a bad mistake to assume that only the broad definition is needed since it logically includes all the others. All this means is that in hindsight we can show how the eventual solution can be classified under the broad definition, but this does not mean that in foresight the broad definition will lead us to the solution.

Concepts of function offer one of the most powerful thinking tools to be had. We need, however, to think in function terms all the time rather than in terms of objects which might carry one function or another. In order to build up this repertoire of functions in our minds we should take an interest in functions and we should observe and comment upon them even when we have no immediate need of them.

The interesting thing about function definition is that vagueness is a distinct advantage. If we consider the function of the brain this is understandable, for too sharply defined a question is only a reflection of one particular answer. If we know exactly what we are looking for we shall find that and nothing else. If we do not know exactly what we are looking for then the broader the range of search the better.

Concepts of value

It might not be easy at first sight to see the value of paraplegics (and even quadriplegics) as a workforce. If we look immediately for value we may not find it – except perhaps in terms of motivation and dedication. If, however, we spell out the attributes of such people: lack of mobility etc. then we can examine these features for their value. Why and how could lack of mobility be a value to an employer? The answer is, if the employee does not stray far from where he, or she, is supposed to be. This immediately leads on to surveillance and video-screen watching as in security and monitoring situations. But the scope is broader. Lack of mobility means that the employee who can operate a telephone is never going to be far from the telephone. So whoever telephones knows that the person at the other end is going to be the same person. This might have considerable advantages, for example in selling property. For the paraplegic there is the opportunity to make contacts and friends and to have a window on the world (in addition to feeling useful and earning money).

I have often thought that one of the most perfect definitions of business value lies in the story of the Monte Carlo society doctor who declared that he had perfected a test that would determine the sex of

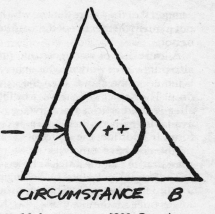

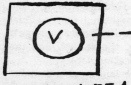

CIRCUMSTANCE A   CIRCUMSTANCE B

the unborn child. For this test he would charge a mere $200. Occasionally, he admitted, the test would go wrong. In such cases he would not only refund the full test fee but – as a bonus – give a superior rate of interest to what could have been obtained on the market. Naturally he made a fortune, since half the time he kept the money and half the time he returned it (with a bit from the money he kept). Yet everyone was happy. He was certainly happy. Where the test was successful the parents were happy. Where the test failed the parents were compensated with their money back, and with a superior rate of interest. As a matter of fact it is quite easy today to tell the sex of the unborn child by taking a cell from the fluid in the womb and examining it for the Barr body that indicates the foetus is female (or male in its absence). This has indeed become a problem in India where parents proceed with the test and then try to arrange an abortion if the child is a girl. Girls go to the families of their husbands, and so are not a long-term investment. To make matters worse a girl, in India, requires a large dowry before she can get married and a number of daughters can damage a family's fortunes. So here we have another concept of value.

It is said that the great Turkish reformer Kemal Ataturk decreed that all prostitutes must wear veils in the street. His intention was to dissuade other women from wearing veils in the street. Instead of forbidding women to wear veils, and so risking fierce opposition from them and from the more conservative members of the public, Ataturk simply altered the value of wearing a veil. The beauty of the procedure was that the value of wearing a veil was reversed. In addition, as soon as a few women chose not to wear veils then the change would spread rapidly, since the fewer women left wearing veils the more possible it seemed that they were the one who had to wear a veil. Of course, it did not matter whether or not the prostitutes actually obeyed the ordinance or not.

A great deal of work goes into producing a magazine. Each writer also puts a lot of work into his or her article. But when the next month's issue is on the stands then the value of all that effort disappears at once. The *Reader's Digest* was a brilliant exercise in value creation. The already used articles were given a further lease of life by being made available again to others who may not have seen them in their original form. In addition, the source of the articles gave the *Digest* a prestige it might not have otherwise built up. Finally, the readers had the reassurance that the articles chosen were the best available.

The James Cook Hotel in Wellington, New Zealand, was built above a municipal car park. This meant that the developers paid a much lower price for the site than if they had built it upon prime land in the centre of the city. Since then 'air rights' have become fashionable in most cities.

There are expensive perfumes and watches that are designed to be given as gifts. The giver buys the value of being able to indicate the value of the gift he is giving. That is the real value to him (or her). There can be nothing worse than to give an expensive present and not have the value appreciated, so the better known the value the better value it is – to the giver and to the receiver.

Value for what; for whom; and under what circumstances?

Imagine that certain public telephones were painted with a distinctive colour because at these phones the caller paid twice as much – for exactly the same service – as he might pay at an ordinary phone. The more these phones were resented, the higher their true value would be for they would only be used by people who urgently needed to make a call and who did not mind paying the premium in order to find a vacant phone booth. So the value is that of being able to make a call at the time one wants to make it. An 'emergency plumber' should charge enough to keep himself available for emergencies.

In the personal computer world the reassurance value of the IBM logo quickly got for them a quarter share of the market within one year of launching. The famous Avis slogan neatly turned a number two position into an asset: 'we try harder'. It seems to be a curious fact that in the service world the notion of 'trying' is rather more successful than that of 'succeeding'. An organisation that proclaims that it offers superlative service immediately suggests arrogance and complacency – if not falsehood. An organisation that suggests that it tries hard gives more value because it implies that the standard of service is not taken for granted. A Harvard business graduate is valued not because of what he has been taught, but because he will probably try to live up to his self-image and because he must have been pretty smart to have got there in the first place.

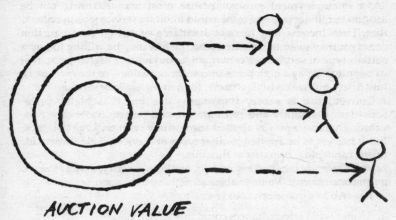

AUCTION VALUE

The toy value of a product is usually more important than the real value. This has certainly been the case with the sale of personal computers. Like many people I have bought a large number of pocket calculators because the newest one seems slimmer or better designed – all of them carry out the same function. This is toy value. It is a very important type of value. *In the developed world, where many of the basic necessities are provided for, it is things like fashion value and toy value which determine industrial growth.* If we only bought what we really needed we should be very much more careful with our spending.

There is the well-known story of the war-time black-marketeer who sold his friend a number of tins of sardines. A short while later the friend came to see him in a very angry mood. It seems that the sardines were all bad. The seller was not at all taken aback. 'You should have told me you wanted them for eating,' he said, 'I thought you only wanted them for buying and selling.' Pass-on value is as real a value as any other. Organisers of conferences do not much mind if the celebrity speaker never turns up. It is enough to have had his name on the conference brochure and to be able to blame him for not turning up.

Auction value

When planes are overbooked some lines in the USA offer cash inducements for passengers to give up their seats. The price of the inducement rises until enough passengers have accepted it. As a tourist bus starts to pull away the price of the goods being peddled to the passengers starts to fall rapidly. Bargaining is an obvious form of auction value.

As unemployment grows, because most manufacturing can be automated, there is going to be a need for more service jobs in order to distribute income and to raise standards of living. Some auction concepts may need to be introduced. People may be willing to buy a certain type of service at a certain price, but not at a higher price. Just as people will pay a high price for emergency values, so they will pay a low price, but seek a high volume, for non-emergency services.

Convenience is a very important value but it is highly price-sensitive. Reliability and price are the two determinants of service value. That concept was applied successfully with package holidays, but it has yet to be applied to other types of service. There is room for much conceptual thinking in this area.

Value seems to imply an end in itself, and yet it is always only a means to an end or a channel. Value enables something to happen.

The two key questions could be:

1. Under what circumstances could this have a value?
2. Under these circumstances (or for this market segment) what could have a value?

The thinking place

Spelling out the concepts
Can children think when they do not yet have the right words with which to think? I am often asked this question and my answer is that children's thinking is often ahead of their ability to verbalise their thinking. This is shown when children are asked to make drawings showing different designs (a sleep machine; how to weigh an elephant; a dog-exercising machine etc). The concepts that are expressed visually are often ahead of what can be verbalised.

Nevertheless the ability to verbalise or spell out a concept is an important part of thinking. This is because it serves to focus attention in a particular area. It is a useful exercise to take different situations and to try to spell out the concepts that are needed or what are involved. For each of the situations given below make an attempt to spell out the different concepts.

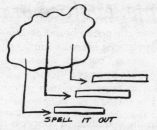

SPELL IT OUT

1. After orange juice has been extracted, the peel is something of a waste product. Is there any way in which value can be extracted from the peel: either as residual flavour or as something else? (A drink called 'Kinnie' is produced in Malta with the flavouring derived from orange peel; in Japan peel has been converted into fuel suitable for car engines.)
2. The age of retirement is getting lower. What residual value might be obtained from lawyers or policemen that retire early?
3. The concept of mini-parks involves turning small areas of the city into gardens or 'park spaces'.
4. Standby seats on aircraft offer an opportunity to those to whom price is less important than time.
5. There is a Swiss company which earns its income by checking whether the cargo that is supposed to have been loaded on a ship has in fact been loaded onto that ship.
6. If you give workers more money as a reward they come to regard that as part of their salary. If, however, you give them a piece of paper called a bonus bond (exchangeable for goods at certain shops) they come to treat it as a bonus which may be given on certain occasions but not at other times.
7. At airports it is not unusual to use some of the walkways for the testing or display of carpets.
8. Consider a toothpaste that claims to do nothing else except polish the teeth.
9. Designer jeans.
10. Bottled water.

In each of these examples there is more than one concept that can be spelled out. The task is to spell out one concept for each item the first time around and then to go back to try to spell out a further concept. In spelling out the concepts, keep in mind the division between function concepts and value concepts.

12

New concepts: evolved or created?

If we firmly believe in the evolution of concepts then we need to do nothing except wait for the concept to evolve and to make itself visible. Then we use it and profit from its use. We could contrast this with the deliberate creation of a new concept. These two contrasting approaches are nicely seen in the haute couture world. There is gradual evolution in a particular direction: perhaps towards longer skirts and more feminine dresses. There may be intermediate stages, but the concept direction is clear. At other times an innovator comes along and establishes a concept directly. For newcomers this may be the only route to attention.

The advantage of an evolved concept is that the market is ready for it and there is less risk. The concept of the five-door hatchback evolved slowly until it has come to dominate the smaller car field. It would be highly risky for a car manufacturer to try a radically new idea. American Motors tried it with the 'Pacer', and the risk turned sour.

Waiting for a concept to evolve does not mean sitting back and then jumping in with a 'me-too' product (as IBM did with its personal computer). It can mean watching trends closely until they seem to gel into a new concept and then moving in with that concept. So one is both following the trend and also ahead of the field. Publishers are always trying to do this because they know that the first away with a new concept is likely to gain the most. Is the trend away from jeans towards white baggy pants narrowed at the ankle a real trend or just one more attempt to break the jeans monopoly? Is the trend towards health foods and light beer going to become a dominant concept, or is it always going to be limited to only part of the market?

At what point do modifications of an old concept suddenly turn into a new concept? This is a matter of vital interest to a designer of services and products. If it is still just a variation of the old concept then there is not much that can be done except to imitate it or try parallel variations. If, however, a new concept is evolving then the ability to spot that concept and to sharpen it up may mean an opportunity to dominate the field.

There are times when a new concept emerges quite soon and for a while there is competition between the new and the established concept. At other times the old concept slowly dies, and for a while there is nothing but confusion to take its place. Gradually a new concept forms and emerges. The new concept is not necessarily an improvement on the old concept. It may in fact be less efficient. It may reflect a shift in emphasis (for example from practicality to femininity). Boredom may play a significant part and so too may the whim of a fashion leader. Attempts to push a new concept through heavy advertising and newspaper comment are probably insufficient in themselves. This is because such attention leaves no lasting impression: there is no mental hook on which to hang the new concept. A concept is not an object that can be designed and sold; it is self-organisation of experience into a coherent thought that then acquires a life and momentum of its own.

Deliberate design

To sit down and deliberately design a concept is not very different from waiting for a concept to evolve – even though at first sight it might seem to be exactly the opposite process. The deliberate design of a concept simply accelerates the self-organising process. The designer assesses whether the design concept is likely to work by noting how it fits in with existing trends. So this sense of judgement serves the same function as evolution. There is, however, one huge difference between an evolved concept and a created one. There is usually only one evolved concept since evolution proceeded in this direction. With created concepts – even when they have to fit background conditions – there may be a number of alternative concepts each of which fits the trends. The creative attitude looks at the trends in terms of both ingredients (towards the formation of the concept) and also in terms of acceptance (the concept must have acceptable benefits).

The difference dilemma

The dilemma is that the new concept must be different and distinct enough to be noticed and commented upon – otherwise it is hardly visible. And yet too sharp a difference may mean that the concept never gets going because the fashion makers are unwilling to take the first step. A sufficiently distinct concept forms its own context of judgement – eventually. This is similar to what happens in the art world. A distinct style, like the impressionists, is rejected at first but eventually becomes the dominant idiom. One cannot, however, draw too many lessons from this. The art world has a profession of people whose business it is to write about and notice what is happening. For such a group rejection is the first logical behaviour. But if the phenomenon does not go away (because artists prefer to starve and drink absinthe rather than abandon their souls) then rejection is no longer logical behaviour for the critics, so they do an about-face and become enthusiasts – rationalising their behaviour as best they can. Most concepts, however, have to survive through their acceptance; so too prolonged a rejection means that the concept never gets going at all. Artists may starve in order to preserve their souls but business executives prefer not to starve. So concepts have to make sense to someone in addition to their designer.

How does a concept make sense?

It might seem to be a simple matter of listing all the benefits and, if these are sufficient, then the concept might make sense. Unfortunately it is not that easy. One particular benefit may be more important than ten listed benefits. This is not because the one benefit is of real importance and the ten are trivial – but because we are dealing with perception. Perception is an organising system, not an adding machine. If you sell a car on the basis that it is the cheapest on the market then that is the concept. Any additional benefits will detract from that main benefit and the concept will be less attractive. A list of benefits does not take into account the organising factor that is so important to the success of a concept.

So a concept makes sense if it 'organises' expectations, habits, desires and needs in an efficient manner. What do we mean by 'organises'? What do we mean by 'an efficient manner'? I do not think there is a satisfactory answer to either of those questions. We can sense organisation just as we can sense efficiency but defining them only shifts the task to other words that also need defining. We could use words like coherent, simple, together, and all of them would point in the same direction without being definitions. The important thing to remember is that a concept is an organising system.

Accidental concepts

Sometimes concepts happen by chance. Someone does something for one particular reason and, unintentionally, a new concept comes about. The intention behind the package holiday concept was probably one of price. In practice the appeal of the concept is the same as the appeal of the concept which started Thomas Cook: someone else takes care of the hassle. The concept of 'twin bar' confectionery has been immensely successful, but no-one quite knows why. There are all sorts of possible explanations (it seems more, can be shared, part now and part later, less guilt etc).) but it must be admitted that the success of the concept was probably accidental. In contrast, the 'designer' jeans concept was a deliberate attempt to add value and fashion to what were utilitarian items. Frozen Pizza is a way of giving people one-step sandwiches, and at a low cost.

Difference

As usual one of the best ways of describing something is to show how it differs from something else. This is particularly so with concepts. *If you want to show how a new concept is emerging it is vital to contrast it with existing concepts.* 'Instead of trying to express their status through cars, people are beginning to treat them as commodities or a transport service.' Sometimes it may be enough to define what people are moving away from without being clear as to what they are moving towards. At other times we can define what people are moving towards (for example towards a greater health consciousness as interpreted by figure shape). Milk drinking has been declining steadily in the UK, although milk is an obvious health item. People do equate good health with a trim figure and overweight with poor health. That is an obvious concept that has evolved. The concept of having 'to do something' to earn good health has also evolved as a result of the commercial pressures for diet books and keep-fit programmes. Original sin has definitely taken a shape form. Would it be possible to create a concept based on the slogan 'fat people are fun'? Probably not, unless a new word was found instead of 'fat' because this word covers the extremes of obesity and ill-health. In any case who would benefit from such a concept?

Spell it out

I do want to emphasise the importance of spelling out concepts if you think you have spotted them. You may well be wrong but at least you can look at something that you have spelled out. Otherwise a concept remains as nothing more than a vague notion that something 'is happening. It is a most useful practice to look around and to attempt to spell out the concepts you see operating in products and in advertising.

Why brainstorming may be dangerous

I want to be fair to brainstorming because it has made an immense contribution to the notion that creative ideas can be sought in a deliberate fashion. We take this for granted today but, before the concept of brainstorming, creativity was a matter of chance, individual talent and some mystical process. To brainstorming we owe the notion that a group of people can sit down at a table with the expressed intention of generating some new ideas on a subject.

Today, however, the general concept of brainstorming is too weak and may be holding creativity back. In some quarters brainstorming has got creativity a bad name: a group of people fooling about and producing crazy, impractical ideas; self-indulgence and so on. There are also other – and much more serious – ways in which brainstorming is holding back the further development of creativity. People have come to believe that, because a brainstorming session is held now and again, nothing more needs to be done about creativity. Brainstorming has also cultivated the notion that creativity has to be a group process. I think this is harmful because I believe that creativity is an essential part of the thinking behaviour of every thinking individual and an individual must be able to use both the creative attitudes and the specific processes as an individual. No-one should have to wait for a scheduled brainstorming session in order creatively to tackle the situation with which he is confronted.

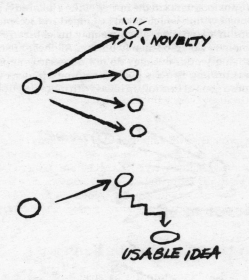

Advertising values

Brainstorming was developed from the pioneering initiative of Alex Osborne who was in the advertising business. It was developed to serve the needs of advertising people. It does this reasonably well. Unfortunately the needs and values of the advertising industry are different from the needs and values in most other areas. Indeed, in some cases the values are unique. For example, in the advertising business novelty is a real value. Novelty catches attention. Novelty may make a dull object into an interesting advertisement. Novelty can provide something catchy and memorable. Novelty can indicate to other potential clients that the agency is bold and creative. Novelty is noticed and talked about. In other areas novelty has nothing like this value. You would not drive across a bridge just because it had a novel shape: you would prefer to be assured about the solidity of the bridge.

In the advertising world 'surreal' reality is as acceptable as ordinary reality. The sight of a white horse standing in the background at a cocktail party is much more acceptable in an advertisement than it might be in real life. In a way advertising admits the logic of the schizophrenic. So long as there is a connection of some sort, then the result may be a striking advertisement. This is a bit like the elephant jokes: 'How can you tell there has been an elephant in the fridge? Because there are footmarks in the butter'. Like a joke, advertising can create the context within which it is to be judged and accepted. Style is also important in advertising, and style may make bizarre demands. Blue-faced gnomes would be merely boring. All these are true values in the advertising world. But they do not necessarily apply to other worlds. Brainstorming is quite good at turning up ideas with these values but not so good at turning up ideas with more practical values.

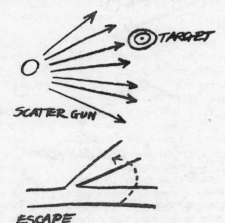

Scatter gun

At the end of the brainstorming session there may be a list of ideas. These are looked at and screened to see whether any of them might be of use. The impression is that of a scatter gun: loose off a large number of ideas and hope that one of them might hit the target. This is just possible when the target is novelty but rather unlikely in most other instances. It is this hit-or-miss aspect of brainstorming which has got it a bad name. It is difficult to believe that a thinker will hit on a good idea in this blunderbuss fashion. I myself am inclined to share these doubts.

This 'scatter gun' approach may be contrasted with the idiom of lateral thinking. As most readers will know, lateral thinking is based on the pattern-forming properties of self-organising information systems. Such patterns have a necessary asymmetry. As our perception follows the main pattern the alternative tracks are inaccessible. If, however, we do manage to escape from the main track then these other tracks become available. So the emphasis is on 'escape'. This means that if we do escape from the main track we have a pretty good chance of finding ourself in another track. This is quite different from a scatter gun hit-or-miss hope. There may be times during the brainstorming session when the thinking approximates to the procedures of lateral thinking, but that is by chance rather than through the use of deliberate structures and tools – as in lateral thinking. It should also be said that it is not a matter of hunting around for these other tracks after escaping from the main track. The self-organising system of the brain makes it quite likely that the other tracks will be entered.

Movement

Instead of screening a large number of ideas for one which might be of use, the idiom of lateral thinking is to take a single idea as a provocation and then to use the 'movement' process to work forward from that idea until the thinker is within range of a useful idea. *The scatter gun approach is analogous to sifting through a mass of sand in order to find a nugget of gold. The movement idiom is more like taking a piece of rock and through a series of steps transmuting it into gold.*

At the end of a brainstorming session there will be a number of ideas: that is the end product. With lateral thinking that would only be the first stage. Such ideas would be treated as 'provocations' rather than as final ideas. The second stage would be to move from these provocations to a new idea. Then there would be the third stage. This third stage would involve 'shaping' the new idea into a practical and usable form. The constraints would be brought in as 'shapers'.

There is a considerable difference between hoping to chance upon a good idea and taking an idea and gradually changing it into a good idea (through the processes of movement and shaping).

It is perfectly true that brainstorming can be a source of the 'provocations' that are so essential a part of lateral thinking, and this may be the most useful way of treating the output from a brainstorming session. There are, however, several formal ways of creating provocations (for example 'reversal') without relying on the hit-and-miss operation of brainstorming. In general, brainstorming involves a lot of messing around in the hope that something useful will turn up. In lateral thinking the process is much more deliberate and much more structured.

Formality

To my mind the greatest advantage of brainstorming has been its formality. There is a time, a place, an agenda, and a group of people have met with the express intention of being creative. This is much better than expecting people to be creative on their own. Most people know, in a general sort of way, the idiom of brainstorming. So they act out the role of creative thinkers on the temporary stage provided by the brainstorming session. Certainly this is of benefit. As I have said before – and will no doubt say often again – if you play-act being a thinker then you will become a thinker. So the formality and idiom of the brainstorming session is useful. It is possible to tell a group of people that you are setting up a brainstorming session to generate ideas on a particular subject. That is a definition of intent. The session then takes place and will always have some sort of output. The overall result is that creative thinking has been applied in a definite manner. This is very much better than expecting it to happen by chance. The word 'brainstorming' provides a convenient notation for such an idea-generating session. The danger is that the generally weak processes of brainstorming will then be used in the session. We may need to develop a new word for such idea-generating sessions.

During a brainstorming session those taking part usually know that they are not supposed to be negative or judgemental. They can catch themselves and say 'I suppose that is too negative', or they might be admonished by someone else at the session. This sort of general definition of the creative thinking role is all to the good. I believe it can be tightened up in an even more formal way and I have a new project which does just this. I shall be announcing it in these pages in due course.

Individual creativity

Brainstorming is essentially a group method. The ideas of others are supposed to trigger your ideas. The atmosphere created by others is supposed to keep everyone creative. Most of the approaches to creativity have followed this group notion. As a result many people have come to believe that creativity can only be used as a group exercise. This is nonsense and dangerous nonsense. *Creativity is as essential to every thinker as the ability to use the reverse gear in a car is essential to every driver*. No-one would consider himself (or herself) a driver if he or she could not use the reverse gear. No-one should consider himself or herself a thinker unless that person is able to use both the idiom and the actual processes of creativity. In this regard the precise processes of lateral thinking are more useful than the loose idiom of brainstorming. An individual should be able to sit down on his or her own to apply a creative tool to a particular problem. No-one else needs to be involved. The process can be worked through in a formal step-by-step manner. At the end there should be some new ideas.

The way a person reacts to an idea, the way a person sets out to find alternatives, the way a person treats a provocation are all part of the skill of creative thinking. It is absurd to believe that a person cannot be creative unless he or she is actually taking part in a brainstorming session.

Because brainstorming has been such a neat way of encapsulating creative endeavour there is a danger that individuals feel no obligation to be creative in their everyday activities, because creativity has been allocated to the brainstorming session – just as stores are allocated to a warehouse. There is also a danger that individuals become lazy about learning and practising formal creative skills because they feel that the idiom of the brainstorming session is sufficient. The result is that they never get much further with creativity.

SANDWICH
I = INDIVIDUAL
G = GROUP

Group behaviour

One of the unfortunate idioms of the brainstorming session is that some people set out just to make people laugh with the outrageousness of their ideas. People try to outdo each other as the joker of the group. It is very satisfying to have people laugh at your idea just as it is satisfying to have people laugh at your wit. I have often noticed that people who have some experience of brainstorming seem to expect me to greet their wildest ideas with enthusiasm. I am all in favour of outrageousness at the provocation stage but thereafter I am more concerned with developing usable ideas. Such people almost always suggest 'helicopters' or 'personal jet-packs' when dealing with the problem of traffic congestion in cities. There are more practical ideas.

I have sat in on many brainstorming sessions where an individual takes every opportunity to push the same idea because he feels it has been insufficiently appreciated by the rest of the group. Such a person has stopped taking part in the creative process and is involved in selling. A dominant feature of all group behaviour is selling.

There are also times when an individual takes over the group and organises its thinking: 'Let's all look at it this way . . . .' In such cases the variety of directions that the individuals might have taken is lost.

Individual thinking

I like individuals to be able to use lateral thinking as a personal thinking skill. I acknowledge that the formality and focusing effect of brainstorming sessions has a value. I prefer a sort of 'sandwich system'. I shall describe the sandwich system in more detail elsewhere, but can outline it here.

In the first type of sandwich we have a group discussion session which may indeed be a brainstorming session. At certain points, however, individuals are asked to develop their own ideas on the defined subject. For three to five minutes individuals work on their own. At the end of that time each individual presents his or her thoughts to the group. In this way individual lines of approach have a chance of opening up. There can also be optional periods during which an individual can break away from the group to go and sit in a corner to pursue a line of thought that has just occurred to him. There do need to be times, however, when the whole group is present and acting as a group. So in this type of sandwich we have group/individual/group.

In the second type of sandwich we have individual/group/individual. The defined task is presented to individuals – perhaps as a task sheet – and the individuals do their own thinking on the matter. A formal group session is arranged and the individuals come to the session bringing their thoughts with them. The purpose of the group session is to have an exchange of views and also the opportunity to carry further ideas which have been offered by someone else. Following the group session there is another individual session in which individuals pursue the lines of thought that appeal to them and also seek to summarize or 'harvest' what has happened in the group session. This follow-on individual session may take place immediately after the group session, or a deadline may be set and individuals required to submit their thoughts by that deadline.

Looseness and structure

Many people believe that creativity is synonymous with freedom and that structure is the very opposite of freedom. They therefore feel that the loose idiom of brainstorming is quite sufficient and that any attempt to use more defined structures must hamper creative freedom. This is a misunderstanding of the nature of structures. There are restricting structures and liberating structures. A rail track is a restricting structure. A bicycle is a liberating structure because it allows you to go further than you would without it (in some ways it is also restricting because it forces you to keep to the roads instead of walking across the fields). A cup is a liberating structure because it makes it easy for you to drink liquids – especially hot liquids. A ladder is a liberating structure because it enables you to climb to higher places. Mathematics is a liberating structure. Language can be both liberating and restricting. It is liberating because it allows us to communicate and to record things. It is restricting because it compels us to view the world through certain traditional concepts. *A key is a liberating structure if it allows you to escape from a prison and a restricting structure if it locks you in a prison*. The structures of lateral thinking are designed as liberating structures inasmuch as they increase your chances of escaping from the established tracks (they act like keys or ladders or cups).

The advantage of a structure is that it allows the thinker to do something definite. For example he might throw in a random word. The thinker now reacts to the situation produced by the structure. It is at this point that the free imagination and creative spirit comes in. Extracting a principle (one of the formal 'movement' processes) is a deliberate logical process, but the incorporation of this principle into a new idea requires imagination and creativity.

The 'freewheeling' of a brainstorming session has the advantage that it enables the thinkers to break off from one approach to pursue another. This is attractive but it does lead to 'messing around in the hope that something will turn up'. It also means that there is less effort to make a provocation work. In lateral thinking the thinker may stay with a provocation for a while in order to get something from that provocation. Unless there is this effort, the thinker will simply take the easiest way out – which means retreating to traditional ideas. For example, with the random-word technique it would be a bad mistake to abandon the first word that turned up in order to try for a better word. Very soon this would degenerate into waiting for a word that fitted into existing ideas. So there would be no provocative element at all.

A key element of the formal application of lateral thinking is that one step can be taken after another. For the moment the thinker is focused on the step that is being taken. An interesting idea that turns up can be pursued, provided the step has been taken. If not, the idea is noted and then returned to later. There is no contradiction between focus and discipline on the one hand and creativity on the other hand.

Catch-22

When I am asked to develop ideas on a consulting basis I often get caught by a Catch-22 which owes something to the attitudes of brainstorming. If I turn up a creative idea which is practical and logical (in hindsight) and capable of being used at once, there is an air of disappointment. Somehow this is not what was expected. If I turn up a wild 'blue-sky' idea then this seems to be what is expected of creativity. Yet the idea is deemed to be impractical. There has developed this dangerous expectation that creativity should be producing wild and way-out ideas that are impractical. This is the fault of the brainstorming idiom which has failed to distinguish between wild ideas as provocations and wild ideas as end products. This is why we need to acknowledge the debt that creative thinking owes to the brainstorming idiom, and then move on to more serious creative processes.

The thinking place

What is there to think about?

In a previous *Letter* I discussed idea-sensitive areas (i.s.a.'s) and suggested that everyone should have a list of pet i.s.a.'s. For those who may have forgotten, i.s.a. is a defined area in which the thinker believes that a new concept would make a big difference. In other words, the area would respond well (or be sensitive) to a new concept. At this point I want to look at the broader issue of focus areas.

If we believe in the power of thinking, where should we apply our thinking? What would we like our thinking to do for us? There is no need to believe that thinking will turn up an answer each time, in order to believe that it may be worth applying thinking to a particular area or problem. The opposite attitude is a sort of fatalism which holds that nothing much can be done and that things will work themselves out in due course with the passage of time and the evolutionary processes that might go with this. So conflicts will be resolved by one or other party triumphing or through a sort of exhausted boredom. There may be some merit in this fatalistic attitude. There may indeed be problems that can only be solved by the passage of time and the working through of the existing system pressures. We could, however, think about such problems and then come to this conclusion. That is a little different from starting out with the negative conclusion and never bothering to do much thinking.

It is easy to assume that, if there are serious problems that concern many people, a great deal of thinking is being done about such problems and that the marginal effects of a little more thinking must be insignificant. This is not so with creative thinking. A hundred thinkers may all be following the same track that has been dictated to them by their background and their position in the situation. The next thinker may come up with a new conceptual approach; it is not a matter of numbers but a matter of difference. A party standing outside of a problem may have a view that is different from all those involved in the problem – no matter how many of these there might be. That is why I am in the process of setting up a supra-national independent thinking organisation (SITO). The foundation has been set up in The Hague and the operating headquarters will be at Palazzo Marnisi in Malta (because of its political neutrality and good East/West and North/South bridges). There are many reasons for believing that such an independent body can have a convenience value. I shall spell out this value in more detail in future issues of this *Letter*.

There are thinking situations that require fuller information. There are thinking situations that require a better analysis of existing information. There are thinking situations that demand a better understanding of the complex systems involved. There are thinking situations that need better designed action plans. There are thinking situations that await the generation of more creative options. What else? If you were to attempt to classify the sort of thinking required by a variety of situations, how might you classify that thinking? It would be easy enough to say that 'better thinking' is required in all cases. It would be easy enough to search for a panacea like 'the proper education of all those involved' or 'the spirit of Christian goodwill' and so on. You might even claim that 'good logic' is all that is 'required', forgetting that logic is only a servicing tool to service various values and perceptions.

For the second part of the exercise make a list of all the special problems and concerns that need thinking about. There might be obvious ones like a cure for cancer or the development of practical nuclear fusion energy or an end to the arms race. List all these obvious ones, but also look for the less obvious ones. De we want to provide employment for all? Do we want to live to be 150? Do we want to be more intelligent? Do we want a greater sense of spiritual values? Do we want better political systems? Do we want better ways of tackling and thinking about problems whatever they may be?

Give some thought to setting out a 'thinking agenda'. In addition, you might indicate what progress you expect to be made in the different areas and the time scale of this progress (for example you may expect a cure for cancer by 2020, or commercial nuclear fusion by 2050).

It may be that improving our thinking habits and methods is likely to make a bigger difference than anything else. If so, why do we have doubts about whether much can be done in this direction?

You might also indicate where you expect the thinking to come from (for example a cancer cure could come from the R&D thinking of major drug companies).

13

General area focus

Where do we set out to apply our creativity and our lateral thinking tools? There are four types of focus area: 1. General area; 2. Specific concern; 3. Review; and 4. Idea sensitive area.

I propose to deal with the General Area focus. This is by far the simplest and is the one I normally use for the practice of lateral thinking skills. It involves a broad description of a general area such as: hotels, retail banking, airlines, hospital care, traffic in cities and so on. It is possible to narrow it down a little further. For example we may want to focus upon hotel restaurants rather than hotels in general. We may want to focus upon bank premises rather than banks in general. Nevertheless these are still 'general area' focus items. The important point is that a specification of purpose must never be used. We must not specify that the purpose of our creative endeavour is 'to increase the profitability of hotel restaurants'. If that is what we want to do then we should use the second type of focus area which is designed for specific concerns. The general area focus is meant to be general. The reason for this is that we want to give ourselves a chance of turning up ideas we have never thought of before. We also want to turn up opportunities.

There is a huge difference between a problem and an opportunity. A problem presents itself. We do not have to go out and search for it. Like an ache or a pain it makes itself felt. There is another type of problem which takes the form of an obstacle or gap which occurs on the road we are taking to achieve something (like an engineer needing to find a metal that will stand up to the great heat in an engine he is designing). An opportunity cannot be seen until after it has been seen. That is why putting a tight specification on the purpose of our creative thinking means that we can only tackle defined problems. We would be unlikely to come up with opportunities. That is exactly what the 'general area' focus is about. It is equivalent to saying: 'I am setting our to look for opportunities in this general area'.

It is perfectly true that with ordinary thinking we need to be very precise and very focused as regards what we are trying to achieve with our thinking. I am very much in favour of that. So some people feel unhappy about the broad vagueness of 'general area' focus. This is a failure to understand that there are many different idioms of thinking and different tools for different occasions. The idiom of 'movement' is, for example, totally different to the idiom of 'judgement'. Each is used as appropriate. The reverse gear in a car is different from the forward gears. A hammer is different from a saw. We use each tool in its proper place.

The difficulty arises with those people who believe that there is a 'general-problem-solving' technique and that it should be used on every thinking occasion. It is possible to define and use such a technique, but then it has to be so broadly defined that it becomes virtually pointless. For example, if the first stage is to define your objective then we would define this as: 'seeking to have new ideas in the general area of hotels'. At this point it all becomes a play with words. We end up by precisely defining something vague. If that is necessary to make someone happy I am not against it. Provided, of course, that the 'general' nature of the general area focus is not lost.

Post-hoc specificity

So we set out to generate ideas in the general area which we have defined. A number of ideas turn up. We note them all. We then elaborate each of them a little bit further. At this point the elaboration has a definite purpose. We look to see in what direction the idea seems to be offering benefits.

The word 'benefit' is the key word in opportunity search. *With a problem we look for a solution: with an opportunity we look for benefits.*

So examine each idea to see in which direction that particular idea may be offering benefits. I list below some of the standard directions in which benefits may be offered, but any thinker can add to or alter this list to suit his or her requirements.

Cost cutting: Savings in general. Ways of cutting out parts of the operation or doing things in a simpler way. Different sources of supply. Different services on offer. In short 'is this idea going to save money?'

Simplicity: This overlaps with 'cost cutting' but need not actually involve a saving in costs. If something can be done in a simpler way it may reduce errors. It may also be possible to have less qualified staff (even if they are paid the same they may be easier to find). Simplicity may also mean less strain on those involved.

Product value: Having a better product (or service) to offer. Having a product which more people will want. Having some USP (unique selling proposition) which makes your product stand out against the competition.

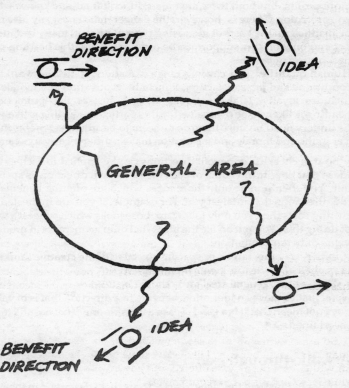

Added value: Adding something to your product or service which gives added value to the consumer or added value to yourself.

Better volume: Anything that increases sales. More people want to buy your product. More people are in a position to buy your product. For example if you find a way of reducing prices you should have a bigger sales volume (assuming some price sensitivity).

Better margins: This means better profit margins. It may arise from raising prices, from cutting costs, from added value or from doing things in a different way.

Promotion and advertising: This covers all those matters which make your product or service more 'visible'. It may be word-of-mouth as people talk about your product. It may be some attention-getting device. Better promotion does not automatically mean more sales or more profits, but both these are rather difficult if no-one knows what you are doing. There is, however, the danger that almost any idea can be justified on the basis of increasing promotion, and many bad ideas depend only on this support. So be careful in using this heading as a description of benefits.

Human qualities: This covers a range of matters. It includes working conditions and job satisfaction. It includes motivation and morale. It includes loyalty. It also includes 'image'. Just as the 'promotion' heading is likely to be overvalued so this particular heading is likely to be undervalued because there do no seem to be any direct profits in it. Yet in the end morale and motivation make a difference everywhere.

So this checklist of benefit directions can be applied to each of the ideas that have turned up. For each idea a 'benefit direction' is spelled out. You then pursue only those ideas which are offering benefits in the directions that interest you. For example, if you are interested in cutting costs then you only follow up those ideas which suggest a way of doing this. You put on file the ideas that offer an increase in product value or better promotion.

In this way the 'target' or specific objective of the creative thinking is applied *after* the thinking has taken place.

That is how 'general area' focus should be used.

Note: Just because an idea offers benefits in a direction that is of value does not mean that it is a good idea or a usuable one. That has still to be ascertained.

A walk-through exercise

In order to illustrate the 'general area' focus that I described in the first section I am going to 'walk-through' a deliberate creative exercise using this type of focus.

General area focus: 'Fast food'.
Lateral thinking technique: Random juxtaposition.

I specify (at random) page 328 and position 7. I then open a tiny dictionary at this page and find the seventh word (counting down from the top of the page). If the word had not been a noun I would have gone on to the next nouns since nouns are, in general, easier to work with.

Random word: 'Mallet' (described as hammer with a wooden head).

Ideas

1. Mallet suggests carpentry and DIY type of operation. What could this mean in the context of 'fast food'? A suggestion that part of a fast food outlet might be made over as a simple kitchen in which customers would make DIY simple meals (eggs, bacon, hamburgers etc). The food would be bought from the outlet. The DIY concept could extend to the whole operation in which only food and cooking apparatus were provided. A simpler DIY version might suggest that students provided service in exchange for meals (for example serving for one evening in exchange for a number of meals during the rest of the week).

2. A mallet operates through repeated blows so there is the concept of 'repetition'. Any food outlet must welcome repeat business. There could be a simple card which every diner gets and which shows the days of the week for the next fortnight (i.e., in two weekly chunks). Presentation of the card within that period results in 20 per cent off the price of a meal. Each time the card is used that date is clipped out of it. There is, of course, the problem of transfer, but that is not necessarily a bad thing. In short, there is always an incentive for someone to return for another meal within a fortnight of his or her previous meal. Another suggestion might be that voucher books of meals at some discount can be purchased in advance. This gives the outlet the use of the money as a float.

3. Mallets are used for hammering in tent pegs. This leads directly to the notion of camping. This could mean a mobile 'fast food' van under the appropriate franchise, which would station itself at camping and caravan sites. This could also be a private enterprise. Using its organisation and bulk buying powers, a fast food operation might also get into the business of packing 'camping food' kits with food to last for a weekend or a week.

4. Mallets are used for setting up cricket stumps, so this creates an association with sport. This, in turn, suggest simple food packs in containers that would be sold at the entrance to sports grounds or race tracks. These would be packed rather in the way airline food is packed (perhaps even by the same people). Perhaps the emphasis could shift from 'fast food' to 'packed food'. Perhaps 'packed food' as distinct from 'take-away' could be a growth area in itself.

5. The mallet has a certain shape: there is a head and a handle. This leads to the suggestion of 'a sort of hamburger on a stick'. In practice what might this mean? It might mean a type of fast food that is easier to hold with one hand. Perhaps something that would be easy to eat whilst driving. Some sort of kebab (or satay) comes to

mind. But there would need to be a mechanism for moving each piece of meat up into the top position. Food on a stick could mean savings in terms of plates, cutlery etc (and washing up).

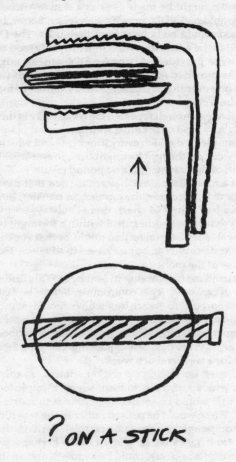

? ON A STICK

6. A hammer (or mallet) is the controlled application of force. This leads to the general concept of 'control'. Obviously control should be applied to every aspect of a fast food operation (particularly when franchised) but no particularly new concept comes to mind. Except perhaps alternating periods of tight and looser control. This might mean that people got into good habits during the period of

tight control, and yet the controls did not have to be so tight all the time.

7. A mallet operates with an 'up and down' movement. This suggests the general principle of fluctuations. Perhaps prices could fluctuate from week to week. More practically, prices might fluctuate during the day. So during hours that would normally be slack the price could be considerably less.

8. The thump of a mallet suggest the time-keeping of galley slaves, and this in turn suggests a training of staff to do everything to a rhythm.

These are the ideas that turned up during a three minute use of the random word. It has taken considerably longer to write the ideas down, and in the writing down some of the ideas get elaborated.

The next stage in the process is to take each idea and to see in which direction it might offer benefits. Often an idea can offer benefits in several directions.

I shall proceed to list the various ideas (there may have been several under one heading) and to indicate possible benefits against each of them.

1. Part of shop as DIY cooking: cost cutting; product value; promotion; human qualities.
2. Total DIY cooking operation: simplicity; better margins; promotion.
3. Students as servers: cost cutting; promotion; human qualities.
4. Repeat business card: better volume.
5. Book of vouchers: better volume; added value (in float).
6. Camp site services: better volume; promotion.
7. Packed camping food: better margins; better volume; new product; promotion.
8. Sports packs: better volume; simplicity; promotion; better margins (possibly).
9. Packed food business: new product; better volume; promotion; added value (to food buying operations).
10. Food on a stick: cost cutting; simplicity; added value; better volume (e.g., for motorist use).
11. Alternating control: better margins; cost cutting; human qualities.
12. Price fluctuations: better volume.
13. Rhythm training: human qualities.

Many of these ideas would increase volume. Without going in to specific pricing it is difficult to say whether margins would or would not be increased. For example, with packed food there is no need for high street premises or serving staff. On the other hand there is the cost of containers and wastage.

If I was only interested in cost cutting then I would pursue only ideas 1, 2, 10 and 11. On closer examination I might even find that they did not really offer any cost-cutting benefits because of hidden costs that only became visible after closer examination (like theft of utensils in DIY cooking or the need for expensive extractor fans).

The other ideas could be put on file. If any of them seemed attractive enough then that idea could be pursued in its own right even if it did not fit in with the defined requirement. For example the concept of sports-packs might seem worth pursuing.

From the whole exercise a single idea might emerge. It might even be that the idea is not usable as originally stated but that the concept put forward in the idea becomes usable. For example it might not be possible to use student help as such (because of union regulations) but it might be possible to have apprentices or trainee staff.

The thinking place

It is sometimes a useful and amusing thinking exercise to set yourself a difficult thinking task. There does need to be a measure of success and a visible measure of achievement. It is best if you can actually try out your ideas to see how they perform. For this reason difficult problems are not much fun because you either solve them or you do not. They can be frustrating. I prefer simple physical tasks: making and achieving something.

For example I once set myself the task of making an object that would climb up a wall, go along the ceiling and then descend the opposite wall. All this had to be achieved with materials that were available around me in the kitchen at that time. It was not a matter of going off to an engineering workshop or ordering special materials. Another time the task was to make a cylinder that would fall over by itself after about 20 minutes (some readers will recognise that I used this as the basis for the experiments in the book *Practical thinking*). Then there was the cylinder that would stand up by itself. On another occasion there was to be a ball that rolled around by itself and when it got into a corner it would find its own way out again.

There is also a very interesting exercise with a postcard and a paper-clip. The object is to design the postcard (you may use scissors but no glue) in such a way that when you drop it (no launching) from chest height it will travel the maximum distance forward. The whole postcard has to go the distance – you cannot discard bits. Three or four quite different aeronautical principles can become involved as you tackle the task.

TOWER
TASK

146

The purpose of the tasks is to enjoy doing them and to enjoy thinking about them. You should also enjoy watching your thinking at each stage. You should verbalise it and spell it out. Do you have a problem: what is it? Are you just going to modify the idea or are you going to move to a different design approach? You could make a sort of log or diary. Getting the answer is very much less fun than enjoying the thinking that you have to do on the way.

You can look back at your thinking and find why you were blocked. You can see how defining a problem in a certain way held you up. You may even see – in hindsight – a route that would have avoided the problem instead of trying to solve it.

The task

I am now going to suggest a task which you might tackle in this way.

Take an ordinary sheet of A4 paper (this should be of average stiffness – about 70 gms).

The task is to make as high a tower as possible out of this sheet of paper. Note that the tower must be quite stable and must be capable of standing on its own for at least one hour.

You are not allowed anything else at all: no scissors; no knife; no ruler or edge; no glue; no rubber bands; no coins – nothing at all.

When I set this task at a seminar I only allow two sheets of paper: one for practice and one for execution. On this occasion,, however, you can use as many sheets as you like (one sheet only per tower) in order that you may try out different design approaches.

What are the priorities? Which things should come first and in what directions should the thinking effort be most directed? Some matters may turn out to be luxuries if we do not get the other things right.

Then there are the sensitive points in the system. This means that an effect at such points could have a spread effect.

14

Eight out of ten for thinking

A few months ago I asked a group of highly educated graduates at a meeting in Florida to give themselves a mark out of ten for their thinking ability. To my surprise the average mark was 7.5. Many people gave themselves eight out of ten and a few even nine out of ten.

THE VILLAGE VENUS

I do not think this was arrogance or conceit, but rather a matter of limited horizons. In *Practical Thinking* I write about the 'Village Venus' effect. The setting has to be a primitive one before the days of television and gorgeous girls in daily papers. To the people in the village, the most beautiful girl in the village had to be the most beautiful girl in the world. If your horizons are limited then your searches and comparisons are also bounded by those horizons.

If you do not believe there to be more to thinking than what you are already doing then you may indeed be inclined to give yourself eight out of ten. If you believe that thinking is a vast field in which our current expertise is only a very small part, then you might award yourself a lower mark. You need to be conscious of what is not there or what could be there. Venuses do no doubt occur in villages as frequently as elsewhere, but to be sure you have a Venus does require a wider comparison.

I put this matter to some of the people who had awarded themselves the high marks for thinking. I said I was rather surprised because it seemed to me that at best our thinking was only a small part of what it could be. The answer was that the person had always come out in the top five per cent at school or university and therefore felt justified in awarding himself/herself a high mark to reflect this 'pecking order'.

In all fairness that person could have said to me: 'when you asked us to give a mark out of ten you should have specified whether you wanted the mark on a comparative basis or an absolute basis'. Even such a statement would not have ended the matter because another person felt that he was awarding marks to his thinking skill relative to his potential thinking skill. He felt he was operating at 80 per cent capacity. In industrial terms this still leaves a lot of unused capacity; so, what seems to be a lack of humility, may be an exercise in humility.

Apart from illustrating the difficulties of communication, the exercise does raise the matter of what we expect from thinking.

What do we expect from our own thinking?

What do we expect from the thinking of others?

What do we expect from thinking as an operation in itself?

There are a lot of obvious end-points to thinking: problem-solutions, decisions, designs, negotiated settlements and so on. I do not want to be as specific as this. I want to examine what we expect from the 'quality' of our thinking irrespective of the purpose towards which it is applied.

Do we want our thinking to be slick, streamlined and decisive – without waffle and with confidence?

Do we want our thinking to be detailed and subtle and exploratory – peeling away the layers of the onion to find further layers?

We probably want both. A rich and sensitive exploration of the matter followed by a clear path to decision or solution. We want to be able to generate alternatives and then to decide easily between them.

I suppose we might want much the same as the carpenter might want from his tools: that he may be able to use them fluently and effectively for the purpose he has in mind. They should be under his command and under his control. Confidence is not enough, because a stupid person only rarely lacks confidence in his decisions or understandings.

What should we expect from creativity?

There is something of a Catch-22 in what we expect from creativity. If I am involved in consultancy and put forward a simple idea that is obvious and logical in hindsight but was derived through the deliberate exercise of creativity, then the idea is treated as practical but not as creative. If, on the other hand, I put forward a marvellous blue-sky concept that has value but might be very difficult to test or put into effect (such ideas also have a provocative value) then this idea is accepted as wonderfully creative – but not practical. It seems that only rarely do people expect a creative idea to be practical.

CATCH - 22

There is a feeling that being creative is a bit like rolling dice. From time to time a double six may come up and if it does this is wonderful (at least in some games); but the dice roller does not really deserve much credit for making it happen.

An idea that might take ten seconds to generate and even less to state can give rise to millions of dollars in profit, but there can never be any proper evaluation of such a creative effort. It is felt that to reward the creator would be equivalent to rewarding the dice cup when someone won a game of backgammon. The analogy works on two levels. The dice cup is simply a container, and similarly the creator's brain is simply a container through which something happens. The other level is that the dice throws in themselves have no value until put into a game strategy by the player. *So an idea has no merit until put into effect by the user.* There is truth in this. A skilful player can make the best out of bad dice and a bad player can waste good dice. Nevertheless a skilful player can do very well indeed with good dice and would be foolish to disregard the roll of the dice.

The dice analogy for creativity is, of course, an extremely bad one. Because something only happens occasionally and seems to be outside the control of our will we tend to regard it as a matter of chance. Well, creativity is a matter of chance – but only up to the point when we start to do something deliberate about it. If we do nothing about it then it does indeed remain a matter of chance.

I have said exactly the same thing about thinking and intelligence. Thinking and intelligence are the same only until we start to develop thinking deliberately as a skill.

Because your use of creativity is a matter of chance does not mean that my use of creativity is also a matter of chance.

The American language provides some neat and useful phrases. One such phrase is: 'where he is coming from'. This is somewhat similar to the 'logic bubble' that I describe in one of my books. It refers to the set of perceptions, concepts, circumstances, experience and expectations that provide the environment 'from which the person is coming'. So in order to understand why some people award themselves eight out of ten for creativity we need to know where the people are coming from. *In order to understand what people expect from creativity we also need to know where they are coming from.*

Sooner or later

As I so often point out in my seminars, any valuable creative idea must always be logical in hindsight. That is because the back-track towards where we are standing becomes obvious in hindsight (the asymmetry of patterns). In a sense our word 'valuable' means that we can see a value in the idea, and that means a logical placement of the idea. It is rarely possible in hindsight to remember how inaccessible an idea was in foresight.

So if an idea is logical in hindsight then we can, truthfully, claim that we would have had the idea sooner or later. It may have been tomorrow or in a week's time or even in a year's time. Or, someone else would have had the idea and we could have copied it. We expect there to be an inevitability about any logical idea. Yet it took ages to invent the hovercraft, which is such a simple and logical idea in hindsight.

New directions

There are many routes by which it is possible to head North. A direction is not a detailed route but a direction that exists through being contrasted with another direction. When you are heading North you are not heading South. There are times when you may indeed head South as part of your general progress Northwards (for example turning off a motorway), but the overall direction is what matters.

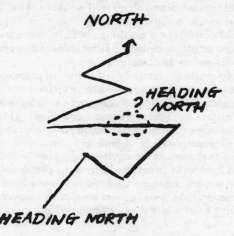

As with compass directions it is best to define a direction by contrasting it with other directions: 'We could move in this direction . . . or in that . . . but we have chosen to go . . .'. This is especially valuable when there is a change of direction. It is often difficult for someone to appreciate a change in direction except by contrasting it with the previous direction. In driving along country roads you might say to your passenger: 'the sun was in our faces before, notice how it is now to our left' (in the Southern hemisphere this might indicate a long journey rather than a change of direction).

For example in a stagnating mature industry there might be a conscious change in direction from 'technology' to 'customer needs'. There might also be a change in direction from 'commodity production' to 'added value product development'.

It is, of course, essential to define where you are at the moment in order to define the change in direction. A broad and hazy view of what is happening at the moment makes it difficult to see why the new direction is indeed new or different. It is usually possible to point to one small aspect of what is now being done in order to show that the new direction is not new at all – and, as a consequence, nothing needs to change at all. In defining directions it is always the broad thrust that matters not the detail. As I mentioned above, unless the road is absolutely straight then any move towards the North will at times involve journeying East or West or even South. To focus on those segments of the journey and to insist that the journey is not truly Northwards is absurd.

A bank may decide that it is going to move away from servicing large corporations (which can often do their own banking) towards serving medium-sized corporations. This could be a conscious change of direction. Such a conscious change of direction is rather different from simply finding that most business is actually coming from medium-sized corporations, whilst the efforts and activities are still geared to serving the larger corporation. To find that the fish dishes on the menu are selling better than the steak dishes is not a conscious change in culinary direction.

Following directions or creating them

If you find that the fish dishes are indeed selling better in your restaurant should you consciously change direction towards that of a fish restaurant? There may indeed be a case for doing so, but this would need to be established in its own right through careful consideration of all that is involved. The mere fact that fish dishes are selling better in your restaurant merely means that, in comparison to other dishes in your restaurant, the fish dishes are preferred. Perhaps the steak or its prices are unattractive. Perhaps fish is the only 'light' dish and clients are weight conscious (in which case you would get much better profit margins by designing other light dishes than by serving fish).

To drift in a particular direction is not the same as consciously choosing the direction. It is easier to do because it removes the responsibility of choice. You might choose the wrong direction, but drift chooses itself.

Defining directions

This is more a creative process than an analytical one. It needs creativity to define the directions. Analysis will simply tell you that more diners choose fish than steak. It needs creativity to suggest the direction change that accounts for this shift. Creativity cannot prove anything, but it sets out possibilities that can then be checked out. It might be a 'health food' direction. It might be a 'light food' direction. It might be a 'price' direction. It might even be that ladies prefer fish to steak and that more ladies are now using your restaurant. It might be a mixture of all these. You might try to analyse what is happening. Are the other cheaper dishes getting more attention? You might want to set up a test. For example, you might create some additional light dishes and provide a special section on the menu for these. You might just count how many ladies are coming to your restaurant, and so on.

As I have written and said so often, there is creative skill in defining directions in a manner that is both broad and yet specific enough. Some definitions can be too broad. For instance in the restaurant example the general direction of 'giving the customer what he or she wants' may be too broad. On the other hand a switch of direction towards 'serving more fish' may be too specific. A switch towards 'a wider choice of lighter dishes' might be specific enough to guide action without being so detailed as to be restrictive.

When I wrote about i.s.a.'s (idea sensitive areas) in a previous *Letter* I said that it was often useful to get a detailed example and then to work backwards from that towards a broader definition of the area. Exactly the same thing applies to directions. Creativity may suggest a specific idea (for example, asking customers to indicate their second choice of menu dish) and then it becomes possible to work backwards towards a broader definition (in this case considering ways of getting customer feedback). A route is only a route, but once we get the broad direction then we can design many other routes.

In an attempt to cut hospital costs there may be a conscious decision to move in the direction of 'segmenting patient needs'. This means seeing exactly what level of care and attention each patient needs rather than supplying the maximum amount of care which is, in fact, only needed by a small minority of patients.

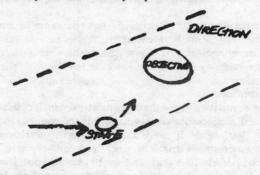

Objectives and directions

What is the difference between an objective and a direction? You could argue that there is a big difference or that there is none at all. What is the difference between the North Pole, the North and moving Northwards? *An objective is usually an end point or an achieved state.* A direction is the type of action that seems likely to take us towards that objective. On the other hand you could set objectives (or rather sub-objectives) which become the markers for ensuring that we are moving in the right direction – like flags on a mountain slope. I tend to think of an objective. A direction might be 'moving towards containerisation in shipping' and an objective might be 'to have a fleet of five container ships by 1986'. As usual, I am not too fussed about tight definitions since these only have a descriptive value rather than an operational value.

It is enough that a person should be able to say: 'in what direction are we moving?' or 'what is the difference between the new direction and the one we have been following?'

Effort or change?

Does a direction imply effort or does it imply change? Surprisingly this is rather difficult to answer. It may seem that any movement must imply change and without movement there cannot be direction. In practice, however, it may be enough to put more effort into the required direction – rather like someone throwing the javelin harder in the same direction. *If there is to be a change of direction then clearly there has to be a change.* This happens first in thinking and is then implemented in various ways (structural etc.). If, however, the direction has been clearly defined and the change of direction has been made, then what may be required may be more effort, effectiveness and efficiency in pursuit of the established direction.

Even so there may be a need for change. You can walk along a road, run along the road, ride a bicycle, catch a bus or drive a car. The road (direction, destination) does not change at all, but your means of moving along the road has changed. This ties in with what I have written in previous *Letters* about levels of alternatives. Even if both destination and route have been decided upon, there is still room for creativity in generating alternative ways of implementing the movement along the chosen route to the chosen destination.

Talk, gradual, step or switch

How sudden should the change in direction be? It always needs to be sudden and complete on the thought level but need not be so sudden on the action level.

The chief executive may talk about the change in direction. This has motivating value. It also gives reporters and analysts something to write about. This rhetoric level does have a practical value. People feel that something is happening. It is not the same drift as before. Even if no practical steps are taken for some time the talk level has a value. In addition, in all decisions or discussions the new direction will exert an influence.

Gradual implementation is difficult because it means keeping on with the old direction even whilst things are moving towards the new direction. This leads to confusion. It is best to talk in terms of new emphasis so that, even when the old things are done in the old way, there is some feeling that there has been change. Just as 'emphasis' in speech means that the same words are said in a different way so a new emphasis can imply switch when the action remains the same.

Step-wise changes need to be designed in a careful and programmed manner. In some cases this is the only practical way. From a motivational point of view those things which are due to be changed go through a depressed period as they await their turn for change. Token actions can change this static limbo into something more dynamic. Even if such steps are not strictly required they have a most useful cosmetic value (and cosmetic values can be real from a motivational point of view).

It is only rarely that a sudden switch can be made. It can be done with the advertising thrust. It may even be possible to do it with marketing (from direct sales to distributors). If thought (change of direction) and action go closely together then there is a danger that some people will be confused and left behind. If there is too long a gap between thought and action then the momentum goes out of it. The best strategy is for some action to show the seriousness of the talk, and then for sequenced actions to bring about the switch-over. This switch-over may be a mixture of emphasis changes and real changes.

Who should know about the change?
Everybody.

The thinking place

Take an idea . . .
A lot of very weak ideas come up in any creative session. A lot of them are produced by people who believe themselves to be much more creative than they really are (this applies particularly to advertising personnel where confidence in one's own creativity is usually more important than the creativity itself). There is also the spin-off from the brainstorming idiom: say something crazy and that must have a value in itself.

The purpose of this exercise is to take a 'weak idea' and then to use *movement* the movement idiom to move from it to other ideas.

The subject of the discussion has been 'toothbrushes'. Someone suggests that the handle be a ball-point pen. The connection is obvious: 'a use for something long and thin like a toothbrush handle'. There could be some merit in the idea if the ball-point contained an ink (washable) with which you could write on the bathroom mirror. You might then market the device as a way of capturing those ideas that occur when you are in the bath or shaving. Otherwise there is a certain inappropriateness in the carrying around of a toothbrush when you need a pen or a pen when you need a toothbrush.

At this point you would have to decide whether you are really interested in toothbrushes as such, or the capability of making toothbrushes or any marketable device of this sort of price and size. Let us suppose that you are not confined directly to toothbrushes.

The next question might be: 'would there be any point in carrying around a toothbrush?'. The answer might be: 'yes in terms of brushing teeth after meals etc.'. Possibly a neat cover completely concealing the brush part could be designed. There is, however, another sort of brush that does need to be carried about. This is a clothes brush, particularly if a dark suit is worn. Toothbrushes make excellent clothes brushes. So perhaps the device could combine a writing function with a clothes brush availability.

If our attention has now shifted to a combination of writing and clothes brushing, we might look around for other methods of brushing clothes. There is the sticky paper concept which is excellent for removing dogs' hairs and fibres. Perhaps the ball-point could contain a tight roll of such sticky paper.

Why does there have to be paper which gets used up? What about a 'wipe-on' tacky adhesive which is applied to the surface of the ball-point which is then rolled over the surface to be 'brushed' and the whole thing is then rinsed off under a tap and dried for use again? At this point this type of adhesive could now be pursued in its own right without reference to either ball-point or to toothbrush.

Let us suppose that we are only interested in toothbrushes. Where does the ball-point idea get us? We might think in terms of a rolling plastic ball at the end of the toothbrush handle for use in massaging the gums. It might also apply some medicament to the gums at the same time.

As an exercise take the following weak idea and move with it in the same manner as I have done with the toothbrush. Try to verbalise or write down the different steps in your thinking.

'Someone suggests that ordinary dining plates should have a flattened portion along one side – instead of being circular.'

Take this idea and see what you can do with it.

15

'The same as . . .'

Most people who have anything to do with creativity know that this is the ultimate killer phrase.

If you put forward a suggestion and a listener claims that it would not work or has no value, then you have a chance to argue the point. You can set out to show how the idea will indeed work. You can point out the value and the benefits. There is at least the basis for an argument. The idea gets attention from all parties: yourself; the objector; and the listeners. Attention is all a novel idea deserves. During that attention opportunity the idea has to show that it is worth examining further.

If, however, the idea is met with the killer phrase 'the same as . . .' then the idea gets no attention at all. It is implied that the idea is not new, that it does not merit any attention time at all. It is even suggested that the outcome of the idea is already known and shown to have no value.

There are many variations of the phrase:

'That's not a new idea . . .'
'That is exactly what we used to do years ago . . .'
'That is no different from what we do now . . .'
'That is a marvellous idea, but we have been doing it.'
'What's new about that?'
'This is the same as . . .'
'We already do that with our xxx system.'
'We have always done that.'
'We used to do that years ago . . .'
'We have tried that and it does not work.'
'We do that all the time.'
'That is the equivalent of what we do with xxx.'
'That is an ancient idea.'

We can look at the motivation behind the use of this phrase. There are several levels of motivation.

Who's the clever chap
If there are any new ideas around in our business we have already had them. We do not need any outsider to come and turn up ideas for us. By

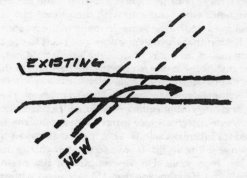

definition any useful idea you turn up is one we already know about or have been using.

You cannot beat experience
Ideas do not matter. Any valid idea will eventually emerge when the conditions are right for it to emerge. The idea will emerge from those who have experience in the business and are able both to form the idea and also to assess its value. If such people have not already had the idea it is because the idea is worthless: it could not possibly work.

There is nothing new
All new jokes are really a variety of seven basic jokes. Any new idea is just a wrinkle on some old idea. It is not new at all but just the same old idea in different clothing. Someone wants to get credit for resurrecting an old idea and calling it new.

New ideas mean hassle
If we can show that any new idea is really an old idea that we know about or that has been shown not to work then we do not have to take any action. We do not even need to evaluate an idea if we can show that it is an old idea which has already been tried or rejected.

Not invented here
If we acknowledge this as a new idea then the fellow will want credit for it (and possibly payment). If we can show that it is not new then he

159

cannot claim credit. Later on, perhaps, we can use that idea in some way or other. After all we are quite capable of generating our own ideas.

In spite of all these reasons there is a further – and perfectly genuine – one. The listener who comes up with the phrase 'the same as . . .' genuinely believes it to be the same. In many of the reasons given here there is the notion that the listener does not want to see any novelty and therefore makes an effort to treat the idea as old hat. What I am indicating at this point is that even with the best will in the world the listener may not be able to see the novelty.

As I have written elsewhere (particularly in my book *The mechanism of mind*) *the brain acts as an environment in which incoming information organises itself into patterns.* Once formed, these patterns are triggered or recognised on future occasions. This is what allows us to survive in a practical sense in the world. If we had to work things out each time life would be impossible. Unlike computers, the brain is able to generalise patterns. That means that, if there is no pattern available, the brain will provide the nearest available pattern. This allows the brain to recognise new things as if they were old things. In time a new pattern may be formed.

The ability of the brain to see new things as if they were old things is a marvellous capacity of the brain. But it does have a drawback. The drawback is that when there is something new which can be seen in terms of something old, then the brain will do exactly this. The result is the 'same as . . .' phrase. The brain genuinely sees the new suggestion as being the same as the old pattern. Under these circumstances it is very hard indeed for the presenter of the new idea to offer it as a new pattern.

EXISTING

NEW

Another problem is that some people prefer to work at a broad function level. At this broad level new ideas can be seen as falling under the same broad heading as old ideas. Imagine that someone is trying to present the Pan-Am Frequent Traveller notion. The listener simply sees it as another discount scheme (which in a broad sense it is). The idea is dismissed on the basis that such discount schemes eventually lead to losses all round. The key point of novelty of the idea would have been missed. The key point is, of course, that in fare discounting the person buying the ticket benefits, but in the Frequent Traveller idea the person actually doing the flying benefits (and is therefore more likely to choose Pan-Am).

At an absurd level we might imagine Christopher Cockerell, the inventor of the hovercraft, trying to persuade someone to take an interest in the vehicle:

'It does not fly, does it?'
'No.'
'It goes along the ground like any car or truck?'
'It goes above the ground.'
'Well yes, but so does a car. The wheels lift it above the ground. We don't need to play with words.'
'It can go across water.'
'So can an amphibian vehicle. They have not been much use to anyone.'

What I do want to emphasise is that sometimes the 'same as . . .' tactic is used by those who want to resist a new idea – but sometimes it is used by those who genuinely cannot see what is new in the idea.

I was once at a senior-level meeting in New York and suggested a product that might fit market conditions. 'That is a splendid idea – but you are too late. We have been using just that idea for two years now.' So I shut up. There was no point in pushing an idea that was already in use. After the meeting I asked one of those who had been present to describe the idea 'that was in use'. He did so. It was significantly different from the one I had proposed. So I outlined my idea again.

This sort of thing happens time and again. At a recent seminar in Holland I put forward, as a provocation, the following: 'Po, insurance should be transferable between clients'.

Someone present said: 'That is not novel. In the shipping business this has always been so.' It turned out that he was referring to cargo insurance which was indeed transferable when the cargo was transferred. Technically he was correct, but the idea of making life insurance and other types of insurance transferable is indeed a provocation.

So we also have to watch out for occasions where something is done under very special circumstances and from this arises a claim that it is done all the time. To transfer a principle from a very special use to a more general use can be a creative idea.

FOCUS ON DIFFERENCE

To get involved in a 'it's-not-novel/yes-it-is' argument is a degrading and futile exercise. Fundamentally there are two elements involved. The first element concerns whether the idea is worth using or not. In this regard novelty simply means that the idea is not currently being used by the organisation in question. The idea need not be original in itself or even original for that organisation (they may have thought of it before). The direct question is: 'are we doing this?'. The second element is to do with ownership of the idea. This is much more difficult. It has to do with both emotional and financial matters. On the emotional level there is the problem of 'not invented here'. On the financial level there is the question as to whether the person suggesting the idea has any right to benefit from the idea. Organisations do sometimes go through marvellous contortions in order to claim that an idea is not novel. They drag out ancient documents which mention something vaguely related to the idea. They claim that at some meeting someone had mentioned something of the sort. Most of this is entirely spurious. It seems to me that the issue is simple. If as a result of someone's suggestion an organisation starts to use an idea which was not in use, then the person who brings that about has made a contribution. It would be absurd to pretend otherwise. It does not even matter if the idea has been transferred from somewhere else.

The position with regard to the patenting of an idea is, of course, different. I do not intend to go into that matter here.

Focus on the different
The answer to the 'same as . . .' difficulty is to focus on the difference.

This is one of the basic ways of getting 'movement' from an idea or provocation. It involves picking out the points of difference and also making contrasts between what is and what is being suggested. To present an idea as a contrast or shift of emphasis in the first place is a good strategy.

Limits of imagination

I have a container and into this container I put an object. The object remains free in the container without being attached or held in any way. Yet I cannot get the object out of the container when the container is open. Nor can I get it out when the container is closed. The object has not changed in any way. How is this possible?

Object A rests on object B. Object B rests on object C. Object C rests on object A. The result is a solid structure.

I start a line on a piece of paper and I proceed with the line. Eventually I am drawing on the underside of the paper a line that follows the course of the first line. Yet at no time have I crossed an edge of the paper. How is this possible?

At first sight the above statements may seem impossible or illogical. Yet in hindsight each of them is so obvious that it almost becomes trivial. The last situation is now so well known that it hardly qualifies as a mystery. Obviously a Moebius strip is involved. I start the line on one surface and simply continue. Eventually I find myself drawing the line on the opposite surface of the paper. Once I imagine the Moebius strip then it all becomes obvious. But to someone who could not imagine the Moebius strip the statement would remain impossible or illogical.

At first sight it may seem absurd for three objects to support each other by resting on each other. How can an object rest on an object which itself has nothing to rest upon? Once we see how it is done then the structure is obvious. I used this problem in my first book *The five-day course in thinking*. Three bottles are placed more than a knife's length apart. The object is to build a platform strong enough to support a glass of water. You are allowed to use four knives. In fact it can be done with only three knives (to the fury of many readers). It is done with an interlocking pattern in which the first knife rests on the second, the second on the third and the third back on the first. There is no mystery at all.

We come now to the mystery container. This happens to be a British Airways document briefcase with a spring-snap brim. The object is the clip-board which I keep on my knee when giving a talk. The clip-board will not fit into the briefcase when it is open (because the aperture narrows), but it will go in when the case is *half-open*. Similarly it will not come out when the case is open – for the same reason. Nor will it come out when it is closed.

These are trivial examples but they serve to make the point. *We cannot accept statements unless we can imagine the mechanism.* And there is no reason why we should be able to imagine a mechanism.

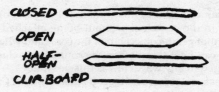

Darwin's theory of evolution may never be proved and may, indeed, be quite wrong in parts. What it did, however, was to offer a feasible mechanism for the variety of species (actually we still need a feasible mechanism as to how the random changes could have given the variety).

In a converse manner we have difficulty in accepting Lamarckian evolution because we cannot conceive how it might work. How can the genes be altered by behaviour that is learned during life? We might possibly conceive that chemical changes in the mother's body affected the foetus (or gene expression in the foetus). This might provide a means for inherited traits.

Imagine an empty cereal carton standing on its corner at the edge of a table. How could it possibly do this without signs of visible support? Perhaps it is suspended by a nylon thread from the ceiling. This is shown not to be so by passing a hand over the carton. In fact a simple wire with a weight at the end provides the arrangement.

When I talk about the teaching of thinking as a skill educators cannot conceive how 'thinking' as such can be taught. Surely we can

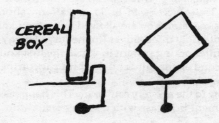

only think about things? How can thinking be taught? Yet when they have watched a simple lesson it becomes obvious to them. Attention scanning tools like the PMI (the first school lesson in which pupils are taught to scan the Plus, Minus and Interesting aspects of a matter) are very easy to teach and easy to transfer to new situations. So the problem of transfer is easily overcome.

At other times *people cannot conceive how it is possible to increase creativity by means of deliberate techniques*. Yet the random word technique can be taught and learned and used in a deliberate, formal manner.

If we had asked an eighteenth century scientist to believe that a person could speak at one point in the world and be heard at thousands of different points without any visible connections, he would have considered the matter totally impossible. Yet we now take radio for granted. Getting to the moon and transplanting a heart would not have seemed so incredible since they might just be extensions of what could could be conceived.

As readers may perceive, this sort of argument can be used to support astrology, telepathy and ESP. Just because we cannot at the moment conceive of a mechanism should we dismiss these phenomena as utterly impossible? Maybe telepathy seems as impossible to us today as radio would have been to the eighteenth century scientist. Obviously such an argument can be applied to anything. Never dismiss anything just because you cannot imagine the mechanism. The opposite of dismissal is not, of course, belief. Non-dismissal stays as non-dismissal until there is evidence to take things further.

We cannot really understand how hypnotism works. What is the communication linkage that allows a word like 'rigid' to bring about a degree of muscle control that cannot be achieved by months of training? Yet hypnotic phenomena can be repeated at will.

I shall not pursue this point about belief and proof because that is not the purpose of this piece. The purpose is to show that imagination is rather limited, and how we are inclined to dismiss something unless a 'type' of mechanism is suggested.

In practice we make use of metaphors in order to illustrate types of mechanism.

If I want to suggest that an amount of something may be good but more of it may be bad I could use the metaphor of salt. Some salt is very good – but a little more becomes bad. This analogy may be totally irrelevant to the matter in hand, but the demonstration of a type of mechanism allows us to understand what is being suggested. The metaphor of a rising tide raising all vessels is a way of showing how economic growth could, conceivably, benefit everyone.

In writing about the behaviour of 'active' self-organising systems, I often use analogies (like the gelatin model) in order to illustrate types of process. Once the process has been shown it can then be translated into the behaviour of nerve networks. At this point it becomes a conceptual model for the mechanism of mind. The important point is that once we can conceive of this type of behaviour then we can examine it, make predictions, and design tools. These must then demonstrate their practical value.

I suspect that there are still a large number of organisational models and mechanisms which we cannot yet conceive. On a more ordinary level we have to use our conceptual imagination in order to design possible mechanisms and processes. Once we can conceive these then we can both explain and take action.

Without this sort of conceptual play, analysis of data is very limited and sterile.

The thinking place

It is well known that problem finding and problem solving are quite different. If a problem is presented to you, then you set out to solve it. We are good at coping with matters that are put under our noses. Problem finding is much more difficult. We have to figure out why a certain area needs attention. We have to figure out the sort of attention it might get. Finally we have to figure out the possible benefits from such attention. In a sense, problem finding is like opportunity seeking.

Imagine you were writing a letter to this *Letter*. You could describe an actual problem or difficulty, or you could conceive of an area that might benefit from attention. The point of this exercise is that the letters be fictitious and need never be sent.

The purpose of the exercise is to set up some mental models for paying attention to the thinking one observes in oneself and in others. It is much easier to recognise butterflies if you have come across butterflies before. In the same way it is easier to recognise phenomena in thinking if you have played around with phenomena before – whether they are real or fictitious.

A fictitious letter is a formula for creating types of attention area.

Dear Sir,
When someone says 'there are three reasons for doing this' is it very much stronger than just saying 'there are these important reasons for

doing this'? Does the adding of numbers means much? Is it just a prop to remind the thinker to find other reasons and to remind him when he has covered all of them? Could it be that he wishes to let the listener know that there are three considered reasons and that he is not just casting around for any reason that comes to mind? Or could it simply be habit because when we visualise 'reasons' given on a sheet of paper they are usually numbered? Is the numbering a convenience of reference so that the listener can refer to 'as to your second reason . . .'?
Yours faithfully,

Dear Sir,
It seems to me that most argument arises not from the mishandling of logic but from a failure to appreciate that each party is using a different set of perceptions. I don't think there is anything very novel in this observation. But what effective method is there for indicating to the other party that he/she is correct 'within a particular framework of perceptions'? How can you switch thinkers from the traditional argument style to what might be called the 'map-making' style?
Yours faithfully,

Dear Sir,
I have found that the most efficient use of thinking is simply 'rationalisation'. Do what you want to do. Decide on any basis you like. Follow your mood. Once this has been done then set to – with your thinking – to prove to yourself and to those around you that you are right. If I am wrong can you tell me why I am wrong?
Yours faithfully,

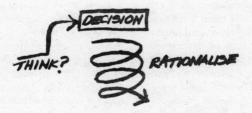

Dear Sir,
Is there any value in actually 'sitting down to think'? I am not referring to the actual physical posture but to the definition of a period of time as being devoted to thinking. I contrast this with the *en passant*

167

thinking that takes place as we discuss something or look at a report. Is there any value in hanging out a label in our minds saying: 'do not disturb, man thinking at this time'?
Yours faithfully,

Dear Sir,
Why isn't thinking more fun?
Yours faithfully,

16

Interesting . . .

To anyone concerned with creativity 'interesting' is a most powerful word. Yet I cannot think of any adequate synonym. There are words like 'rich' or 'fertile' but they only cover part of the meaning. I suspect it is because ordinary language, like ordinary thinking, wants to reach certainty as soon as possible. The purpose of thinking is usually recognition. We want to identify a situation so that we know what to do with it. We want things parcelled up and labelled. 'Interesting' goes in exactly the opposite direction. 'Interesting' opens things up and leaves bits trailing out of the parcel.

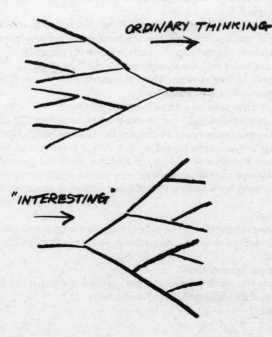

'Interesting' is a signpost to nowhere and yet a signpost to everywhere. 'Interesting' is a gate to a mystery garden in which there is much to be found – but we do not quite know what. 'Interesting' is a beckoning word which leads us further in our exploration and our thinking. 'Interesting' is a temptation to keep on thinking. It is a promise of excitement and of 'interest'.

It is easy to think of 'interest' in terms of multiple leads, triggers, paths and connections. There is richness and fertility and more to come. An interesting person has a background to be explored or a wealth of experience to be passed on. An interesting idea is one that offers much. We can see leads going off in a number of directions, even though we may not see any one direction in detail.

A creative person needs the sort of sensitivity that can recognise 'interest' in an area.

'I think walking sticks should be bowed or sabre shaped.'

'That's an interesting idea.'

'Why do you say it is interesting – is it just because it is different?'

'That's part of it. Also it seems so natural for a walking stick to be straight that a change could open up lots of ideas.'

'For example?'

'It could be made more "springy". Then there are four ways you could hold it: convex forward, convex backward, convex inward and convex outward. We can explore each of these for benefits.'

'There have to be real advantages over a straight stick.'

'Differences to begin with. Then we work with those differences and work towards real advantages.'

'A curve for the sake of a curve is only a gimmick.'

'Convex outward would curve away from your legs. That would leave more space for carrying a briefcase in the same hand. Now that is "interesting". You cannot hold a stick and a briefcase in the same hand because the stick would jut out and not reach the ground. But if there was a curve then this might be possible. A slight curve wouldn't do. There would have to be a sort of indentation to accommodate the briefcase.'

'What else?'

'If you were sitting down the point in contact with the ground could be right under your seat – something that is not possible with a straight stick.'

'And the purpose of that?'

'If you use the stick to help you get up then the point can be more under your centre of gravity. That could help.'

'What else?'

'If the curved handle was in a different plane from the curve of the body then it could never lie flat on the ground. So you could pick it up much more easily.'

The important point is not that these observations are 'interesting' after they have been made. There is a sense of 'interest' which leads the creative thinker to dwell on a point or an observation and then to look around that point to see what can be found. It is the same sort of feeling which youngsters might have when they come across a cave: 'this is an interesting looking cave, let's explore it.'

There has to be a sense of curiosity.

But why is one point more interesting than another?

Unusualness, contrast or difference are contributions to 'interest'. When we can contrast something new with something usual then there is interest. Immediately we look to see what could arise from this difference. Since the starting point is different we rightly expect to end up somewhere different. A kangaroo is immediately interesting because it proceeds in a different way from a horse. *It is a natural habit of the mind to explore things that are different and unexpected.* One of the main purposes of provocation in lateral thinking is to create ideas that are unusual enough to encourage exploration.

It may be that there is a sudden similarity to something else. For example the curved walking stick might have suggested a leaf-spring, a bow, a boomerang, a scythe. Such suggestions add connections or richness. These parts of memory are activated even if we do not consciously pursue the comparisons.

Another source of interest is the hint of a direct benefit. For example a curved pencil might fit behind the ear. The curved walking stick does not immediately offer such a benefit (at least not to me). The benefit may come to nothing, but it is enough to make us pause at an 'interesting' point.

Glimmer or hint

The notion of 'interesting' suggests that there is a glimmer or hint of what may be found if we but pause to look. It is a matter of suggestion or suspicions. It may come to nothing. The trained creative thinker is, however, sensitive to such hints and willing to pursue them. The trained creative thinker knows that once interest is pursued it is very unlikely that nothing at all will be found. Occasionally a creative thinker will be forced to admit: 'that should be interesting – but I really cannot see how.' To be able to say that is useful creative practice. To be able to note points of 'interest' even if such points are not pursued. This type of noticing is very much what all the classic detectives have done: 'now that is a very interesting observation. I don't quite know its significance at the moment. But it will fit into place in due course, I don't doubt.'

Over-indulgence

Is there a possibility that for the highly sensitive creative thinker *everything* will be so 'interesting' that the result will be confusion or paralysis? There is such a danger. The trick is to be able to pursue a point and then to crystallise its 'interest' into a concept or point of difference and then to get on with other points. Unfortunately we cannot just deal with the most interesting points. This is because the most obviously interesting points are, by definition, closest to our present ideas – and therefore less likely to stimulate fresh ideas. It may not be possible to explore all the interesting avenues that arise. This does not matter. It is never possible to use all available random words either!

Concept differences

I want to give readers of this *Letter* a challenge.

The challenge is this:

How would you define a concept?

It is not easy, although we can all recognise concepts when we see them. A convenience package, a grouping, a clustering, an assembly for a purpose, all have some of the flavour of a concept. In the end a concept is made up of other concepts until we get down to raw experience. Perhaps we could define it – in attention terms – as a sort of town with the various roads leading to and from the town. We look at the town as the junction or node point for those roads. Its existence is made up from the roads and yet it exists separately from the roads. There is a convenience in talking in terms of towns or junctions.

The simplest way to describe or to contrast one concept is to contrast it with another concept in the same area.

There was a time in the fast-food business when the 'operating concept' was speed. How quickly could you serve the customer and get him or her out again. The faster the throughput the greater the profits. Everything was calculated down to the last second. Any delays meant a loss of business. The concept was 'get them in and out as quickly as possible'.

Then (in the USA) the fast-food business grew and grew until there were a great number of people selling fast food. There were not enough customers to go round.

So the concept changed, virtually overnight.

It was not necessary to keep a customer there *as long as possible*. The idea was to try and get the customer to spend more: some cheese, some dessert, another drink, perhaps some cigarettes and so on. You could no longer be sure that when the customer left there would be another customer as replacement. So the concept became: 'keep the customer there and try to sell him or her as much as possible'. The contrast between the two concepts is obvious.

In health care the concept of 'treatment' can be contrasted with the concept of 'prevention'. The concept of matching care to real needs can be contrasted with the 'hospital' concept. In the hospital concept sick people are taken to hospital and stay there until they are fully recovered. The cost of a bed in a hospital is very high indeed because of all the support staff which is needed for really sick patients. The concept of 'matched care' means that as soon as the patient is well enough he or she is moved to an annexe where the level of care is rather less than in the hospital but still adequate. This frees the expensive hospital bed for another patient.

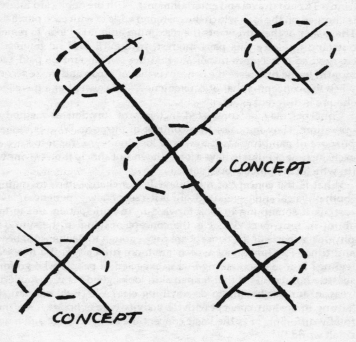

When the twin-bar confectionery was introduced it quickly became a success. No-one is quite sure why: it may have seemed more; there was the possibility of sharing; the eater felt less guilty eating one piece at a time etc. etc. The twin-piece concept can be contrasted both with the single bar confectionery and also with a bag of sweets (many pieces).

The frequent-traveller-mileage-bonus concept can be contrasted with the normal discount concept. In the discount concept the purchaser of the ticket gets the saving. In the frequent-traveller schemes the user of the ticket accumulates the mileage towards a free ticket. There is also an additional aspect of the concept because the loyal passenger accumulates mileage, whereas in the normal discount method there is no special bonus for being loyal – each ticket stands on its own.

The concept of an auction is obviously different from the concept of a sealed tender bid. A tender bid is a one-shot guess whereas an auction allows for a continuous interaction. Both are different from a fixed-price sale.

Although they may seem similar in use, a debit card is quite different from a TE card (travel and entertainment). With the debit card interest is charged on the loan which the customer adds to with each purchase. The issuer of the card wants the maximum amount of loan to remain outstanding since this pays interest. In the TE card no interest is charged so it becomes important that the full amount be paid each month. In the first place the concept is that of a loan and in the second place the concept is that of convenience. The concept of a traveller's cheque is different again.

Concepts may be contrasted in terms of function or method of operation. They may also be a contrast of purpose. What is the real purpose of gambling? Is it to win or lose money? Or is it to have an exciting time? Or is it to have a long-drawn-out anticipation of winning (in which case Bingo would suffice).

What is the concept of a holiday? Is it a change in surroundings (both physical and psychological)? Is it a set of new experiences? Is it a rest? Is it something to look forward to in anticipation and to talk about in retrospect? What is the concept of lying in the sun? The physical aspects of the concept are easy enough to define: sun, beach and time. The functional aspects are more difficult. Is it a nice lazy feeling? Is it just something that is expected of people who go for a seaside holiday? Is it that tanned skin looks good? Is it a wonderful 'reason' for not having to do anything else? We could contrast the 'sitting in the sun' concept with the activity type of holiday. Are they totally different, or is the basic concept the same: change and a new small world?

In science (as I have written before in these *Letters*) there are the 'lumpers' and the 'splitters'. The lumpers look for common characteristics that will lump different things together. The splitters look for differences that will separate apparently similar things. In practical terms, which is likely to be the more useful? The splitters are likely to find new markets, new market segments and new needs. The lumpers are able to transfer the experience and idiom of one field to another. On the whole the lumpers will do better in science (perceiving basic groupings and rules) and the splitters are likely to do better in the commercial world – especially in a saturated market. When the tobacco companies started to differentiate between men and women smokers in a serious way they succeeded in increasing the amount of smoking done by women (to compensate for the reduced smoking by men). A concept which encouraged women to drink more beer could make a big difference to that market. There is a big difference between the concept of an 'occasion' drink and an 'occasional' drink. The success of the wine cask arose from its ability to combine these two concepts.

Multi-purpose concepts often seem to fail. It seems as if they should do better but in practice they lack the specificity of a single concept. Multi-purpose cars are less successful than cars which seem designed for a specific purpose but are capable of being used more widely.

Whenever we look at a concept or seek to define a concept it can be very helpful to contrast it with parallel concepts. The 'discussion' method of teaching thinking can be contrasted with the 'tool' method. The concept behind a popular newspaper can be contrasted with the concept behind a serious newspaper.

Why should we bother to spell out a concept if we are using it successfully without ever having had it spelled out? There is something to be said for operating on a sort of intuitive basis while things are going well. *But when they start to go bad then it becomes very difficult to escape from the old concept.* It is also difficult to assess a proposed new direction if we cannot really tell how new it is.

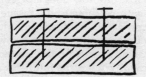 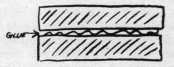

CONTRASTING CONCEPTS

███████████████████

Why is this interesting?
I am going to put down a number of situations. I want the reader to take each situation in turn and, as a creative exercise, to indicate why it is an 'interesting situation'. Some of the situations may appear interesting at first sight. With some of them the reader will need to make more of an effort in order to demonstrate 'interest'.

You can do the exercise on a piece of paper or in your head. I shall 'walk through' an example to indicate what is required.
Situation: A pigeon with a broken wing.
Interest: It might be more interesting if we knew where the pigeon was. We shall assume it is free rather than in a cage. How might a pigeon get a broken wing? Could a pigeon break its wing by flying into something, maybe a telephone wire in the dark? Perhaps someone tried to grab the bird and it got away. Why should someone try to grab the bird? Perhaps it was a dog, a cat or a fox. But how does a pigeon with a broken wing escape? Perhaps something came to the rescue. Could it be that other birds 'mobbed' the predator – as some birds are known to do? How does a pigeon with a broken wing survive? How does it get food? Do pigeons feed on the wing or only on the ground anyway? Will the wing ever mend on its own? What is the future for a pigeon with a broken wing? How do the other pigeons react? Do they notice? Do they care? Would it be a kindness to catch the pigeon and kill it? If you were the pigeon would that be a kindness?

Situation: A banana skin on the pavement.
Situation: An almost empty Jumbo 747 crossing the Atlantic at night.
Situation: A voice-activated telephone.
Situation: A life insurance policy where the premiums get smaller as you get older.
Situation: A car salesman who is deaf.

As you go through the exercise you will find yourself using a variety of 'frames' of interest. Many of these were mentioned elsewhere in this *Letter*. You may, however, find additional frames. There are frames of 'explanation'. There are frames for carrying something forward in time in order to watch what happens.

In some ways the frames of 'interest' are similar to the operation of the 'movement' mode in lateral thinking. The difference is that with interest we do stay close to the subject whereas with movement we can use it as a stepping-stone to move on to something else.

17

Idea flavour

Noting the 'idea flavour' is one aspect of the harvesting that needs to be done at the end of every creative session. Without such harvesting everything except a completed idea is wasted. I have often sat in on creative exercises and listened to the ideas being put forward. Then I have listened to the report-back stage. I am always surprised by how little of the idea flavour comes through in the report stage. An idea, which sounded exciting when put forward, seems dull when summarised or reported. It is not that the idea itself was dull, but the extracted essence of the idea lacks flavour.

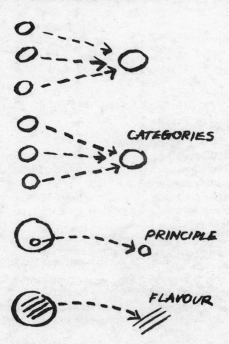

There are wine tasters and tea tasters and cheese tasters. There are whisky blenders and tobacco blenders. In each case the palate or nose of the expert is highly sensitive to different flavours. A flavour is sometimes so subtle that a novice nostril may miss it altogether.

We can often categorise ideas and group them under broad headings. An idea flavour is much more subtle than a category. Suppose we are trying to discourage smoking; we might collect the following suggestions:

- raise the price of cigarettes
- restrict advertising
- advertise harmful effects
- lower tobacco strengths (tar contents)
- restrict smoking in public places
- publicise expense of smoking
- publicise anti-social aspects (bad smell etc)

In all these suggestions there is the 'flavour' that smoking is a form of 'sin' and therefore should be made expensive and difficult. What other flavours might there possibly be? There could be a flavour of 'silliness'. There could be suggestions (perhaps through cartoon characters) that smoking was just plain silly – and definitely not smart or heroic. There could also be a flavour of 'old-fashioned'. People who smoked were not with it. They were wearing out-of-date habits just as they might have been wearing out-of-date clothes.

Let's take a single idea to do with leisure. For example, 'Everyone gets "leisure vouchers" as part of the pay packet. These can be converted into time or a cash value.'

The following flavours may be detected:

A 'transaction' flavour which allows leisure to be traded in for cash.

An 'option' flavour which allows a person to decide to have time, or to buy entertainment, for leisure.

An 'earned right' flavour so that leisure becomes something which is specifically earned through work. Anyone who works has a leisure credit balance.

A 'concrete' flavour so that leisure becomes something definite rather than just a gap between working periods.

A 'limit' flavour to leisure. It is not free; there has to be a voucher for it.

A 'control' flavour. Every bit of life is organised and controlled.

An 'accounting' flavour. Vouchers are issued and redeemed and can be counted. So the expenditure can be accurately measured.

A 'hoarding' flavour. The vouchers can be stored. They do not have to be used all at once. So vouchers can be hoarded and then used at one time for a very long holiday (the option flavour comes in here again).

A 'trading' flavour. Vouchers can be bought or sold and auctioned. Markets might be established (this is similar to the 'transaction' flavour but profit oriented).

A 'value' flavour. Leisure might be valued much more if it is actually paid for by vouchers. Instead of being a 'nothing' time it becomes a 'bought' time.

A 'conflict' flavour. Who decided how many vouchers are issued and how much they are worth.

In some cases the 'flavours' seem to be principles. There is no sharp division between a flavour and a principle. In general flavours are less definite than principles. The 'transaction' flavour might well have been regarded as a principle. The 'value' flavour is less of a principle and more of a flavour.

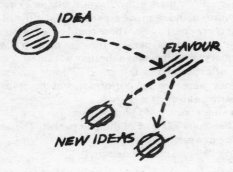

Before and after

In the cigarette smoking example we saw how a flavour can be decided upon first and then ideas found to carry that flavour. In the leisure example we see an examination of an idea for its various flavours.

There is a further possibility. This is where a flavour is detected in a particular idea and then an effort is made to strengthen the flavour by finding another idea that has an even stronger flavour (same flavour but stronger). For instance, in the leisure example the 'hoarding' flavour could be accentuated with a notion of an 'interest rate' so that vouchers used later would actually increase in value – a sort of saving scheme for leisure. Conversely, a 'buy now, pay later' concept could be suggested.

In general the use of flavour as an aspect of ideas follows the basic rules of creativity. We may want to note the flavour and to become directly aware of it in order to escape from a particular flavour.

'All these ideas have the same flavour – can we try something different?'

There are times when we might not even be aware that the ideas have the same flavour, unless we are paying direct attention to idea flavour.

'Let's "taste" these ideas for flavour.'

At other times flavour is used in order to generate fresh ideas. This is using flavour for its movement value as suggested earlier. Here we note the flavour for a single idea in order to work towards a better one.

'There is a faint flavour of "achievement" here; can we work with that? Can we get an idea that makes that flavour very much stronger?'

Just as some people are much better at tasting the subtle flavours of wine, so some people find it easier to pick out the different flavours of an idea (a single idea may have several flavours). *Like any tasting, skill improves with practice.*

When looking for principles we more towards the most definite principles that are expressed in an idea. With flavours we look for the most subtle flavours. We aim to extract as much as we possibly can from the idea.

The words 'tinge' and 'hint' also express the flavour concept.

'This idea has a hint of cost consciousness about it.'
'There is a tinge of showmanship in that offer.'

The flavour habit encourages us not just to look directly at the idea but also at various aspects of the idea. Instead of just looking at a flower, we stoop to sniff the scent.

Questions asked about creativity

Question: How do you quantify and evaluate the different routes, approaches and alternatives that result from the exercise of lateral thinking?

Answer: You need to drive to a certain destination. You look at the road map and examine alternative routes. How do you pick the best route? The procedure is very similar. It depends on what you have in mind. You may want the faster way. You may want to avoid holiday traffic. You may want to see a part of the country you have never visited. You may want to call in on a friend. Experience and knowledge come into the selection.

Once an alternative has been created there is nothing special about how it is selected. We can apply perfectly logical criteria of judgement. These can include cost, difficulty, dangers, risks, use of known channels, benefits, motivation and many other factors.

Quite often people do not want to set out to find alternatives because they do not want the task of deciding between them. There is some sense in this if the outcome does not much matter (for example the point at which you cross the road). If the outcome is important, then it is absurd to settle on the first approach through fear of indecision.

The purpose of lateral thinking is to achieve insight. This means finding a way of looking at things which immediately makes sense – once it has been found.

We can also use a simple rule of thumb. Think first of the obvious or traditional approach. Then look for other alternatives. If these are not obviously better than the first approach, stick to the first approach. If, however, you have the time, and if the other approaches are sufficiently 'interesting' then you may want to spend more time exploring them to see if they improve on further examination.

I am not too much in favour of spurious quantification which can mean assigning weights and probabilities which are conjured out of the air and then treated as mathematical certainties thereafter.

Genuine quantification can include actual costs and times and resource needs. Sometimes an estimate has to be used but this is different from assigning values to things like 'importance' and 'convenience'.

Question: To what extent does experience help creativity?

Answer: Everyone has stories of how children sometimes come up with fresh and original approaches to a problem. There is also the story of the housewife who suggested a pencil sharpener to solve the problem of putting a point on the carbons used for carbon-arc lighting. Innocence has its value. *If you do not know how something should be done you have a better chance of coming up with an original idea.* With children there may be the added factor of 'daring'. This is the willingness to have ideas and to suggest them.

Experience in a field means that we know why something cannot be done in a particular way. We know why an idea will not work. We can marshal our experience to demolish an idea we do not like.

So it is commonly suggested that experience in a field may be a disadvantage rather than an advantage.

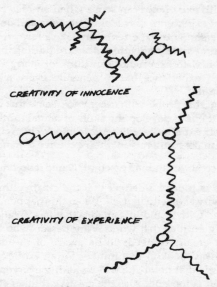

CREATIVITY OF INNOCENCE

CREATIVITY OF EXPERIENCE

We do, however, need to keep a sense of perspective. We always remember the instances where innocence produces a solution but we often overlook the instance where a mixture of experience and creativity has provided the answers.

The more experience you have in an area the more difficult it becomes to be creative: because you know so well how things 'should' be done. But if you do succeed in being creative then your creativity will be much more effective.

An innocent person can more easily switch to a new pathway but he (or she) is unable to proceed very far along that new path because experience has not extended the path. If a person with experience switches to a new path then he (or she) can move a great distance along that path.

So the answer to the question is complex. First of all it depends on the field you are in. In design and in advertising innocence may be an advantage; in engineering it may not be such an advantage; in politics it may be fatal. In the second place it depends on how the experience is used. A lot of experience used in a negative and destructive way can provide a formidable barrier against creativity. Conversely, the same experience used in a constructive way can get a far higher yield from creativity.

A person with experience can sense when an idea has benefit – a person without experience may look at the idea and be unable to see the value. A person with experience can take a raw principle (or idea flavour) and immediately provide a means of putting that principle to work. A person with experience can think of many alternatives. A person without experience has to generate every alternative in a speculative manner.

It is important that people with experience realise that it is even more important for them to develop the skills of lateral thinking. Without such skills their experience will tend to block creativity. With such skills they can make further use of their experience in new directions.

Question: Is all creative thinking practical? Could it become too abstract?

Answer: There is indeed a danger that the creative thinker starts to think of creativity as an end in itself. When this happens the thinker is more concerned with fashioning an idea that has 'creative value' than with providing an idea that works. Any person who has built up a reputation for creativity needs to be aware of the danger. People around will always look to that thinker for an exotic 'creative' idea. The thinker feels that he or she will be letting everyone down if the solution offered is too dull. Also the creative thinker starts to feel an aesthetic urge to fashion an idea which is both startling and effective. This becomes the direction of achievement. Whilst it can be useful to practise creativity in this manner, when it comes to applied creativity then the practicality of the solution must be the first priority.

To some extent our expectations of creativity are false. We are inclined only to acknowledge exotic ideas as creative – and then to condemn such ideas as practical. Very occasionally there can be an idea which is both exotic and also very practical but applied creativity is not restricted to such occasions.

On the whole it is better to have practical ideas and to risk others complaining that they are not very creative, than to have creative ideas which are never practical. If we go back to the car driving analogy, we find that driving along an exotic road that leads nowhere is only fun from time to time.

Question: Creative thinking is supposed to solve problems, but does it sometimes create problems?

Answers: If there is an obvious and straightforward way of doing something then setting out to find other ways may seem to be creating a problem. This is rather like a politician saying something straight-forward and yet his listeners ponder for hours to understand the hidden significance of what has been said. Matters can be over-intellectualised. The inappropriate application of creativity can turn something simple into a heavy task. The simple rule is to think of the obvious way first and then to spend a little time seeing if there might possibly be a better way.

There is, however, a completely different way in which the question may be answered. It can be the legitimate role of creativity to 'find problems'. Looking for an i.s.a. (idea sensitive area) is an exercise in problem finding. If we only react to problems that present themselves then we shall miss many opportunities.

From time to time we de need to challenge things that we take for granted and to 'create a problem' out of them. For example we might look at a car door. There is no problem with a car door. It works perfectly well. Then we say: 'We take it for granted that a car door swings open, can we escape from that idea?' At once we have created a problem that needs thinking about. Suppose we consider some sort of sliding mechanism. We have created a further problem: how might we get a practical sliding mechanism to work?

If we take 'routine' as the opposite to 'problem' then it is the role of creativity to create problems. The difficulty is really one of language. We are used to the word 'problem' meaning a difficulty, an obstacle or a gap. We would rather be without such problems so that we can get on with whatever we are trying to do. *The problems created by creativity are 'opportunity problems'.* We do not have to think about them – unless we choose to think about them. Someone who is perfectly happy with routine need have no creative problems.

There is even a further sense in which the question can be answered. Sometimes a creative idea can deal with one part of the situation in a new and effective way, but this upsets all the other parts of the system and the thinker has indeed created problems. For example a new idea on efficiency in a factory may upset demarcation lines and established practices. There is now the problem of dealing with these matters. It may be that such matters have to be tackled sooner or later, nevertheless they are problems. It is always worth looking around to see if a creative idea at one point might have created problems at other points. This is likely to happen in complex situations where matters have settled down over time into some sort of stable system.

Question: Where does inspiration fit in?

Answer: Inspiration can be either a starting point which leads eventually to a valuable new idea, or it can be a flash of insight. Any stimulus can act as a trigger for inspiration. It could be an event or a remark. It could be an apple falling on someone's head.

Many of the deliberate techniques of lateral thinking are ways of provoking inspiration instead of just waiting passively for it to come along. We could say that 'inspiration' is the sort of lateral thinking that occurs naturally without any special effort on the part of the thinker.

We use 'inspiration' in a broad way to mean something that is marvellous and out of the ordinary. That is the intended purpose of lateral thinking. Inspiration can occur without lateral thinking or during lateral thinking.

For practical purposes 'inspiration' does not tell us very much. It indicates that 'creativity has happened'.

It may just be that inspiration is some sort of manic state in the brain. It may be that the brain chemicals are different from the normal state. It may be that the brain is giving itself a 'high' with one of the many internally generated drugs. This is looking at the state of creativity rather than any fact of creativity.

The thinking place

The following is an imagined part of a creative session that is seeking to make postal services more economic.

'Why do people expect their mail to be delivered? Why don't they go and get it?'

'They could go to the pub in the evening. That would be welcomed by the pub because it would bring in more custom. People would go down to the pub to collect the mail and stop for a drink whilst there.'

'You could have home delivery if you wanted it, but it would be much more expensive.'

'Instead of being more expensive it could be much less frequent. The mail would go to the pub and at the end of the week it would be collected from the pub and delivered to homes. So there would be a home delivery once a week. If you wanted your mail sooner you would go and collect it.'

'People would probably adjust to their own frequency of mail. Someone might go along every evening. Another person might go mid-week. Another person would simply wait for the week-old mail (some of it) to be delivered.'

'Why the pub, why not the supermarket or the corner newsagent?'

'Because the pub stays open later. Perhaps you could choose from a small number of choices where you wanted it delivered. The supermarket might be best for someone who shopped most days.'

'Perhaps the receiver of the mail should pay for it.'

'You would not know if it was junk or not until you had paid. You would also resent paying to receive a bill.'

'But if you live far from a post office it is not unreasonable that you should pay more to get your mail delivered.'

'Perhaps there could be "receivers" licences. In your window you would display a special sticker which meant that you had bought a licence "to receive mail". The postman would only deliver to houses which showed licences. The rest would have to pick up their mail.'

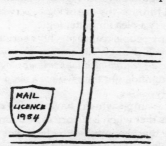

'That is like the early days of the fire brigades which were organised by insurance companies. If your building did not carry the right "disc" then the fire brigade would not put the fire out.'

'We may already be moving towards very expensive courier services for letters that simply have to be delivered directly the next day. If it really is so important, then people do not mind paying a high price.'

The thinking exercise is to read through the various ideas put forward and then write down some of the 'idea flavours' that you notice. Group the ideas under different flavours. One idea may, of course, turn up in several groupings.

Take just one of the ideas and try to extract as many flavours as possible from that idea. With these different flavours in mind, look around to see which other ideas have the same flavour.

Verbalise the different flavours and write down your verbalisation. It is not enough just to be aware of a particular flavour. You need to be able to identify it and to describe it. Wine tasters get into very poetic language as they seek to describe flavours that are obvious to their tongues but difficult to capture in words.

18

The great creativity dilemma

Any valuable creative idea is always logical in hindsight.

That statement gives rise to the great creativity dilemma. If an idea can be shown to be logical then it is logical to claim that the idea could have been obtained through the use of logic. So what is claimed to be creativity is really only a plea for better logic.

I wonder how many people realise just how serious is this dilemma. Perhaps I should spell it out a little more clearly. *We are unable to recognise as valuable a creative idea which is not logical in hindsight.* If that idea is logical in hindsight then we see a need for better logic but no need for creativity.

Let us take an old example which I have used in one of my books.

'The suggestion is that when a factory is built on a river we should make it compulsory that the input to the factory is downstream of its own output. In this way the factory would be the first to get a sample of its own pollution and would tend to be more careful about cleaning up the effluent.'

'It may not always be easy to do it in practice but that is a sound and perfectly logical idea. The logic is simple: let people suffer from their own mistakes. It is an obvious idea. What is creative about it?'

Now the idea is not all that obvious except in hindsight. I remember discussing the matter with the person who was in charge of the environmental impact agency for a major US state. The person had never thought of it and considered it to be a valuable new idea. If a person in that position had not heard about it then it was not such an obvious idea. How did the idea come about in practice?

'Po, the factory should be downstream of itself.' This was the deliberate provocation. This was a 'stepping stone' type of provocation. It was also a provocation of the 'wouldn't it be nice if . . .' type. I might have said: 'Po, wouldn't it be nice if the factory was downstream of itself?' From this provocation the idea arose.

Let us take another well-known example.

'The man gets into the lift and travels to the tenth floor, then he gets out and walks up to the fourteenth floor. What is the reason for this behaviour?'

People tend to think in terms of exercise or malfunctioning lifts or a special tower which does not have a lift etc.

'The simple answer is that he was a dwarf and could only reach as high as the tenth floor button.'

'That is a very logical answer. Any logical person would have got it. The line of reasoning would have been as follows. The man either does not want to press the fourteenth floor button or wants to but cannot. We could then go through the reasons why he might not want to press it. Next we come to the reasons why he cannot press it. Surely the short height of the man would have come to the surface at this point?'

Possibly. Why then do so many people have difficulty with this problem? The answer is that they have an image of a full-sized man. If the problem had been posed using the word 'person' then the listener might well have thought of a child. But with the image of a full-sized man then all the logical thinking that subsequently takes place does so around this ingredient of the full-sized man.

As I have said on so many occasions, logic is a servicing tool for perception. Logic has to have concepts and perceptions to work with. If the creative solution involves cutting across these starting concepts and perceptions then logic is unlikely to reach the solution.

How does one cope with the dilemma? How do you respond to someone who says that, since all valuable creative ideas are logical in hindsight, all that is needed it better logic – not creativity?

It is very difficult to answer that challenge without going into the background of perceptions and self-organising systems. It is easy enough to say: 'If it is logical then why don't more people get that answer?' or, 'If the logic is so simple in hindsight why didn't you get the answer?' This is only a partial response. The true response must come from examining the nature of hindsight. That is not easy to do in a casual conversation.

That is why in my seminars I spend a certain amount of time looking directly at the background to creative (lateral) thinking. It is from the logic of this background that the answer must come.

In perception we are looking at an active information system. This is in sharp contrast to the passive information systems we use in the processing part of thinking. When we make a mark on a piece of paper or on a magnetic disk we are using passive systems which preserve the information passively. In an 'active system' there is an environment in which the incoming information can move about and organise itself. In fact it organises itself into patterns. I have gone into this process in detail in my book *The mechanism of mind*. The concepts of self-organising information systems put forward in that book are now very much at the forefront of information technology. (Neuro-computers.)

So we end up with a pattern which is a sequence in time of different states of activation of the brain cells. We can represent this with a 'track' type of notation. Quite simply, the probability of our proceeding along the track is higher than jumping over the side. Such perceptual patterns are immensely valuable and without them life would be impossible. When we cross the road, drink a cup of coffee, or read, we are triggering perceptual patterns.

What happens when there is a side pattern? The architecture of the nerve cells in the brain is such that the less established pattern is temporarily subdued and the main pattern is pursued. Why this happens is explained in *The mechanism of mind*. For the purposes of notation we can show the side track as having a very narrow joining neck with the main track.

If, somehow, we managed to get to the side track then we can easily find our way back because from the outer point the track is not narrowed at all. I have tried to show this in the diagrams.

This asymmetry is the very basis of humour as I have said in many of my books. With humour we are suddenly snapped over to the side track and then see the 'logic' of humour in hindsight.

'What goes ninety-nine, bonk . . . ninety-nine bonk?'

'A centipede with a wooden leg.'

The mechanics of lateral thinking are very similar to the mechanics of humour. We use techniques of provocation and movement in order to help us escape from the main track in order to increase our chances of reaching the side track. Once we have done so then 'the logical track' may become obvious in hindsight.

If we were to jump out of the main track and reach a point for which there was no 'backtrack' then we should have an unrecognisable idea. It would be a mad sort of noise. In order to recognise an idea as valuable we have to see the backtrack that fits the idea in with our existing patterns of experience.

At this point we begin to see the solution to the dilemma.

We can only *recognise* those creative ideas which are logical in hindsight.

Other creative ideas we should simply be unable to recognise as valuable. So it is not that all creative ideas are logical in hindsight but that our recognition of value is limited to recognition of logical value. So, by definition, a valuable creative idea will be logical in hindsight.

Because such ideas are logical in hindsight does not at all mean that we could have reached the idea by the exercise of logic. The asymmetry of patterns means that what is visible in hindsight may not be visible at all in foresight. When you have won a large sum of money with your first bet at roulette you can boast of how easy it is to win. Those who know how the roulette game works know that hindsight success is not at all the same as setting out to win.

In the end the dilemma is as simple as that. *Because something is obvious in hindsight does not mean that it is obvious in foresight.*

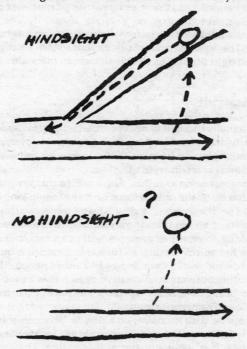

But we need to go further. Someone will claim that with a complete and comprehensive logical scan it should be possible to pick up any logical solution that exists. Here we come to the mathematics of combination. You can juggle around the existing perceptions in all possible combinations in order to achieve a logical scan. But these perceptions are themselves made up of other perceptions. These in turn are made up of still others – and so on. We do not need to go very far to realise that the mathematics of combination soon yield astronomical figures. We must also realise that there is no such thing as a unit of perception waiting to be juggled with. There are perception patterns with attention flow so we may not even be aware of what is being taken for granted in any given perception (until after this has been demonstrated).

People are prepared to accept creativity when the final value is going to be appreciated aesthetically. They are reluctant to accept creativity when the final value has to be proved logically. This is because they cannot see how a provocative process can produce a logical solution. Yet there is no mystery about it. The 'logic' of patterning systems clearly indicates why provocation has both a place and a value. The logic of asymmetry explains why an idea may be logical in hindsight but not accessible to logic in foresight.

Action creativity

Creativity is usually thought to be concerned with ideas and concepts. There are many brilliant concepts which never get implemented. Too often the creative thinker believes that it is enough to have the idea: implementation is someone else's business.

There are many reasons for this. The creative thinker may have so many ideas that he or she cannot focus on one of them long enough to be effective. The challenge of a new idea is more exciting than the implementation of an old one. It may be that the creative thinker is happier thinking in terms of concepts with an arena that is entirely within his or her mind. Puting an idea into practice requires time, energy and dealing with messy things like other people. There may simply not be the motivation. A creative person may be motivated by the challenge to find a creative solution but once it has been found then the challenge comes to an end.

I do not believe that it is simply a divide between thinkers and doers. I do not believe that creative people are incapable of putting ideas into effect. It is more a matter of motivation. They may not be particularly interested in the hassle of convincing other people. Some are so motivated. Indeed some are remarkably persistent.

What I want to write about here is the direct application of creativity to doing rather than the doing which may be needed to put an idea into effect.

We are very used to creativity in its problem solving aspects:
'We need a concept that will do this.'
'There is as yet no known way of doing this.'
'How can we lower interest rates without fuelling inflation?'
'How can we increase employment?'

That is only one aspect of creativity. There is another aspect which is less glamorous but probably more practical.

'Is there a simpler way of doing this?'

'This is the traditional way – is there a better way?'

'Can we make this more convenient?'

'We know that we can do it – but can we do it in a much better way?'

'Can we find a more efficient concept?'

There is less need for creativity because when we do have a usable concept: we can do what we want to do. On the other hand the risk is much less. We are free to look for a better way. If we find a new way we can compare it with the existing method. We can even test it. If we do not like it we do not need to use it. *There is no reason why creativity should only be used in 'desperate' situations when nothing else will do.*

In the London Underground railway system tickets have to be bought for each journey. Monthly tickets are available for commuters but for those with unpredictable patterns of use there is a need to queue up for a ticket or to have the right amount of change to operate a ticket-dispensing machine. If tickets were not dated then a ticket bought one day could be used another day. A passenger travelling to Heathrow could buy a return ticket to use on his return. It must be just about the most inefficient way in the world to issue a ticket for each journey.

In the USA there has been developed a stand-alone terminal that will issue cinema tickets against credit cards. The user can call up all the available films in the neighbourhood and then punch in his requirements. A ticket is issued at once.

There will also be video-shops consisting of a screen on which merchandise can be displayed. The catalogues are stored on laser-read discs. Purchases will be made using credit cards. Is this any better than mail order from a catalogue? It could be quicker, more convenient, more suited to impulse buying and better able to display the goods (especially those that could not properly be displayed in a shop – for example, a lawn mower in action).

It is clear that electronic technology will change a lot of interface transactions as it has already done with automated tellers in banks. But creativity is not just a matter of using new technology. With regard to the cinema-ticket dispenser I would have thought that an automatic telephone information system would be far more useful. You dial a number and get broad cinema information. You then dial other numbers to get details on particular films or you can dial for a genre of films or even for a certain actor. The ticket dispenser only gives convenience once someone has decided to go to the cinema. The telephone information system makes the cinema more available as a casual purchase. Another way might be to make a restaurant receipt a voucher for part payment of a cinema ticket or the same with a parking lot ticket.

There is a danger in assuming that action concepts have to depend upon or to use new technology. If computers and telephone lines had not been available I think we might have been more imaginative as to how we handle air travel. There probably would have been no reservations at all and a tiered level of pricing so that those willing to pay the highest prices could get a flight at the time they wanted. A passenger would hold a 'universal' London/New York ticket and would go along in the morning to be assigned a flight.

The one queue system for banks is an obvious example of concept efficiency. Everyone goes in one queue and the person at the head of the queue goes to whichever window is vacant. Putting a charge on one serving window might also be interesting. People in a hurry would regard this as a proper cost in order to save time. Business users would treat it as they might a taxi fare. People at other windows would know that if they were impatient they could always put a price on that impatience by moving to the more expensive window.

What are the steps to be taken to make something happen? What are the best steps? What is the proper sequence of these steps? The design of an action path can make use of creativity. This may be no more than spelling out the alternatives available at every point. There may be no 'new' concepts as such.

It may be that some steps can be dropped, combined or short-circuited. It may be that the insertion of further steps can segment the market and cater to different buyers: for example the sale of unfinished furniture in parallel with finished furniture. The video-taping of secretaries might cut down on interview time. So might the creation of some 'capability' index which gave more information than typing and shorthand speeds.

What is the most efficient way of mowing the lawn? Perhaps the lawn should be shaped so as to make it easy to mow.

What is the best way to send a letter? Send two if the mail is unreliable. At one time it was cheaper to send bulk mail into Australia from New Zealand than to mail it within Australia.

How can management reward workers? What are the methods available? Is money the only method? Is it the best method?

How can management signal dissatisfaction to workers? What methods are likely to be effective without causing resentment? How can competition be implemented?

The people factor

Getting things done does not have to involve other people (robots, automation) but it usually does. People do not change easily. People are only briefly impressed by the 'cuteness' of an idea – after that the idea has to offer real convenience. People are highly suspicious and fearful of being tricked, ripped-off or cheated. People are lazy, people place a very high value on convenience. People have different tastes, needs and motivations. People are very subject to category thinking. People are heavily influenced by fashion, fad and their peers. Getting a new customer is said to be four times as expensive as holding an old one. People may say one thing and do another. We do not know nearly enough about people to be able to tell with any certainty whether a new idea will work or fail. It is usually easier to tell that an idea will fail than that it will work.

To prevent credit card fraud we could have the photo of the card holder placed on the card. An even simpler device would be for every person to have an identity number tattooed somewhere on their hand. This would make the use of stolen cards or cheques very difficult since the number on the card or cheque would need to match the identity number. The idea is effective but would probably never be accepted. It smacks of identification in a concentration camp and it seems to be an invasion of privacy. People are not cattle and so on. The acceptance of the idea would also be affected by such detail as to how the tattoo was applied. If it was done by means of a dye-impregnated strip which just had to be worn on the hand overnight then it would be more acceptable. If the number lasted no more than six months and then faded away it might also be acceptable. If there was some very great advantage in using it then again that would help acceptance.

If you reward people with extra money then in time they come to expect that extra money as part of their salary. So when the reward is not forthcoming they complain and feel cheated. If you reward them with 'bonus bonds' which are pieces of paper with a certain value that can be exchanged at stores for goods then workers feel rewarded and do not feel cheated when they have not earned the reward.

It is very important indeed when developing creative ideas to do with people to realise that things which may seem functionally, or logically, the same, may not be treated in the same way at all. If you raise school fees parents do not object too much. If you leave the school fees as they are, but start charging a lot of extras, then parents do complain. The amounts may be the same. But one seems finite and the other seems open-ended. If you give people a chance to work on their own ideas, they may never use that chance. They will, however, appreciate having the chance. People logic is very much tied up with security, appreciation, anticipation and solidarity. The designer of ideas needs to keep these in mind.

With people the context within which a new idea is put forward will have a huge effect on its success or failure – quite apart from the merit of the idea itself.

The thinking place

Obvious in hindsight

I want to continue the theme of the first article in this *Letter*. We do really believe that any idea turned up by creativity could have been found by clever logic. It is obvious to us now that dividing the whole twenty-four hours into equal divisions is a much simpler way of recording time than trying to divide daylight into equal units and night-time into equal units. This concept delayed the satisfactory measurement of time for many centuries. Since day and night are continually varying in length, except on the equator, the task is technically difficult.

Why didn't the American civilisations invent the wheel or the arch? These are quite obvious in hindsight. There are said to have been religious taboos since a circle represented the sun god. The 'zero' was an immensely powerful invention in mathematics but the Greeks and the Romans had to do without it.

There are many many concepts that we take for granted today that we shall regard in a hundred years' time as quaint and primitive. The concept of 'money' may be one of these.

Try to make a list of basic present-day concepts which you feel might be obsolete in a hundred years' time.

We can divide this task into two sections.

In the first section put down those concepts which you feel will become obsolete because new technology offers a different way of doing things or looking at things. For example, the idea of 'going to work' may become obsolete because much work will be information work and we can do that at home through computers.

In the second section put down those concepts which you feel will become obsolete *without* any new technology. For example, the same water clock that had difficulty in measuring time when day and night were divided separately was perfectly adequate when the whole twenty-four hours were divided up. In other words, find concept changes which do not depend on new technology. For example, marriage may become a contract for a limited duration.

In this task you do not have to suggest a wonderful new concept to replace the existing one. It would be enough if you indicated why you felt the present concept was antiquated, quaint, primitive, or heavily dependent on continuity for its survival.

Look around and take the most obvious concepts. Look at them with fresh eyes. Imagine you were walking through an anthropological museum in a hundred years' time and you read about this strange concept. To you it would seem as strange as the concept of slavery seems to us today.

Thinking need not only be a reaction to events or a matter of problem solving. A thinker should be able to stand back and to look objectively at things that are both taken for granted and regarded as the ultimate. Towards the end of the last century it was recommended that the US Patent Office should close because all that could be invented had already been invented. Very often we think exactly that way about those features of society and civilisation that we now take for granted.

Historically one hundred years is hardly long enough for this exercise. In view of technological change and the steep path of geometric change which we now seem to be riding, one hundred years should suffice.

19

The idiom of creativity

Four quarters of melon are lying on a plate at an open air lunch in a sunny garden. There are lots of flies around and one of the guests spends most of his time waving flies off the melon. Of course there should be some sort of cover but there is not. Another of the guests up-ends the melon quarters so that two hemispheres are formed – facing downwards on to the plate and so protecting the melon from the flies. This is the idiom of creativity.

Is the present situation satisfactory?
Is there another way of achieving the objective?
How might it be done better with minimal cost, effort, hassle?

Someone else might have gone to fetch a fly cover – if there was one available. Another person might have tried to devise a fly cover or to cover the melon with a cloth. The eventual solution was very simple and very neat.

In following through the thinking used it is worth noting that the solution used *was not* a general solution. It could only have applied to the melon quarters. Consider the following starting points:

'How can I keep the flies off the melon?'
'How can I provide a cover for the melon?'
'How can I arrange the melon so that the flies cannot get at it?'

Keeping the flies off

This might have involved moving the melon back indoors or into the refrigerator. It could be a matter of taking the melon away from the presence of the flies. It could also have meant killing the flies by means of a spray or swat. This is a very general statement of the objective. Logically it includes both others. In practice, however, the neat logical tree that would start with this broad objective and then move on to various sub-sections (ways of keeping the flies off) does not work. The starting point of 'keeping the flies off' tends to move in two directions:

removing the flies
removing the melon from the flies

I am not suggesting that it is not possible to work from a general need and then to consider sub-section needs as in a logical tree. What I am saying is that in practice we tend to follow the implementation of the general need rather than follow the logical tree.

In my books I have often advocated following the logical tree – for example in the 'working backwards method'. Here I appear to be saying that it is nice in theory but does not work in practice. This is not the case. The method does work, but we have to set out to use the method deliberately in the first place.

If we do want to use the logical tree method, then we need to spell out the tree in all its various parts *before* using any one of them. This means that before setting to work on the general need 'keeping the flies off' we should have spelled out the logical tree – in writing or at least verbally to ourselves. If we do not do this but start to work on the general need, then we cannot subsequently move on to the logical sub-sections.

For quick action creativity, as opposed to a deliberate structure, it is useful to list general needs and sub-sections of them as parallel ways of viewing the problem, forgetting that some of the ways are logically just a sub-division of a more general approach.

Providing a cover for the melon

This would be a very traditional approach. The problem is the possible contamination by flies. So we need to protect something from the flies. That means a cover of sorts. We might first think of a formal cover. Then we move on to improvisation. We might end up with a napkin placed over the melon.

If we want to be practical we must come down in favour of this practical approach. This is because such 'transferable approaches' have a much easier application than approaches which only suit a particular situation. *In the end the purpose of creativity is to be practical rather than exotic.*

The creative mind is stocked with a number of general-purpose needs and applications. This aspect is not unlike the mind of an engineer which is stocked with 'ways to do things'. When a need arises the engineer searches his 'ways and means' file and comes up with a stock answer. The obvious dilemma is that the better we are stocked with these standard 'ways and means' the less likely are we to come up with a solution that fits the current situation even better. We are also unlikely to look for anything else. The attitude of 'this is adequate', of 'this will do the trick' removes the motivation for seeking something better.

The dilemma is a real one. The fixer or repairman wants to move on to the next job. He needs to apply the standard solution and to move on. Competence and completion of the job is his task. The creative designer has a different motivation. He is not interested in completing it quickly and moving on. He (or she) is interested in doing something better. He is interested in improvement. That implies innovation.

At this point the creative person has the choice between a 'creative fix' and a 'creative design'. The temptation is to go for the fix because it is quicker and more certain. But if we always go for the fix then we are never going to get a creative design.

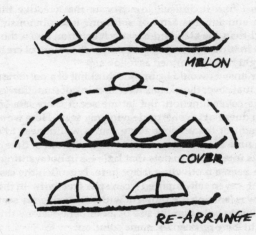

Arranging the melon

The creative person might have had a sort of 'vision' of the melon portions forming themselves again into a complete melon. Before the melon was cut, the flies could not get at the interior. He might even have thought that it would have made better sense to leave the slicing of the melon to the last minute – as it would. Such a solution might serve for a future occasion but it was too late for this occasion. Perhaps the pieces could somehow be re-assembled? Ways of doing this with a band round the middle might have come to mind. From there it is but a small step to realising that there was no need to re-assemble the whole melon. It would be enough just to put together two halves. Each half would face downwards on to the dish and so exclude the flies.

The virtue of this solution is that it is extremely neat. The word 'neat' is itself neat. It is a simple way of describing a solution to a problem but it encompasses a great deal. 'Neat' implies an exact fit with no extra frills. 'Neat' implies an economy of effort. 'Neat' implies a low-cost solution.

Compare the effort required for the hemisphere solution to the effort required for other solutions. There is no need to remover the melon or to get up in order to search for a cover or fly-killing spray. There is nothing extraneous required. There is no soiling of a napkin used to cover the melon. Any solution which requires no more than the re-arrangement of the existing components is likely to be neater than other solutions.

Nevertheless I find it difficult to advocate that creative thinkers should always aim for this kind of solution. It is obviously more difficult to find than the standard approach solution (even though it seems obvious in hindsight). This is all part of the idiom of creativity. That idiom might have performed as follows:

'The sensible answer would be to start thinking of a possible cover. If there is no actual cover then I shall have to think of something which could fulfil this cover function. But let me see if there is a simpler solution which does not involve me leaving my seat.' Here we see the acknowledgement of the obvious route, but a willingness to invest some thinking time in a simpler solution. That amount of time can be quite small. It is interesting to note that laziness in not wanting to get up might have been a motivating factor here. It is often the case that some constraint – even self-imposed – can spur creativity. In this case the constraint was 'solving the problem without leaving my seat'.

It is interesting to note that the use of a deliberate lateral thinking technique might have reached the same solution:

'Po, the melon became whole again.'
'Po, the melon protected *itself* against the flies.'

The melon example happens to be a true story. It also seems very trivial. But it does illustrate what I call the 'idiom' of creativity. That is to say, the actual way creativity gets to be used on a day-to-day basis.

Part of the culture

'You know, we always assume that a lubricant must be a liquid. Just suppose we set out to use a gas.'
'Like what?'
'I don't know yet. It is just a thought.'

'If you do not know what you would use, how it would work, how it might be possible or what advantages it would offer, then what is the point of your remark?'

This exchange illustrates why creativity needs to become part of the culture of an organisation.

The first person is using a provocation. Indeed, he is using the classic 'escape' method that is one of the deliberate techniques of lateral thinking:

'We take it for granted that lubricants are liquids. Let's escape from that. Po, liquids are a gas.'

The second person is not familiar with the idiom of provocation. He expects that a remark is made because there is a good reason – or at least some reason – for making it. That is the normal scientific and rational approach. We move with reason from one position to another. We can have speculative hypotheses, but there does have to be some reason for the speculation. A completely random provocation is not permissible. Yet in lateral thinking it is not only permissible but actually necessary.

The definition of a provocation is simple and clear:

'There may not be a reason for saying something until after it has been said.'

Where lateral thinking has become part of the group culture then the remark would have been taken for what it was meant to be: a provocation. The listener would immediately have set about getting 'movement' from the provocation. What does the idea lead to? What might the special characteristics of a gas be? How might a gas be used for lubrication? Could a gas interact in some beneficial way with existing lubricants? Could something be a liquid only where required and a gas as it moved around? Could a gas under pressure dissolve in the liquid and add certain qualities? The purpose of any provocation is to open up such avenues of thought. The next idea that emerges may have nothing to do with gas, but may arise from a thought track that was opened up by the gas provocation. For example, there might be a concept of a changeable lubricant which changed nature or characteristics according to demand or according to some outside signal.

The purpose of the new word 'po' which I invented many years ago is to symbolise a provocation.

'Po, wheels should be square.'
'Po, water flows uphill.'
'Po, planes land upside down.'
'Po, lubricants are gases.'

Obviously the po symbol can be used to indicate something which is totally illogical (square wheels) or something which is merely unlikely. In between these two extremes there is a range of likelihood.

Of course 'po' has no value to those who do not already know what it means. And, it might be said, there is no need for 'po' for those who do know what it means. There is some truth in this. Nevertheless po acts as a crisp signalling device even to those who do fully understand the nature and purpose of provocation. For those who do not then the insertion of po – and the subsequent explanation – can be a simple way of explaining provocation.

'Normally statements are supposed to fit reality. A provocation does not have to fit reality. It is meant to jerk our thinking out of its usual ruts so that we can move to new patterns. A provocation can be totally illogical, like "po, wheels should be square". The word "po" used before a statement means that it is put forward solely as a provocation. See what this idea stimulates. Instead of judging the statement move forward from it, see where it takes you.' Just as a white flag of truce allows a negotiating party to enter the castle walls, so under the banner of po a statement may be allowed to enter the mind instead of being rejected at the judgement gate.

Because culture and climate are intangible we tend to give them less attention and less value than such tangible things as cost and production. Yet we know that confidence and morale have extraordinary effects. When the Normans exploded out of their home country to invade England and to journey as far south as Malta, it was a burst of energetic confidence that got them going. When one particular laboratory has success after success for a brief period, then again it is a matter of morale and confidence. The same applies to those periods in a country's history that give rise to an efflorescence of writing or painting or music (plus the additional factor of critical mass and inter-stimulation).

The creative culture is one that understands the nature of creativity and the value of creativity. There is a constant search for better ways of doing things. It is accepted that ideas will be generated and discussed and treated with appreciation. This does not mean that every idea is going to be acted upon. That would be impossible. When an idea is not acted upon, it is made clear that the idea is not developed enough, not suitable at the moment, does not fit the needs, or that the benefits of the idea are not sufficient to warrant change.

There are organisations in which creativity is regarded as an aberration. Since it involves risk and uncertainty it is best left to others. If the idea works for others then it can be copied with a 'me-too' effort. If a trend is established then the trend can be adopted. Such strategies can work for major ideas, but they are useless for day-to-day creativity. No-one is interested in improving the way he or she is doing something if the culture is such that any suggestion will be treated as 'disruption'. There are organisations in which the culture implies that certain people are to do the thinking and the rest are to do as they are told. In such a culture any attempt to alter a procedure must be regarded as rebellion.

There are other organisations that pay a lot of lip-service to creativity because they feel that it is of value. It is felt that this lip-service and some of the cosmetics of action are sufficient. Creativity is supposed to produce some fantastic ideas. Anything short of that is regarded as inconvenient. This is especially true with successful organisations who know that future success depends on creativity – and yet they are doing so well at the moment that any change must seem for the worst.

Many organisations want to be 'overwhelmed' by creativity. They want a new idea to be so splendid that everyone at once sees its virtues. Anything short of that is more bother than it is worth. *If you have to prove that a new idea has value, then its value cannot be sufficient for the idea to be used.*

I am not too much concerned with the level of acceptance of new ideas. I do not much mind if only the very best ideas are accepted and acted upon. We must, of course, assume there is a way of selecting these. Without such a method then only a fraction of the really good ideas will be selected, since the rest require a little more attention or are ideas whose value cannot really be predicted before trial. Even so a severe selection procedure is not a major problem.

What is much more important is the culture that encourages people to have ideas. It is this generative attitude that is important. If people are willing to have ideas and to go on having ideas then a strict selection does not matter. But the method of selection does matter. There are ways of rejecting an idea which kill creative motivation and there are ways of rejecting an idea which actually encourage it.

Most people who do not want to act upon a creative suggestion go to a lot of trouble to show that the idea won't work. They want to show that it is a bad idea. They want to show that the creative effort has produced something useless. Labelling an idea as a 'bad idea' absolves anyone from acting upon it or giving it any further attention. Other labels which are just as useful in this respect are 'crazy' and 'impractical'. Another label (which I have mentioned in a previous *Letter*) is 'same as . . .'. This method of rejection is most de-motivating.

The alternative approach is to acknowledge and to encourage the creative approach even whilst indicating that the output is not usable. This encourages the creative person to go on trying and even to try harder – instead of turning him, or her, off.

'There is one point I cannot understand about that idea, could you explain it to me?'

'I can see how it will work, but where do you see the benefits coming from? And how big are those benefits going to be?'

'That's a great idea but it just does not fit our circumstances. It might be a great idea for someone else.'

'I can see that you have used a very different approach. That might lead to some very useful ideas in the future. For the moment I feel that the idea does not justify a change. But I do like the approach.'

'That's a nice idea and, if we had more of a problem in that area, I would suggest using it.'

'I like that idea as an idea. It is effective and it is neat. But the cost of changeover would not justify our using the idea.'

In this way the *effort* of creativity can be encouraged without having to accept or act upon the products of the creativity. This is a very important point in practice. If the only way we have of encouraging creativity is to act on every creative idea, then it does become difficult. So there is this need to develop a culture in which the generation of ideas is given a value quite separable from the use – or even utility – of the ideas. This may be the most important part of a creative culture.

Suggestion schemes often fail because the reward is too remote. Any idea put forward has to be passed through a number of appraising committees and only if the idea is used and saves money does the originator get his reward. This can be a long time off and, as a result, many people feel that they are never going to have that sort of idea. It makes much more sense to clear the suggestion box every month and to invite for a drink all those who have put in a suggestion. This may mean that a certain amount of drink is wasted on the perennial crank who will always put in mad ideas – but that is a small price to pay for creative motivation. Reward the effort not just the result. *After all creativity is more valuable as an effort than as a result.* This may surprise some people but I have no doubt at all about this in relation to corporate culture. That there should be people ready, willing and eager to have ideas is most important. That sort of climate provides the sort of motivation that can also be provided by Quality Circles. It provides an interest in what is being done.

Contrast this culture with a culture that feels threatened by creativity and which insists that all useful ideas will eventually evolve without the need for the 'hit and miss' process of creativity.

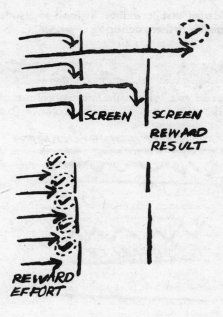

I encourage organisations to send people to the various public seminars that I hold. I think it is very important for senior people to understand what I call the *logic* of creativity. It is this understanding that takes creativity from being a luxury and something of use only to artists and the advertising department , and places it where it should be – as an essential ingredient in all thinking. The logic of lateral thinking arises from the behaviour of perception which acts as a self-organising information system. Such a system creates the patterns which allow the mind to make sense of the chaos around and to work competently. Nevertheless we need a method for escaping from established patterns and moving across to new patterns. That is the logic of creativity.

It is, however, very difficult for an individual to carry the message back to the organisation and to create, single-handed, the creative culture. For that an in-house seminar, involving as many as possible of the core group in the organisation, is important.

Creativity is an idiom, a habit, an inclination and a group culture. From the culture comes confidence. Confidence that an idea can be had and confidence that it will be listened to. Nothing is more important for creativity than confidence.

The thinking place

Take a look around you. What is the 'creative culture' of the place in which you work?

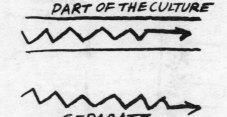

Are people encouraged to have ideas?
Do people try to have ideas?
Are people willing to discuss ideas?
Is there a conscious focus on matters that need ideas?
What sort of reception does a new idea receive?
Who is likely to have new ideas?
Who do you go to if you need to discuss an idea?
Can you recall some specific ideas that were used?
What sort of status does an 'ideas person' have?
Is there any suggestion scheme?
Do people ever meet specifically to find ideas?

Do you know where it would be most useful to have some ideas?
Is this the sort of area where a constant flow of ideas is needed?
Is there a feeling that only information can produce new ideas?
What is the risk acceptance level?
Is there an ideas policy?
Is there an ideas liaison person?
How much time do *you* spend looking for ideas?
When was the last time you had a creative idea?

It is obvious that an advertising agency needs more ideas than an engineering firm producing bearings. In an advertising agency each new idea is an enterprise in itself. The idea does not detract from what is already being done. With the engineering plant any new suggestion may mean a change in existing procedure. This means moving away from what is known and established in order to try something new. That means interruption, disruption and risk.

How would you classify the business you are working in with regard to its need for ideas: on a scale from 1 to 10 where 10 implies a great need for ideas?

As I have often stressed in these *Letters* creativity does not only imply the great big invention. It also covers small, day-to-day improvements. A slightly different way of doing something. A realisation that things need not be done in the same way. An understanding of how new technology can be used to its fullest. Human relations are also an area for new ideas.

Creativity is often more of an attitude of mind than a stated intention. Some readers might therefore find it difficult to carry out this exercise in self-awareness. They might claim that no-one in their organisation makes a song and dance about creativity but that it quietly takes place nevertheless. From experience I have come to be a little bit suspicious about this attitude. It usually means that people have such a low expectation from creativity that the occasional idea (one every three years) is judged to be enough. There are, indeed, organisations with a high creative atmosphere but no formal attention to creativity. This happens when there is a strong creative leadership. Without such leadership I doubt whether such an atmosphere can emerge.

20

Escape

There is no doubt that children can come up with very original solutions to a problem. This is not just because they are cute and therefore we make allowances. It is partly because they are uninhibited and unfettered by too much knowledge of how things work; and partly because they tend to think in function concepts.

The main reason, however, is that if you do not know the established approach to a situation you have a very good chance of coming up with an original approach. This is the creativity of 'innocence'. Adults in their own fields have no chance at all at this sort of creativity. It is impossible to be ignorant and innocent if you are not. It is just possible for an adult to be innocent in a field about which he or she knows very little. But even this is difficult, since adults are sensitive about making a fool of themselves and showing their ignorance. In any case, an innocent idea produced by an adult is likely to be scorned when the same idea produced by a child is likely to be appreciated – because an adult is expected to know and a child is not.

In general, in lateral thinking we have to use the creativity of 'escape'. This is why we have provocation and the word 'po'. This is why we have the idiom of movement. One of the broad techniques of lateral thinking is even more specifically concerned with escape. I am going to be dealing with that aspect of lateral thinking and with some aspects of the 'escape' mode.

General-area focus

The 'general-area' type of focus we might start with is some new ideas for breakfast foods. This is a typical general-area focus. We just state the general area and our need for ideas. We do not state exactly what we want from the ideas. At the end we hope to have some new ideas in this general area.

'Take for granted'

The first stage of the escape idiom is to 'spell out' what it is that we are going to try to escape from. There are various ways of doing this. For example, there is a check-list method which covers points such as 'dominant ideas', 'boundaries' etc. The simplest technique of all is to use the phrase 'take for granted'. What do we take for granted in this situation (or problem)? It seems very simple but in practice it is difficult to do. It is difficult to be aware of the obvious things that we do not even notice because they are so obvious. It is not enough to have a general awareness of the whole situation. It is not enough to suppose that this general awareness must automatically include all aspects of the situation. It is essential to single out some aspects and to 'spell it out' verbally. If we are going to escape from something, then we need to know what we are going to escape from.

We take for granted that we have *orange juice for breakfast*.

Note that this is not true of all breakfasts. In fact, outside the USA, it may be rather rare. Nevertheless it is a valid starting point, since many people do have orange juice for breakfast.

The escape

The simplest form of escape is just to drop the concept. So we might just drop the idea of orange juice for breakfast. We might say: 'Po, we do not have orange juice for breakfast'. This might lead us to think of the other times of the day when we might try to formalise the taking of orange juice. But that is not the purpose of the exercise – so we resist that temptation.

Since orange juice is just another addition to breakfast – rather than an intrinsic part of the concept – dropping orange juice is not a powerful provocation in itself. We might just shrug and say, 'So we do without orange juice'.

At this point we move to another variation of the escape idiom. Instead of just dropping the concept we alter it. We keep one feature of the concept and then find an alternative which also has this feature. So we might keep the 'juice' feature but drop the 'orange' part. This brings us to consider juices other than orange juice. We might think of tomato juice, prune juice, mango juice, water melon juice and many others. In each case we might pause to see whether there is a business to be built out of promoting any of these juices.

It is obvious that in the 'alternative' type of escape we must keep something constant. Otherwise we could say anything. We could escape from orange juice in order to suggest fried squid or roast beef. Such suggestions may have a provocative value in themselves, but they are more part of the random entry technique than the escape technique. By keeping the 'fruit juice' part constant, we then escape from the need for it to be orange juice. We could call this a 'partial escape' to contrast with the 'total escape' when a concept is simply dropped.

TOTAL ESCAPE

PARTIAL ESCAPE

We might try a different approach. This time we will keep the 'liquid' aspect and then look around for alternative liquids to orange juice. There could be a glass of milk. What about soup? What about a breakfast soup? At this point we have an idea that could be interesting. We move to the next stage.

In practice the stages flow into one another without need for a formal pause, but in illustrating the procedure it helps to break it down into stages.

Movement, interest and benefit

The provocation we have created at this point might be: 'Po, we have soup for breakfast'. We now pursue this line of thought for its movement value, its interest and its benefit.

'Movement' is the classic way of using a provocation. We use the provocation to open up some line of thought and then pursue that line of thought. We may end up quite far removed from the provocation. For instance, the above provocation could lead to the notion of a totally liquid breakfast. Because soup is salty another line of thought might be towards a breakfast which was non-sweet. This itself would open up a whole number of suggestions.

'Interest' and 'benefit' are more directly concerned with the provocation as an idea in itself. Instead of using the provocation as a stepping stone to move on to something else we look for benefit or interest in the idea that is being suggested. What is interesting in the idea of soup for breakfast? What is of benefit in the idea of soup for breakfast?

It is interesting to note that the Japanese always have soup for breakfast. This could be a useful promotion point since Japanese matters tend to be in fashion and there is a notion that they are fit and work a hard day. In any case if a whole nation always had soup for breakfast then there might be something in the habit.

There is something of an anti-caffeine movement because caffeine in excess is thought to be bad for health. Yet people do want something hot to drink when the weather is cold and they have to brave the outer world. So a hot soup – without any danger of caffeine – might be a habit with appeal.

Then there is the health trend and the diet trend. It is easy to make all sorts of diet soups which contain minimal calories and all the right vitamins and minerals. People jog a lot and when you jog you tend to sweat. This may mean a need to put back into the body some of the sodium that has been lost. That is another argument for soup. Perhaps we could market 'the joggers' soup'.

Consolidation

This is the next stage. It overlaps with the previous stage. We try to take what we have got and to consolidate it into an idea.

The idea seems to be that of promoting a breakfast soup. There are several different avenues of product promotion. There is the Japanese approach. There is the diet/health approach. There is the 'jogger' approach. There is the 'caffeine-free' approach. Each of these ideas could be developed further. We might even change the name from

213

'Breakfast soup' to 'Breakfast-sip'. In this particular case the idea has already formed itself in the second stage of the procedure.

Find a better way
This is the final stage. At this point we have the idea or concept. We now look around for a better way of implementing it. This does not apply in all cases, because the idea may be valuable enough in itself – as it may be on this occasion. Nevertheless we can try. We have the idea of marketing a breakfast soup so that it can become an essential item of every breakfast. At this point we may start thinking of another liquid which could become essential at breakfast.

What about a special 'cereal liquid'? Most people put milk or cream on to their cereals. Perhaps we could design a special liquid that would taste better and be much better for health? If we were to succeed with such a liquid, then it would piggy-back on cereal sales. It would have keeping qualities so that you could buy a large jar and keep it. There could also be different flavours so that different members of the family could choose their own flavours. This would increase sales. Of course all the ingredients would be 'natural'.

As a result of this exercise we now have two ideas:

– the breakfast soup
– the cereal liquid

Each of these ideas could be pursued and could lead to multi-million dollar businesses.

What I have tried to do here is to show how the simple 'escape' technique can work. There is much more to the technique than I have shown here and I shall be returning to different aspects of it from time to time in these *Letters*. I have tried to show how a creative person's mind might work as he sets out to develop some ideas in a specified area.

Is concept evolution enough?

Those who do not believe in creativity believe in concept evolution. You can always believe in both. But if you do not believe in creativity then you are forced to believe in concept evolution.

Concept evolution means that concepts evolve to meet needs. A concept emerges to meet a particular need and, when that need is strong enough, a concept will emerge. The concept that emerges is formed from ingredients and methods that are available at the time.

The next step is that concepts adapt and adjust to changing needs and changing circumstances. This implies that the pressures and needs will adjust the concept as required. This also implies that concepts are living organisms that alter and grow.

The third element in the notion of concept evolution is the Darwinian one of survival of the fittest. Concepts emerge and the best survive. Concepts change and those that do not change drop out.

These three elements make up the notion of 'concept evolution'. It is probable that few people consciously spell out a theory of concept evolution – yet the vast majority of people, in business and outside it, implicitly believe it. *There is a belief that needs will create concepts and that concepts keep up-to-date through adjustment and competition.*

If we followed this theory there would never be any need for creativity, lateral thinking or, indeed, any conscious effort to generate concepts. All we would need to do would be to sit back and allow concepts to emerge and adapt. Which is precisely what most of us do.

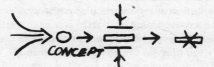

EMERGENCY ADAPTATION ? SURVIVAL

In science there is a belief in steady concept evolution. Evidence and experiment provide the environment in which concepts emerge and adapt. Occasionally the pressure of evidence is such that a new concept is born. History does not quite bear this out. Very often the new concept has required a conceptual leap and can only be seen as part of evolution in hindsight.

Danger
There is a great danger in this belief in concept evolution. The danger is that it is a passive attitude. We do nothing because we believe that nothing needs to be done – evolution will always do it for us. We not only believe that we do not need to generate new concepts, but we also come to believe that any attempt to introduce a new idea must be wrong because the natural course of evolution would quietly introduce the idea at the right time without any effort on our part.

So there is the danger of passivity and there is also what we might call an 'anti-creativity' bias that arises from the passivity. These dangers are serious enough. We must also multiply these dangers by the dangers to be found in the very process of evolution.

Evolution is not always for the best

There is a notion that evolution is always for the best. We believe that, if something changes from what it is to something different (without interference by man), the new must be an improvement on the old. This is not necessarily so at all. *The new evolves from what is under some pressure of change*. That is all. In the animal world, if the change is positively harmful then the species may die out. If it is not positively harmful the species may survive encumbered by quite unnecessary attributes.

Female birds might select brightly plumed mates. The offspring will carry the genes for such a selection. In time male birds will come to be brightly plumed. There is no necessary connection between bright plumage and other important characteristics. Indeed the bright plumage might make the birds more visible to predators. So a biological whim has caused evolution along a particular pathway.

With animals the environment is harsh and competitive. With human concepts there may not be this independence of the environment. The concept itself may set the environment through which the concept is judged. That is why in science an old idea may set the frame through which a new idea is rejected – until years later the new idea breaks through. In matters of belief the old concept can survive indefinitely. *In business the habits of the market-place may sustain an old concept beyond its true value*.

All we can say about evolution is that the next step is not negative when viewed through the current environment. Step by step an out-dated concept may lead us to great inefficiencies and errors.

Evolution is very slow

If a concept is adequate and satisfactory it survives. If a concept is inadequate, but we have adjusted to it and can live with its in-adequacies, it also survives. If a concept is deficient, but we cannot immediately see a better alternative, it likewise survives. If we were to make an effort we might find a better concept – but in the evolutionary idiom we do not make such an effort. Furthermore, if the judgement system operates from within the old concept then a new suggestion may be judged ineffective until it has had a chance to prove its worth – and it will not get that chance.

If ingredients are comfortably locked up in an old concept then it may take a very long time for a new concept to evolve. When it does evolve we look back and realise that it could have come about a long time before.

The principles of self-organisation ensure that once a pattern has been formed then it will drain other potential patterns and prevent their formation. Once there is the concept of 'profit', with its connotations of capitalist exploitation, then the concept of 'added value' is much harder to establish.

Even if we were to accept that evolution does eventually produce the required concepts, we still have to ask how quickly that happens. Is the new concept born as soon as it becomes possible? The answer has to be a definite 'no'.

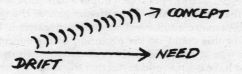

Blind alleys

There is nothing to say that evolution cannot take us down blind alleys. As evolution proceeds down a blind alley it does not know that the alley is blind. Right until the moment of discovery evolution assumes that the pathway is beneficial. This happens with animal species just as it happens with concepts. With animals the species dies out. With concepts there is no problem unless the concept is a dominant one. If so, we refuse to accept it as a blind alley. The concept just becomes less and less efficient and eventually chaos ensues. *There is no way that a blind alley can change to a useful path by a process of evolution.* That has always been the political justification for 'revolution'.

So a belief in concept evolution must imply a belief in the value of revolution. The alternative is a belief in creativity which can lead to the generation of new concepts, thereby making revolution unnecessary.

Changed circumstances

In a way this weakness of the evolution model includes several of the other weaknesses. A concept evolves under a particular set of circumstances and then keeps going. If the circumstances change radically then the concept may continue and may not be negative in behaviour. An example of this could be the evolution of the concept of trade unions. This was at a time of gross exploitation of workers. On the whole unions have been so successful that the situation has changed. Yet the structure and culture of the unions may not have changed.

Another example may be the attention to figure analysis that was necessary when business was very much a seat of the pants operation. So figure analysis was a necessary concept. But once the balance has been redressed then the continuation of this as a dominant concept may be stifling. There are numerous examples of situations where a concept is needed but continues beyond that need – or at least in a dominant position. A doctor may give a medicine to cure an illness but once the illness is cured there is no need to go on taking that medicine all the time.

Altering concepts

Once we accept that evolution does not give us perfect concepts then we can make an attempt to escape from existing concepts. Sometimes the escape may be total. We may shift from one concept to a different one. Here I am more concerned with a partial escape in which we operate the same concept but perhaps in a different way.

As a concept emerges the way it is carried out depends very largely on the technology available at the time. If the technology of polls, telephones and interactive TV (which is coming) had been available then the concept of democracy might have evolved in a different way. So in examining any concept we try to get an understanding of the circumstances prevailing when that concept emerged. We may then find that the function or purpose of the concept can now be achieved in a different way. This process is very similar to the well-known engineering process called value engineering. Do we still have to do it this way? Is this still essential? For example, something may be done in a particular way because at the time of invention there was not a metal able to withstand high temperatures: there may be such a metal today.

The basic concept of insurance is that those exposed to the risk should pay premiums and that whoever suffered the risk should be compensated from these premiums. The idea of sharing risk is the basic concept of insurance. An intrinsic part of that concept was that those exposed to the risk should eventually pay for the losses. Yet the whole concept of Lloyds of London is that people who are not exposed to the risk may eventually be called upon to bear the losses: that is to say, the names at Lloyds do not actually own ships that may sink, and yet they may be called upon to compensate an owner for a lost ship. Such names are, of course, at risk but in a very different way. They choose to be at risk and get compensated for that.

This is an example of how a basic concept can yet be altered.

There is no concept that is immune to challenge. We can look at a wheel and challenge the concept of a wheel. We can look at a banknote and challenge the concept of physical currency. What is important is that the challenge is never a criticism. The challenge is a creative one.

Reverse of evolution
In a way the creative challenge is the reverse of evolution. Instead of supposing that evolution has given us the best possible concepts, we suppose the opposite. We acknowledge that evolution may have given us the concept in front of us. Because of the serious deficiencies of evolution we consider that it is extremely unlikely that the concept is in its best possible form or able to take advantage of technology that is now available. We therefore challenge that concept in order to escape from it, to substitute another for it, or to improve it.

The question every thinker must ask is simple: do you really believe that evolution is adequate for the generation and development of concepts?

Sales commission
What is the basic concept of 'sales commission'? It is usually part of the basic concept that the reward is proportional to the value of the sale (ranging from 1% to as much as 30%). That seems a basic enough concept. How might it be altered?

One possibility is to challenge the proportionality. Instead of the commission being a constant percentage of the sales value, this percentage might start quite low and then increment with every further sale. Suppose the salesman started on a 2% commission and as he neared his usual performance this increased progressively until he was at 10%. Then the commission increased dramatically as he exceeded his own average performance until if he doubled his average performance, he might be on 30%. Perhaps the salesman could set his own scales on the basis that for his average performance the total earnings would be the same as before, but on further sales the commission could be much more.

Another possibility would be for the commission to be related to group performance. One rate would be applied if the total group output reached target and another rate if it did not. Or the rates could be based on comparative performance within the group: the top salesman would be on rate A, the next on rate B and the rest on rate C.

Another type of challenge would be to allow the commission to be in some form other than money. For example a good salesman could accumulate 'time off' instead of money.

In another idea each sale would give the salesman (in additon to normal commission) a 'ticket' in a lottery for some large prize. The more tickets he held the better the chance of winning the prize.

At this point it should be clear that the concept challenge attitude links up directly with the escape technique described in the previous article. Any aspect of the normal concept can be 'escaped from'. Although the escape technique is for generating new ideas and the concept challenge is for improving existing concepts, there is an overlap in the type of thinking required. The starting points are quite different.

With the formal escape technique the starting point is the value of provocation, and the escape technique is one way of getting a provocation.

With the concept challenge there is a realisation that concept evolution is far from perfect and that challenge of the existing concept can lead to a better one.

The thinking place

The thinking place is intended for brief exercises in thinking. The 'escape' technique depends rather heavily on the thinker's ability to be very definite as to what he is escaping from. If we are using the simple 'take for granted' approach then we need to spell out quite clearly what it is that we are taking for granted. Consider the following examples.

What do we take for granted about a restaurant?

There is a chef.
It is a place for eating.
There is a menu.
There are tables and chairs.
There is cutlery and china.

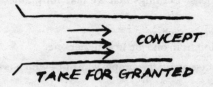

CONCEPT

TAKE FOR GRANTED

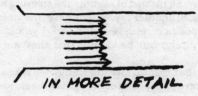

IN MORE DETAIL

There is a fairly straightforward list of things we take for granted. We could, however, have a rather more subtle list.

The chef is employed by the restaurant.
It is the same chef every day.
The chef is not usually known to the diners.
The price of the food is the same all the time.
The waiters are provided by the restaurant.
The diner does not choose the waiter.
Each table partakes of the same decor and background noise.
The diner has no choice of cutlery of china.
You are expected to pay at the end of the meal.
Each table is a separate unit on its own.
Food is brought or you serve yourself from a buffet.

For almost every one of these 'take for granted' items there is an obvious escape that leads to a new idea. There could be different chefs

221

who are advertised. You could bring your own waiter or at least choose your waiter. The diner could choose his china or a corporation could keep its own crested china at a restaurant. The expectation that diners should pay at the end of the meal did lead, historically, to the invention of the 'Diners Club' card (two advertising executives in New York challenged the need to pay in cash).

As an exercise, take each of the two following examples and write down a list of at least 15 things that we take for granted about each item.

Item 1.: a car steering wheel
Item 2: promotion from one job to a higher one.

In doing this exercise avoid the simple way out – which is to put down a lot of negatives.

We take for granted that a steering wheel is not a lobster, not a frog, not a brake, not a radio antenna and so on. Obviously there is an infinite number of things which something is not. So that version of the exercise would be pointless. In general, it is best to put things down in a positive way. So instead of saying: 'the steering wheel is not movable from one seat to another', we might have 'the steering wheel is usually in a fixed position relative to the car'. I would not like to exclude negatives entirely, but be careful that they are used in a constructive way.

You will probably find that just listing things we take for granted will automatically open up new lines of thought and new ideas. That is not, however, the prime purpose of the exercise.

21

Background creativity

There are those who believe that creativity is all mood, ego and attitude. This approach has two consequences. The first consequence is that we seek to identify those people who seem to think and behave in a creative manner. The second consequence is that we seek to create the right environment for the encouragement of the creative attitude.

The creation of the right environment can range from a corporate culture that welcomes and appreciates new ideas to the micro environment of a brainstorming session. Those who find the left brain/right brain notation useful would say that there is a need to create an environment in which right-brain thinking can rise to the surface instead of being dominated by left-brain expectations.

I think that these approaches have a certain merit. I am much in favour of a corporate culture that makes it clear that new ideas and new approaches are an expectation and not just an interference with routine. I am much in favour of a corporate culture that goes beyond the maintenance role of management.

I do not accept that the 'attitude' approach to creativity – and the various formal ways of encouraging such attitudes – is enough. As readers of my books and participants at my seminars will know, I favour a more structured approach in which specific thinking tools can be used in a deliberate manner. Such tools (like 'po') are designed to operate in the 'active', self-organising information universe of perception. I regard 'creativity' as the changing of concepts and perceptions. In order to avoid disagreement with those who have a different view of creativity, I introduced the term lateral thinking to mean precisely the changing of patterns in a patterning system. I do not intend to deal with such matters at this point, but I do want to indicate how the formal and deliberate use of lateral thinking meshes with background creativity.

'I want to develop new concepts in this i.s.a. (idea sensitive area) and I am going to use the random entry technique' as a declared intention to use deliberate lateral thinking. But what about background lateral thinking?

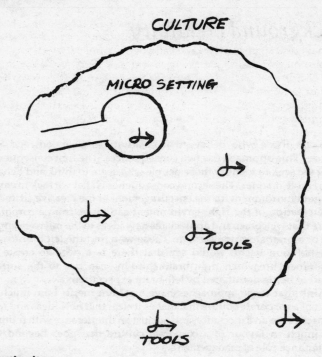

Continuity

Things are done the way they are because it was the best way at the time and is still the best way. Is this very likely?

It is just possible that after careful examination of a broad range of alternatives some approach was chosen because it was indeed the best. Even if this were so there is no reason to suppose that it is still the best. Changing needs, changing circumstances and changing technology may mean that a better alternative is now available (perhaps even one which was rightly rejected at the time).

It is far more likely that there was no thorough examination of alternatives, but that the first adequate idea was fastened upon and has remained in place because it has never been a problem and our thinking is only 'problem oriented'.

If we believe in an evolutionary theory of concepts then we believe the following:

'Any particular way of doing things has evolved through repeated pressures and needs and is therefore likely to be the best way'.

If we really believed this then there would be little point in background creativity. We should then only direct our creativity at areas which were obviously inadequate and performing poorly.

Evolution is not, unfortunately, linear and there are many blind alleys and dead ends. The pressure of events can indeed modify a stem idea but is unlikely to change it competely. We may end up with a well-adjusted poor idea rather than a good idea. Again, I do not want to go into the matter of concept evolution at this point.

The point I do want to make is that an appreciation that many things may be done in a particular way for no better reason than continuity is a powerful motivator towards background creativity. This motivator enables a thinker to look at any object and to say: 'Is this really the only way to do this?' Note that I did not write 'Is this the *best* way?' If we assumed that we could immediately find a better way that would not be creativity but modification. The only way we can be sure of finding a better way immediately is simply to remove the faults in the existing method. True creativity will seek a different approach. This may indeed prove better, but is more likely to be worse on final examination. So the ultimate aim is to find a better approach. But this may only happen after the generation of a number of new approaches, many of which will have to be rejected.

Benefit

Another motivator for background creativity is a belief in benefits. 'All ideas are much the same. They get the job done. The additional benefits are not worth the hassle, disruption and cost of change'.

It is obvious that a creative ego likes to see change. It is obvious that a creative ego likes to see his, or her, idea put into action. It is always nice to 'make things happen'. But those who have to put the change into effect and to live with it do not have these 'ego-benefits'. So they are very much more inclined to believe that creativity may lead to change for the sake of change. They are therefore justified in asking for the real benefits.

The truly creative person should also be seeking the real benefits rather than ego-satisfaction (nothing wrong with ego-satisfaction as a motivator but not as a selection criterion). So there is a tendency for a person to believe that whilst a new idea is indeed possible – as an intellectual exercise – it may not make much difference in practice.

So background creativity demands a conviction that ideas can make a real contribution. The direction of the contribution may be in terms of simplicity, cost saving, productivity, time saving etc. It is useful for the creative thinker to have *one* of these directions in mind as a habit.

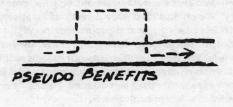

PSEUDO BENEFITS

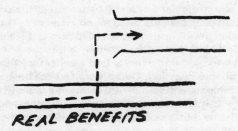

REAL BENEFITS

This needs to be more specific than the general notion that a 'better idea' can be produced.

The perfect creative thinker should always be striving to design an idea where the benefits are so visible and communicable that those required to act upon the idea will be eager to do so. In new product design the 'advertisability' of the new product is a key feature. Perceived value is even more important than real value. So it is with background creativity. *The communicability of the benefits arising from an idea is even more important than the benefits themselves.*

Too many people ask me how they should set about 'selling' a new idea. I admit that there are many situations where a very good idea needs selling because the benefits are long term and possibly out of tune with current thinking. In general, however, I would consider the total setting – including the people who were going to 'buy' the idea – as part of the creative design process. In other words, the selling of the idea should be designed into the idea in the first place.

In my seminars on opportunity search I talk about 'benefit sensitivity'. This is an attitude of mind that senses benefits of any sort and to any party. Just as some people have very sensitive judgements, so it is possible to develop sensitive 'benefitment' (a word invented at this moment and for this purpose).

There are many other aspects regarding background creativity and I intend to deal with them in the next issue of the *Letter*. For example, one key element is 'what to do with the ideas generated'. The motivation for background creativity depends a lot on this point. Will people be willing to keep on generating ideas even if none of them are ever used? The answer needs to be 'yes'. So how is this to be achieved in a practical manner? What sort of structural encouragement should be provided for background creativity? Is it enough to create a climate, or should individuals get some training as well?

Lip service to creativity

Who could be against creativity? Creativity is a wide enough word to cover change and benefit. Anything new that turns out to be worth doing can be called creative. Of course, it is permissible to suggest that in some circumstances strict cost control is going to be of more value than creativity. It is also permissible to point out that some creative accountants end up in jail. The answer in all these cases is to accept that we need efficiency, problem-solving and motivation – and then we need creativity in addition. Creativity is not a substitute for anything else. Conversely, nothing else is a substitute for creativity (with the possible exception of 'me-too' and copying).

So it is indeed easy to pay lip-service to the need for creativity. Then what happens? There may be some training in brainstorming or one of the parallel technologies, and then the mood passes. The great things that were expected fail to materialise. Exhortation has a limited life. Everyone is happy that something has been done about creativity, and therefore we can move on to the next fashion: communication? motivation?

Would we treat financial management in the same way? Would we be content that we had *done something about it* and therefore could get on with other things? Or would we stay with it until we were convinced that we had done enough? Unfortunately we can be aware of poor financial management, but we cannot be aware of poor creativity.

In a previous *Letter* I mentioned the Catch-22 of creativity. It runs as follows: 'For me to marvel at a creative idea it must be blue-sky and impractical. If it is practical and logical in hindsight, then I shall assume that it could well have been reached without creativity'.

This leads to the absurdity that we only believe creativity to be working when it produces much of amusement and nothing of value. This leads on to the serious problem of the 'creativity dilemma' with which I have dealt in a previous *Letter*.

The only way to overcome this dilemma is to have a clear under-standing of the *'logic'* of creativity. That is why I stress this point so strongly in my seminars. Even so, there are those who feel that understanding this logic is a luxury and that creativity can be worked just with a set of attitudes and techniques. It cannot.

Once we have understood the logic of creativity then we have no choice but to see it as a fundamental and essential part of our thinking. That is why a short talk I once gave to 1300 Ph.D.s in the 3M Research Department was said to have had more effect on their research thinking than anything else they had ever done. Once these highly technical people could see the 'logic' of creativity then it stayed with them. It was no longer a luxury. It was no longer a god to which occasional lip service should be paid.

An in-house seminar to a large number of people in an organisation is possibly the best way to acquaint them with this 'logic' of creativity. For those who are motivated, reading a book can also be helpful.

Preaching to the converted

I am well aware that my seminars, books and indeed this *Letter* are all instances of preaching to the converted. Those who are already motiv-ated to be interested in my work in lateral thinking (and thinking in general) are already pre-disposed to being creative. There are others who pay not the slightest attention to what I am about and are more than content that their thinking habits are complete and sufficient. I can only hope that what I write here and elsewhere, and what I say at my seminars, will provide arguments and insights which can be used by others to make an impression on the complacent.

I ought to add that complacency is not confined to the uncreative. I am always coming across people who give themselves very high marks for creativity, without much justification. Such people see the value of creativity and want to be creative. The contrast with those who do not even want to be creative is so strong that these 'creative' people are content to regard that as sufficient. Such people do not consider that there is very much more to creativity than they can imagine, for any enlargement of the scale of potential would only reduce their position along that scale. Humility is never a measure of talent but of horizons.

Taking both these aspects of complacency together, we need to develop methods for reminding people that creativity is important and an open-ended challenge. It is a language at which you can get better and better but never arrive at complete fluency.

If you want someone to learn French then you might send them off for an immersion course in French or for a visit to France. We could do the same for creativity, and I have in mind to set up just such an immersion course some time in the future. But there will always be the fear that anything as encapsulated as an immersion course would remain a rather specialised game played under certain circumstances and confined to those circumstances. That would not be much use.

I would like creativity to be usable at the three levels that I mention so often. The 'background' level, where it is part of the thinking attitude with which everything is approached: there could be an alternative way of doing this. The 'focus' level, where an effort is made to find a creative alternative at a specific point: right here we need a new idea. The 'tool' level, where the thinker uses a deliberate technique: let us use the stepping stone method here. Between them, these three levels cover both the background use and the specific use.

How can these idioms of creativity be put across to those who are not interested in acquiring them? I have mentioned the in-house seminar as one possible way. This *Letter to Thinkers* is another possible way. There are organisations which make sure that all their senior people are given a subscription. This ensures that each executive

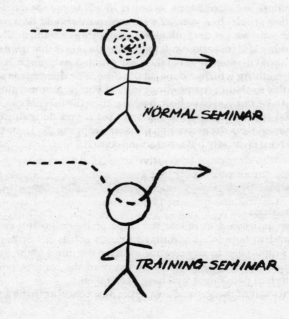

229

above a certain level has a continuing exposure to the idiom of creativity. It is more like a series of mini-visits to France than an immersion course. That is what I would really like creativity to be: there all the time as a continuing part of the life of every thinker. It should not be a fashion that comes and goes. It should not be a slimming camp which you visit and then leave. It is not a toolbox which you buy and then put in the garden shed alongside the other tools. It should be a permanent part of thinking. People need to be reminded about that, because there are very few situations which have a label attached: 'please be creative about this'.

Creativity is indeed a luxury in the sense that no one is ever compelled to be creative. But it is not a luxury in the sense that we can do well enough without it.

Less fuss about it
In a way I would like there to be less fuss about creativity. So long as there is a magic and mystique about it, then creativity will continue to be regarded as something extra – like a good wine at a meal. I would like creativity to be regarded as a sober and natural part of thinking. It is said that if you have to think about your manners then they are not really manners but affectations. *Manners should be the natural way of treating other people.* In a parallel way, creativity should be a natural part of the way we get to think about something. Paradoxically this means making less fuss about creativity. The danger is that if we make less fuss about it then it gets taken for granted as though it were already something which is done all the time. The dilemma is somewhat similar to that of 'name dropping'. If you do not mention the people with whom you have been dealing, then the listener can never know what sort of background there is. But if you do mention the names, then there is the accusation of name dropping. So I would like less fuss about creativity but more attention to it.

The thinking place

About bus stops
The reader is invited to follow the steps of the following creative exercise and to note what additional branch points his or her own thinking might take. In any creative exercise the mind of the thinker has taken one particular path. Yet at many of the concept points a totally different path might well have been taken.

The focus was of the 'general area' type: new concepts in the general area of 'bus systems'. The particular lateral thinking technique that was to be used was the 'random entry' (by means of a random word). The word was obtained from a dictionary by someone selecting a number to give a page and a second number to give the word position on the page. The word turned out to be 'picket'.

'Picket' suggested a group of people (from the strike sense of picket). So we imagine a group of people standing at a bus stop.

If there were more people at a stop, then perhaps the bus should preferentially stop there rather than at another stop. This brings to mind taxi auctions in Tokyo or Moscow. Empty taxis go past until the hopeful traveller learns to hold up two or three fingers indicating a willingness to pay twice or three times the fare. The notion is that a group will thus gain preference over an individual (it is illegal). So, somehow, the busier stops would get more bus attention. Perhaps an electronic sign would light up to show the driver how many people were waiting there. Perhaps people would move to where there were many people waiting, if this then became a preferred stop.

If more people waited at fewer stops, this could have a value in that buses would have to stop less often. Journey time would be lessened and traffic flow improved.

How could people be induced to choose their stops more carefully?

Perhaps there could be 'cheap' stops and 'expensive' stops. If you got on at a cheap stop you would pay less than at an expensive stop – irrespective of distance (or even flat-rate systems).

This might mean that people would walk a little way to a cheap stop instead of waiting at the expensive stop. Those who wanted to use the less central stop would pay extra for that convenience.

So we begin to see a principle emerging regarding convenience, pricing and efficiency of the system.

The trade-off between price and convenience is an old one. There are, of course, many problems. For example old people might be induced to walk too far to get to the bus stop (since they may be the group most likely to want to save money). This could be overcome by having the senior citizen pass over-ride fare differences.

The overall principle is that, if you help the system operate better, then you may benefit from that better operation It then becomes a matter of creating practical ways in which people can choose to help the system operate better and, at the same time, benefit themselves.

As a general point, it is interesting to note that there are times in transport systems when there is an advantage in 'bunching' and there are times when there is only disadvantage in bunching (peak-time travel). If airline travellers could be induced to bunch their travel so that all aircraft were full, then airlines might make more profits. If passengers could be induced not to bunch their travel, then peak hour congestion at airports like La Guardia in New York would not occur. Should there be penalties for peak-hour use or a bonus for off-peak use? Should systems fit people, or should people fit systems?

What if the bus fare system suggested here did not make for any extra efficiency in the system but was simply used to increase profits by charging people for convenience (after all, you pay more if you take a taxi)?

22

Coal, conflict and concepts
(written during the miners' strike)

I do not intend to analyse the motives and the developments of the prolonged miners' dispute in the UK. That in itself might be a worthy task. So might the apportionment of blame and righteousness. What I want to do here is to explore the 'design' of concepts that are relevant or could become relevant.

The traditional concepts of *confrontation, battle, victory and defeat* clearly set the mood. It could indeed be said that the dispute has continued because both sides *are in a state of victory and neither side wishes to terminate this state of victory*. I do not mean that both sides think they are going to win. It is that both sides are at this moment in a state of victory. The government is winning by not giving way on its policy and economic intentions. Arthur Scargill and the NUM are winning inasmuch as the strike continues and a substantial number of miners back their leadership: they are not being cowed. There is no advantage for the leadership on either side to give way. This brings up the question of those types of dispute where neither side wants to end the dispute – although both sides may wish that it were over. There is a clear need for some outside mechanism or commission that is set up to cope with such a situation. It may be thought that Arthur Scargill has much to lose from the continuation of a conflict that might eventually lead to a drift back to work. Up to a point this may have been so, but once that point is passed (which may now be the case) defence remains heroic. This is like a captain going down with his ship or a defending general in a long siege. Circumstances and the 'weak will' of supporters will preserve the heroism of the loser. The very prolongation of the dispute is already a victory which cannot be cancelled.

To expect individual miners to run the gauntlet of substantial numbers of pickets and to risk violence at home is an unreasonable demand for heroics which many individuals cannot offer. The threat of intimidation must be real enough in the minds of miners who may want to work – intimidation for the moment and for future relations with their comrades. The expense of police protection and the media-feast of the violent confrontations may have a public relations value for the government but it is expensively bought. Suppose that miners could register for work (post or telephone) but stay at home. Their wages would be held in escrow. When more than 50 per cent at any pit had registered for work, then the miners would be expected to go to work. If this happened then the wages held in escrow would be fully paid. If it did not happen the wages would not be paid. If the number did not reach 50 per cent then the wages would not be paid, unless the men went to work (as at present). In a way this would constitute a sort of implicit national ballot.

On the other side we need to examine the concept of an 'uneconomic' pit. It is perfectly true that coal is not the same as steel. There is no point at all in producing steel uneconomically with no hope of selling it at uneconomic prices. But coal is a resource and the expense of reopening a closed pit is prohibitive. So there is some point in producing coal, even if the cost of production is higher than momentary economics suggest. Future energy costs are difficult to predict. It is perfectly conceivable that what is not economic today may be so in the future – if oil prices rise. So in its own right the concept of 'uneconomic' needs careful handling. Add to this the special nature of mining communities and the shut-down of a community rather than just a pit and one has a sort of 'special case' which mining has always claimed for itself. Should the acknowledgement of these principles deliver the sort of 'blank cheque' which Arthur Scargill seems to demand with the notion that there is no such thing as an uneconomic pit? Presumably there could be some statistical definition of 'uneconomic'. Suppose we said that uneconomic meant that the cost of production was more than 1.75 standard deviations from the mean cost of production (or some other figure). Clearly the investment in a pit would have to be factored in and also related to the mean investment.

I recently completed a book on the *Design approach to Conflict Resolution*. The basic concept is that there are three roads. The first is fight/litigate/conflict. The second is negotiate/compromise. The third road is design. The design view is that a conflict is a situation with different perceptions, principles, needs and emotions and the task is to design an outcome. After all, the design of a jet fighter is an immensely complex process involving trade-offs between weight, cost, manoeuvrability, robustness, etc. Yet it can be managed through the proper use of the design idiom.

The point is that the design idiom starts from a point that is completely different from the conflict idiom.

In the conflict idiom the participants try to reduce the concept to its *basic confrontation simplicity*. So in the miners' dispute we reduce matters to the clash between socialism and capitalism. The socialist principle is that people come first, and that subsidies to preserve uneconomic mining jobs are worth while and particularly worth while if we consider the real and psychological expense of unemployment and the destruction of communities. The capitalist view would claim to be just as caring for people, but would maintain that it is only through the principles of economic and competitive production that there can be produced the wealth that allows an improvement in the standard of living and the provision of those welfare services to which people are entitled. Capitalism would say that there has to be a 'negative cash-flow' of hardship in order that the eventual investment will pay off. Socialism mistrusts this negative cash flow and believes that the ultimate benefits will not flow to those who have borne the hardship. When a conflict is reduced to these conflicting principles then it seems that only victory and defeat can offer a solution.

CONFLICT IDIOM

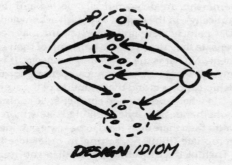

DESIGN IDIOM

The design idiom goes in exactly the opposite direction. Instead of reducing the matter to fundamental warring principle there is an attempt to complicate and enrich the situation so that a design can be made.

For example, the definition of an 'uneconomic' pit can be richly elaborated to take into account a host of factors. Indeed the dispute could be ended whilst a special commission works out this definition.

We could imagine that the NCB would have every right to close an uneconomic pit – provided certain conditions were met. These would include the immediate provision of other means of keeping the community alive. So pits could be shut down but not communities.

Conversely the NUM might have the right to keep any pit open – provided certain conditions were met. For example, that 25 per cent of the additional subsidy required was contributed by the NUM in any way they liked.

The NCB could keep its position as judge and jury on the matter but the NCB itself would consist of both managers and union representatives working within a defined framework of social and economic responsibility.

It could be that for a given pit the miners at that pit would vote for its continuation or shut down. They would vote under circumstances that offered special conditions. These would go beyond simple redundancy payments. For example, there could be a three-year notice of closure, and during that three years wages would be substantially increased (perhaps by 50 per cent) in addition to a final payment being given.

I am not suggesting that the ideas I am putting forward here offer a solution to the dispute. But I am suggesting that the design approach is different from the conflict approach. For example, in the conflict approach Mr. Scargill and his followers should be defeated and taught a lesson in order to preserve a basic economic principle – and a political one (governments are democratically elected and thereafter can operate autocratically). In the design approach acknowledgement is given for the NUM point of view, and some 'reward' may need to be designed to compensate the miners for the hardship of their strike. Is this not appeasement? No – it is the *design of the way out*. It is hardly likely that this 'reward' would in any way compensate for the very considerable hardship on miners and their families of the strike.

The key question is whether continued conflict-style confrontation is the way out of whether design-style thinking is now more appropriate. If it is the latter then there does need to be some outside agency providing the appropriate 'thinking' setting in order to effect this change in mode. Each of the disputing parties has got itself into a win-lose posture from which it is virtually impossible to escape.

Strength, determination and leadership are admirable qualities. They become even more powerful when supplemented with the imagination of design.

Expectation and motivation

At a recent seminar I gave on 'Opportunities' there were two interesting and relevant comments from the audience. At one point I was mentioning various factors which influenced opportunity search within a corporation. Someone claimed that only one thing mattered: the corporate culture. In the end this is true. But corporate culture is only a summary. It is a summary of what may have happened historically. For example, the organisation may have been started by a creative entrepreneur who quickly established a style of creativity. That entrepreneur might also have chosen lieutenants who shared this attitude. In turn those executives would choose others – in a sort of Apostolic succession. Such successions (always to be found in universities) preserve the existing culture, whether it be good or bad. The effect of such continuity is that an organisation may indeed have a 'creative' culture even though there is nothing very definite at this point in time to show why it could be so. The result is that analysts point at the organisation and praise this intangible culture. What is not realised is that this type of culture cannot suddenly be grafted on to an organisation. Such cultures have to arise over time from an historic base. Executives in such an organisation get to know the style of thinking that is expected from them. They get to know the rules of the game and become good at playing according to those rules.

The second comment came from an executive who was involved in a new division at Ericsson (the Swedish electronic organisation). He related how 10 per cent of the employees spent 10 per cent of their time in direct creative endeavour. This provided a very tangible structure and expectation. Apparently this had come about when a member of that corporation had attended a previous seminar of mine. The point I want to make is that in order to introduce a culture or bring about a culture change there does need to be some *tangible commitment*. Exhortation and leadership are not enough. Such things need to be anchored in a tangible way. There needs to be time set aside for creativity. There needs to be an expectation. People need to be asked for their creative ideas – and they should be expected to have an answer of sorts. It is not realistic to demand that people have brilliant creative ideas. But it is realistic to demand that they make a creative effort and produce a creative outcome of some sort. You can put a problem under someone's nose and ask that person to come up with alternative solutions.

As I have mentioned so many times in these *Letters*, it needs to be made clear that creativity is *part of the rules of the game*. People are very good at playing the rules of the game as soon as they perceive what these rules are. So if creativity is part of the rules then that game will be played. In time, confidence and skill will improve and so will the calibre of idea produced.

What are the changes that have been made?

What are the changes that are being made?

What are the changes that need to be made?

What are the areas that need focused creative thinking?

Change is not always a matter of creativity. For example, a change may follow from a new technology or in response to a price change. Nevertheless the awareness of change and the possibility of change is a sufficient focusing motivation for creativity. The concept of 'change' is less threatening than that of 'creativity' and yet a conscious effort to change requires creative thinking.

The merit of creativity depends not on the total novelty of the new idea, but on the new benefits that follow from the idea. The application of a known idea to produce new benefits also ranks as creativity. *The purpose of creativity is benefit, not ego-satisfaction.*

The creative person

I need to say that I am not in favour of labelled 'creative people' or a 'creative élite'. Some people are more creative than others, either through talent or through motivation – or possibly because they have learned the sort of techniques I write about. Nevertheless such people should not be treated as if they are wearing a special halo. I believe that creativity – or more correctly 'lateral thinking' – is a basic part of everyone's thinking.

If I was given the choice of adding logic and experience to a 'creative person' or adding some creativity to a person already equipped with logic and experience, I might well choose the latter.

In a future *Letter* I shall deal more directly with this point. At this moment I am concerned with how the creative person sees himself (or herself) and the role that he or she seems expected to play.

If the creative person turns up something that is simple and even logical in hindsight, then those around profess to be disappointed. What they seem to expect from creativity is a sort of impractical fireworks with ideas that are startling but never practical. Such ideas are useful in order to encourage people to dream more widely. They are also useful in order to illustrate the role of provocation. But they are not what steady-stream creativity is all about.

Instead of playing up an idea for its unusualness, the creative person needs to play it down so that it seems matter of fact, logical, obvious and practical. That way the idea is more likely to get acted upon.

There is also an additional advantage in this down-playing. The advantage is that many people who have no confidence in their 'creativity' will feel able to contribute this quasi-logical type of idea.

To be fair there is a danger in this down-playing. The danger is that if the ideas are too logical and reasonable then, after a while, there may arise a feeling that nothing needs to be done about 'creativity' as such because the flow of new ideas can take place without it. The dilemma is that if creativity is not seen as something special then nothing will be done about it – on the basis that current thinking habits are quite sufficient. If creativity is seen as something *too special* then its relevance and practicality are doubted.

The trick is to keep the right balance. There needs to be a mixture of ideas which range from the logical and immediately practical to the more extreme. The more extreme ideas can always be treated as 'concept directions' rather than finished ideas. In other words the idea provides a direction in which to look rather than a plan of action.

As I have indicated on many occasions the truly creative person can carry out his or her creative thinking internally and then come out with a final idea that seems very logical.

Rejecting ideas
For there to be a successful creative climate there has to be a way of rejecting ideas. Many people complain that when creativity has become a corporate by-word the truth of the culture change is belied by the fact that all the new ideas are rejected. This is a difficult point. There is no way an organisation could possibly act upon every new idea put forward. In many cases such ideas are inappropriate or even unworkable. Yet there is a need for the ideas to keep flowing.

It is certainly the task of the person who is responsible for introducing the creative culture to make quite clear that the exhortation to have ideas does not mean that any of these will be acted upon. There has to be acknowledgement and recognition of the ideas. This is essential. But it should also be made clear that an idea will not be acted upon unless defined benefits are demonstrated on behalf of the idea. Novelty is enough to get an idea noticed but not enough to get it acted upon. The type of idea that is *usable* should be clearly defined so that creators seek these types of ideas (for example, cost cutting and simplification ideas).

This leaves the difficult question of ideas which are not finite money-saving ideas but ideas that open up new directions. A lot more work and a lot of testing may need to be done on such ideas. Yet the potential can be huge. Are such ideas to be discarded?

It may well be that in the beginning (of the introduction of a creative climate) such open-ended ideas should not be encouraged. When the climate is firmly established then a limited number of such ideas may be pursued. Any innovator needs to realise that the potential of the idea as he or she sees it may be very different from the risk/reward ratio as seen by others.

There is a point which I have mentioned before and which no doubt I shall mention many times again. An innovator should be encouraged to *sell benefits not novelty*. This applies in virtually every situation outside of advertising. In advertising the very novelty of a campaign may attract attention to the product and indeed to the advertising agency itself. In all other situations what is going to matter are the benefits: is the idea workable; if it works, what are the benefits? Novelty is never a substitute for benefits. If novelty itself leads to benefits that is fine but it is the benefits that have to be assessed. This is one of the reasons why many of the traditional habits of creative thinking do not work so well in practice. It is because they are largely derived from the ambience of creative advertising which has demands that differ from most other situations.

Sell benefits rather than novelty

This should be inscribed in the mind of every creative person. Of course it goes against the creative motivation. Any creative ego wants to come up with something which is novel, original, exciting and startling. His or her measure of creative achievement derives exactly from this 'newness' or 'difference'.

In a previous *Letter*, I distinguished between small 'c' creativity and big 'C' creativity. In the introduction of a creative corporate culture it is the small 'c' creativity that needs to be built upon.

Very few creative ideas can be acted upon. The creative spirit should take pride in the fact that on any matter 'a large number of new ideas have been created'. That is the measure of achievement. It is rather like putting good quality wine into your cellar. You can only drink the bottles slowly, one at a time, but you take pride in your cellar.

It may be that a certain creative idea has a value under certain circumstances and those circumstances have not yet occurred. So the idea is a good idea but not applicable at the moment.

The person rejecting a new idea should put emphasis on this matter of 'inappropriate'. It is a convenient type of judgement because it means that the idea may be good in itself but not suitable at the moment or for this particular organisation.

The other strand of rejection is to put the onus back on the innovator:

'Could you explain to me exactly how this would work?'

'What sort of further work needs to be done on this idea?'

'Can you spell out the benefits for me?'

'Would the benefits be sufficient to compensate for the cost of changing over to this new idea?'

Such questions should not be used in a negative way ('prove to me that your idea is any good') but in a genuine exploratory way ('I would like to convince myself that your idea is going to offer benefits, can you help me on this?').

Creativity should neither be oversold or undersold. The key requirement is that a definite commitment should be made to do something about it. Thereafter it is a slow and steady build-up process. The temptation to produce something startling as quickly as possible should be resisted.

It is perfectly in order for a creative person to say, 'We are still doing it in the old way but now we know about several other possibilities. Some of them we are exploring. Others we have in readiness should the need for a change become apparent.' Such an enrichment of the conceptual map is of value in itself. It means that we do things in the old way because *we choose to* and not because we have never conceived of a different way.

The thinking place

I intend to set out here the rules of a simple two-person word game. I have not come across this game before and so I shall claim to have invented it. It is quite possible that some reader will write to tell me that the game is, in fact, an old one that is well-known in certain areas. That is a risk any inventor takes.

I want readers to look at the game as I have set it out. There might be additional rules or ways of making it into a more interesting game.

Play
The first player puts down a word: for example, TWIST.
The next player has a choice of three possible operations:

1 Add or insert a letter at any point.
2 Delete a letter.
3 Change the position of any letter.

Only one of these operations can be carried out. *The result must make a word in its own right.*

If the player cannot produce a new word in this manner, then a second or third operation (and more if required) may be carried out. Again, these operations must come from the list of three choices of operation.

Each one of these further operations must be paid for, either with 'points' or with a pre-agreed sum, for example 10p a point (or much more).

At the end of the game the different points are added up and the winner is the person with the least number. If the game is being played for money then the appropriate financial adjustments are made.

Example

1st   T W I S T

2nd   T W I T (delete letter)

1st   W I T (delete letter)

2nd   W A I T (insert letter)

1st   W A I S T (insert letter)

2nd   W A I T S (change letter position)

1st   W A I S T S (insert letter)

(note that it is not possible to go back to a word that has already been used in the same form)

2nd   H O I S T S (three purchased operations: remove W; insert H; remove A; insert O – one operation is free as usual).

1st   H O S T S (delete letter)

2nd   H O S T (delete letter)

1st   P O S T (this is really two operations: delete H and insert P – so one purchased operation)

The substitution of a new letter for one which is there needs to be two operations otherwise it becomes too easy.

The skilled player will do more than just survive. He, or she, will attempt to set up a word that is difficult to modify so that the opponent has to 'purchase' several operations in order to proceed.

The use of plurals or a change of tense in a verb seems rather feeble and it might be possible to exclude this type of change.

Another suggestion might be to give 'positive' points for the addition of letters. Such positive points could cancel the negative ones. So the change from P O S T to P O S I T would gain a point, whereas from P O S T to P O T would not.

M O A N

M A N

M E A N

A M E N

N A M E

23

Does lateral thinking work?

It might seem strange that after years of writing and working in this area I should pose the title question? So how is lateral thinking being used today?

First, the 1984 Los Angeles Olympic Games. These were no doubt a huge administrative success. I think they were a triumph on almost every level. But on some levels they are more open to subjective judgement. As regards the administration there can be no doubt. Things worked very well indeed. The staging of Olympic Games is an expensive procedure, and the host city/country usually loses up to $500 million. In Los Angeles the city voted not to spend a cent of taxpayers' money on the Games. Yet the Games made a *surplus* of $215 million. Much of the credit for this extraordinary feat must go to the organiser, Peter Ueberroth. No doubt he had a team of very capable and motivated people working with him, and all of them must share in the success. Nevertheless Peter Ueberroth was chosen by *Time* magazine as US 'Man of the Year' because of his achievement. In the 30 September 1984 issue of the *Washington Post* there is an interview with Peter Ueberroth, in which he is asked about the secret of his success. He answered that it was due to lateral thinking.

When Peter Ueberroth was chosen to head the Olympic organising team, his name seemed vaguely familiar to me. But the Ueberroth I had known had been running a travel agency called 'Ask Mr Foster'. This Olympic Ueberroth had indeed owned a travel agency, so I wrote to Peter Ueberroth and asked him if he was the person I thought I remembered. He was.

Peter Ueberroth had been my faculty host at the ninety-minute talk on lateral thinking that I had been invited to give to the Young Presidents' Organisation at their Boca Raton (Florida) meeting which was held in 1975. So it would seem that the exposure of Peter Ueberroth to lateral thinking was for only ninety minutes, nine years before. It says much for this remarkable man that he developed his skills in the technique and put them to such good use. In the *Washington Post* interview he describes the classic provocative techniques of lateral thinking.

One of Peter Ueberroth's imaginative concepts was the running of the Olympic torch across America a few kilometres at a time. This kept attention focused on the Games for very much longer in the build-up period. This in turn helped get the sponsorship which made such a big difference.

Further examples

In Sweden the Pharmacia Company has been immensely successful in its field of pharmaceuticals and speciality chemicals. Only last week they reported a further 24% increase in profits for the last year. A few years ago Gunnar Wessman was appointed chief executive. He has been interested in lateral thinking for a very long time. I have worked with him at Perstorp AB and also at Uddeholm AB. In Pharmacia he had a company in which he could put his lateral thinking talents to work. Within three years he had increased the profits of the company by a factor of *ten*.

Gunnar Wessman has given me permission to quote him in print. He says that *lateral thinking was an essential tool in being able to escape from the perceptions and concepts of the past and in order to develop new ones*. On a number of occasions I have now given in-company seminars to about 500 key people in the Pharmacia organisation.

Michael Johnson, the president of the New York investment bank, Paine Webber Blyth Eastman, is another advocate of lateral thinking. He told me how, after coming to a short talk that I had been invited to give to a meeting of the Institute of Institutional Investors in Bermuda eight years before, he had continued to use lateral thinking in his daily business.

Lateral thinking seems to be associated with all kinds of successes. The well-known group 'The Eurhythmics' on the side of an album that was in the charts for months had the inscription: 'Thanks to Edward de Bono'. Why I do not know.

There are numerous other examples of success associated with lateral thinking. One such is the case of the famous Australian film producer, Pat Lovell. She once told me that she switched from being a TV host to being a film producer after reading one of my books. She had been interviewing me on TV in Australia and, after the interview, decided to read the book. She had always wanted to be a film producer. After reading the book she simply said: 'Why not?'. She produced *Picnic at Hanging Rock* which really started the very successful international Australian film industry. She was also the producer of *Gallipoli*.

Why do I mention these things here? It is because those who subscribe to this *Letter* are those who are really interested in creative thinking. From time to time they try to persuade others that the concept part of thinking is indeed important, that the analysis of figures is not by itself sufficient. Such persuasion can – and should – be done on a direct level. Nevertheless there are listeners who will accept the argument on an intellectual level but will then leave it on one side as 'something of interest'. This is why some examples are useful to show how the direct use of lateral thinking has made a difference.

A sense of value and benefit

This taxi driver does not know the way. So what does he do? He uses his radio. He consults his map. More likely than either of these actions would be a question directed at the passenger: 'Can you tell me how to get there?'

Many people would never reach this conclusion because it is not sufficiently comprehensive: many taxi users have not the slightest idea about how to reach their required destination (for example taxi users in any foreign city). But when we are using 'movement' on an idea we never do it to be comprehensive. Some taxi users might indeed know the way. Indeed taxi drivers often ask their passengers the way.

The question is, how many thinkers would perceive a value in the taxi driver asking the passenger for directions on how to get there.

What are the links? Well, the passenger would have to know his way about. He, or she, would have to be a resident. So only residents could use this type of taxi. We now begin to see some value. Residents often have trouble getting taxis in the high tourist season. This way there would be a type of taxi reserved for residents. We now imagine non-residents hailing such taxis and then finding that the taxi driver did not know the way. So the non-resident should know in advance. Perhaps these special taxis would have a big question mark on the roof or would be a different colour.

At this point there is some value in having a dual taxi system since town residents would not always be competing with visitors. The major value in the suggestion, however, would be in a city like London where taxi drivers are not given a licence until they can pass an exam which tests them on their knowledge of streets, hotels, restaurants, monuments etc. This apparently takes eighteen months. As the learner is not being paid over this period, there are not many people who want to do this. In the dual system the learner gets paid at once, and continues to get paid as he learns his way around. So more people may want to become taxi drivers, and there would be more regular taxi drivers in the end. In addition the learning process is more attractive to the learners.

Suppose the city is not London and drivers can get a taxi licence without having to pass any special exam. What then is the value of the idea? Perhaps experienced drivers could drive specially-marked taxis – and charge a higher fare. Even if they did not charge a higher fare, they might get more business. Any complaint might lose them the 'super-knowledge' label.

If the resident is directing the driver, he might as well be driving the taxi. This suggests available cars which residents get into, drive to their destination and then leave for the next driver. Such cars might have a 'caretaker' who might collect fares and prevent theft.

At this point there is a clear concept of a taxi system geared to residents. The taxi is no longer there to provide street knowledge but merely to provide a car only when required and one which does not have to be parked. What is the value of this concept? If residents did not drive their own cars into the city there would be much less traffic congestion. So a taxi system especially geared for residents might reduce traffic problems.

Where is the benefit? Who enjoys the benefit? Under what circumstances would this be a benefit? These are the questions that are used – consciously or unconsciously – to ferret out value.

At this point we come to a difficulty. One of the things that has got creativity a bad reputation is an apparent inability to tackle the specified problem. For example, in an effort to improve an umbrella someone suddenly discovers that a proposed shape would have a value as a photographic reflector. Should this value be pursued or not? The answer is not simple. I would not like to suggest that ideas that turn up out of context should be rejected. Many an excellent idea has turned up out of context. Nevertheless an effort must be made to tackle the specified problem. Is this suggestion of value in the field of umbrellas?

In a recent session with some police chiefs one of the areas for consideration was 'the improvement of relations between the police and the public'. The escape method was being tried and 'police uniforms' was the basic 'take for granted item' from which the escape was to be made. One escape could be 'Po police had no uniform'. A partial escape was 'Po policemen had half a uniform'. From that came an idea of a 'police jacket' which would be the only item of uniform to be worn. With this jacket could be worn any type of shirt, trousers, shoes or hat. What value would this be? Plain-clothes police seem sinister and to be spying on the public – so a complete lack of uniform is far from 'friendly'. The solo jacket might serve to give this casual/ friendly air and yet to identify the person as a policeman. It could be a sort of half-way position between the public and full police operation. In fact all police might spend one or two weeks a year in this sort of role. Here the value might not be that of the role itself but of the 'training' the police would have in public relations whilst they were in the solo jacket role. In other words, the suggestions would have a double value: a less remote type of police; a training method to improve public relations.

The appreciation of value involves the shifting of perspective: looking at things from different points of view. Any proposed change is likely to have a variety of effects. Many of these are likely to be negative but some of them are going to be positive. It is rather unlikely that all effects of a change will be negative. It should also be remembered that there may be many different values in an idea. We always need to go beyond the first obvious value no matter how dominant this may be.

It can happen that a value that arises from a particular suggestion then 'takes off' on its own. For example, another of the police concerns was with 'increasing the number of police so that they would be more visible to the public'. A wishful thinking type provocation was used: 'Po policemen could be in two places at once'. This led to the idea of mobile police offices as vans or caravans. So policemen doing routine work could have their computer terminal in the van and would thus go on working and also be visible at the same time. From this concept of 'visible working' might then come the idea of policemen working from home with computer terminals. Such policemen would be known to work from home and in this sense would be highly visible.

This ability to sense value is a very important part of creative thinking skill. I have seen people on the brink of a good idea but unable to go forward because they could not see the different values in what they themselves had just said.

The thinking place

The story is told about Gauss as a young boy. It is said that the teacher set the class a tedious problem so that he could go on reading an interesting novel. The task was to add up all the numbers from 1 to 100. To the teacher's surprise – and disbelief – the young Gauss offered the answer of 5050 after a few seconds.

It is said that Gauss reckoned the middle number to be 50. The extra one in the number above (51) could then be transferred to the 'deficient' one in the number below the middle (49). The same argument would apply for 52 and 48, for 53 and 47. Finally the 49 would be transferred from 99 to 1, making both 50. So now there would be 100 × 50. The 100 figure would transfer 50 to the zero position and leave 50 in place. This would now make 101 columns of 50. So 50 × 101 = 5050.

Another way to look at it (which I refer to in my seminars) is to add 1 to 100, 2 to 99, 3 to 98. Each time the result is always 101 since we add one on this side and subtract one on the other. The end result is that we have 50 × 101 to give 5050.

The simplest way of all is really a visualisation of the preceding approach. Imagine a staircase. At the first step you rise one unit. At the second step you rise two units. Three at the third step and so on. When you have taken 100 steps you will have risen 100 units. You might imagine the staircase as a drawing. If you now put an identical staircase upside down over the first one you will obtain a rectangle which is 101 units high and 100 units long. This is twice as many units as are needed so we divide by two to get the result 5050.

These are largely variations of the same concept. Nevertheless the starting perception is different.

The task I want to set you here is to ask you to figure out some further approaches to this task.

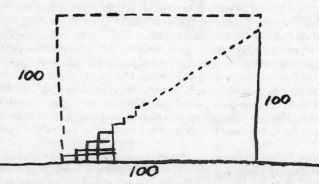

Since you know the answer will be 50 × 101 you can work backward from this point to figure out what perception might give this result.

24

If unemployment is not the fault of the Government then they should do very much more about it

This seems paradoxical. Surely if unemployment is caused by government policy then the government should do something about it. But if unemployment is not caused by government policy, why should they do even more about it? The reasoning is simple. If unemployment is really caused by government policy then the government only needs to defend that policy or to change it. If unemployment is not caused by government policy then the government has no control over it. Therefore the government must make *an even bigger effort* to do something about it.

Of course, quite a lot is being done – but not nearly as much as could be done. In this piece I intend to point out what else could be done.

At a recent ministerial meeting in Venice the US Secretary of Commerce (Mr. Baldridge) lambasted the Europeans on the failure to create any net new jobs since 1975. He pointed out all the structural rigidities and inhibitions in the system.

These presumed *causes* of unemployment are all well known. There is over-regulation and protection of service industries. There is a lack of venture-capital investment. There is a lack of incentive for entrepreneurs. There are restrictive union practices. There is lack of training and lack of job mobility. Workers are unable to move to where the jobs are because they cannot sell their homes in order to buy new ones. Industrialists do not want to take on more workers when an economic upturn comes because of the difficulty and high cost of getting rid of them again later. Welfare and unemployment payments (transfer payments) mean that in some cases it is not really worth a person's while to work: what he will receive will only be slightly better than what he already gets.

Then there is the other batch of *causes* of unemployment. More women than ever want to work. *There are more jobs than there have ever been in the UK, but still over 3 million unemployed.* Increasing automation means that fewer people are needed to do a job: a ditch digging machine replaces many people. Most large organisations are investing heavily in people-shedding equipment. About twenty five per cent of people work in offices. Office automation equipment will have a huge impact on the need for office personnel. The high cost of wages, partly caused by higher taxes to pay for higher health and welfare expectations, makes industry less competitive with the newly industrialised countries (NICs). It used to be said that a Korean car company could never produce the Italian style of cars. Of course they can: they just contract an Italian designer. Any NIC can buy a turnkey

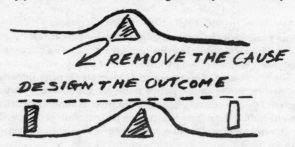

plant with all the latest equipment from the West. Sulzer textile machinery is to be had for the buying. I find it difficult to think of anything which is now made in Europe that cannot just as easily be made more cheaply elsewhere. I would, of course, exclude such things as Scotch Whisky (although an ersatz Philippino whisky once won the prize for best tasting Scotch whisky).

Now most of the above things are very well known and in many cases very true. From time to time there are protests that something is not true. The City of London always claims that there is a good deal of venture funding available in the UK. Venture funds are run by people on 'performance' salaries which immediately kills any sense of venture. Only individual capitalists can have the risk/agreed sense of venture. In the USA the second generation of such capitalists have made their fortune the first time around. The government often claims it is trying to help enterprise and small business. Any small business venture knows the mass of regulations that still exist. Furthermore the imagination of the US tax system (sub-system S companies etc) is unparalleled anywhere in Europe.

In short there is a great deal of lip-service given to the problem and a lot of political exhortation.

Are the causes going to go away? Maybe yes and maybe no. My bet would be on the 'no' side. Talk is cheaper than any action which would interfere with so many vested interests. *The decline of any nation occurs when the power and complexity of vested interests mean that any new idea is likely to inconvenience more people than it benefits.*

Having written thus far about the *causes* of unemployment what have I new to offer? The above list of causes is very well known. I would say let us forget about the causes.

Our traditional thinking method (and the one used by government and its civil service advisers) is simple: identify the cause and remove it and that will put things right.

This is the idiom of the doctor: find the bug, kill the bug and the patient is cured. It is the idiom of the car mechanic: find the cause of the breakdown, put it right, the car goes again.

It is the idiom of the problem solver.

It is not the idiom of the designer.

The EEC Commission and every government has given a great deal of problem-solving thought to the growing unemployment problem. This is fine and as it should be. I have no quarrel at all with this and with what is being done. But it is not more than *half* of the required thinking. The other half is the design aspect of thinking.

The design idiom says: never mind the causes, what can we do about it?

Now that requires a great deal of conceptual, creative and lateral thinking. I do not see any government department equipped to provide that.

So I am going to make a specific proposal. I suggest the calling of an international (European) meeting specifically for the purpose of focusing creative design thinking on the problem of unemployment. I will offer the services of SITO* for the organisation and *creative focus* of the meeting.

Now who should be interested in such a proposal? Not the trade unions. I do not believe the trade unions are at all interested in unemployment. Why should they be? It is not their job. They are set up to extract the best working conditions for their members. They are indeed concerned about losing members to unemployment. But once the loss has occurred the interest of the unions necessarily ceases. They are nothing if not logical – in a local sense. Should governments or political parties be interested? The answer must be 'yes'. Is something likely to happen? The answer must be 'no'. No government can conceive that it is not already doing all there needs to be done.

---

*SITO stands for Supranational Independent Thinking Organisation. This is a body set up to encourage and focus thinking outside national and political boundaries. The emphasis is on the creation of additional options and the design approach to matters (including conflict resolution).

What do we mean by designing new concepts? Surely the analysis of information can give us all answers we need? The short answer is that information alone cannot design the concepts we need. For that we need creative thinking.

Many years ago I put forward (in my book *Future Positive*) the concept of the 'work packager'. I see this as a deliberate and skilled profession. Work does not simply appear as a need. Only the most crude and obvious work appears in that way. Property developers are the most expert at packaging. They put together land, finance, tenants, municipal benefits etc. in a package that makes sense and offers value to all around. The profession of work packager would work in a similar way to find things that need doing, to find values that people would be willing to pay for, to package the lot into work, pay and value. It may not be easy but it is a direction in which we must move.

The concept of 'voluntary unemployment' seems bogus and highly dangerous. The working public will strongly resent the existence of a group of people who have chosen not to work and still receive payments (from the people who do work). This bare concept can be worked upon and put into an acceptable form. It may be that the voluntary unemployed would have to undertake some community or social work in return for their benefits. This is very much a design task once the direction has been set.

Then there are a whole range of concepts that arise from the basic concept of the 'brown economy'. This is quite distinct from the normal economy and yet it is not the illegal black economy (French taxi drivers and pastry cooks do not declare 52% of their incomes). The brown economy is a new type of economy with an interchange of values and services controlled by a targetted currency. It is an approach which is quite different from both the free market approach and the Keynesian public works pump priming.

New types of industrial organisation (like the 'trinity system') and new types of profit motive (like profit per head) are only some of the new concepts that can be explored.

I certainly do not intend to give instant solutions here. There are many concept directions that can be explored. Some may turn into useful practical ideas. Others may turn into ideas that can never be tried because they can never be tested. Other concept directions may peter out. Yet others may end with ideas that are so fraught with political dangers that they could never even be considered (let alone originate within government thinking). All these are normal aspects of the creative design process.

The summary question is this: do we really believe that the only answer to unemployment is to identify and blame the causes?

I say that is only half the answer. The other half is creative conceptual design.

That is why I propose this international conference on unemployment with emphasis totally on creative design.

Sense of purpose

A strong sense of purpose is one of the most important aspects of thinking skill. People who know what they want do far more effective thinking than those who drift about and hope that they come across something useful.

A sense of purpose gives an immediate sense of priorities.

A sense of purpose makes decision and choice much easier. *If you know exactly where you are going then you have an easier time avoiding roads which do not get you there.*

In the book *Tactics: the art and science of success* (Collins and Fontana in the UK, Little Brown in the USA) the interviews with successful entrepreneurs and other successful people all showed this strong sense of purpose. These successful people knew at each moment what they were trying to do. To a large extent they were single-minded.

Just as a mountaineer has a very clearly defined aim so too does the successful person. The mountaineer can see the peak towards which he or she is heading. In his mind so can the entrepreneur. Sometimes there may be two objectives – but these have to be aligned. When Peter Habeler made the first ascent of Everest without oxygen, he and his companion had the peak of Everest as one objective. The second objective was to see if it could be done without oxygen. There might even have been a 'personal' third objective. To see how far they could push themselves and overcome this ultimate mountaineering challenge.

At this point I want to bring in the dilemma. If we have such a strong sense of purpose how do we deal with the opportunities that arise along the way? Does an entrepreneur who has set his mind on some objective, recognise a better opportunity when it comes along? The answer is that he or she probably does not. Much depends, of course, on how the objective is set up. An entrepreneur who is building up a computer company may not recognise an opportunity in typewriters. But a real estate developer who is in the middle of negotiation for some major project may well recognise and take advantage of some other opportunity that comes along. The objective of the real estate developer is 'to recognise and make use of good deals'.

At the other extreme is the person who is going in so many different directions at once that no one direction is ever pushed far enough for success.

In this piece I want to focus most directly on the relationship between sense of purpose and creativity. This is where the dilemma is most acute. If we stick to the accepted tracks, then we are never going to have any new ideas. The whole purpose of 'brainstorming' was that you could take off in any direction that occurred to you. So if you were brainstorming about traffic congestion in cities you might find yourself discussing helicopter transport. This 'cartoon' type thinking is very irritating to some people because it is obvious to them that mass helicopter transport would never be very practical. I call it 'cartoon thinking' because in a cartoon anything which is remotely logical and which the cartoonist can draw becomes a reality.

To what extent should the sense of purpose include a sense of practicality? In discussing traffic congestion in cities should we put as part of the purpose *practical* alternatives? This is a difficult point because of the danger of restricting the thinking to humdrum approaches that are already known.

There are two ways around this dilemma.

The first is the defined use of a provocation. In lateral thinking the concept of 'provocation' is deliberate and defined. We are allowed to use a temporary provocation because it is clearly understood that the provocation is only going to be used for its *movement* value. We are going to move on from the provocation to end up with useful ideas. The provocation is only a temporary phase. We use the new word 'po' to indicate the defined nature of the provocation.

In brainstorming sessions someone might say, 'Why don't we use helicopters'.

In a lateral thinking session someone would say, 'Po we use helicopters to transport the people'.

At first sight the two may seem similar but in practice they are different. The mention of helicopters in the brainstorming session simply opens up that idea. In the advertising world this would have a value in itself because in the advertising world 'cartoon thinking' is not only acceptable but often very useful. If you can show something in a picture then it has validity. We must remember that brainstorming was designed for the advertising world. In almost every other world this is not so.

The use of 'po' indicates that the temporary intrusion of helicopters is only in order to trigger different ideas. From the helicopter we may get the idea of moving across the tops of roofs. This might lead to the concept of elevated roadways. Once we have this concept then we can look at this in its own right. The elevated roadways do not have to move across roofs (though in some cases they might) but they may simply be another tier elevated above the existing roads. This might be especially useful if a long stretch of road has a lot of side junctions. Instead of underpasses we have overpasses.

A helicopter might also give the idea of vertical movement up and down. That might even suggest going up towers for cable car transport across different points (like rivers). The helicopter could also suggest some over-view system that could alter traffic lights and traffic flow according to the over-view of the state of the roads.

The stronger the sense of the ultimate purpose of the thinking, the more easy it is to use a provocation because the thinker knows what he or she wants to get from the provocation. When you use a stepping stone to get across a stream you have a very clear idea of where you want to go: the opposite bank. It is not a matter of getting on to the stepping stone and then saying: what now?

What about the interesting ideas that turn up that are not directly relevant to the matter in hand? Should they be wasted? They need not be wasted. They can be noted briefly on a piece of paper and then put aside.

Creative people always have the fear that a strongly defined end point will limit them to that. For example in the traffic congestion problem if the problem setter had said: 'I want ideas for speeding the traffic along the roads', then the creative thinker would have felt restricted to that solution approach. He or she might have preferred the freedom to come up with ways of encouraging sharing or improving the attractiveness of public transport. Personally, I feel that one of the best approaches to the problem is to have a very good, very plentiful and very cheap taxi system.

There are times when it is quite in order for the problem setter to ask for ways of achieving a particular desire: like speeding up the traffic on the roads. When I discussed different alternative levels in the *Letters to Thinkers* I did indicate that there were three levels (implementation, route, destination). To ask for ways of speeding up the traffic is to ask for second level alternatives: ways to achieve this speeding up.

At other times the sense of purpose can be just as strong but it does not have to be defined in detail. We may say we want a practical, low-cost, easily implementable, way of coping with traffic congestion. If possible, it should be attractive to all parties. The creative thinker can have these requirements in the back of his or her mind throughout the creative thinking exercise.

Once the sense of purpose is very clear, then we can move as far outside it as we like – because in the end we are going to make the effort to come back to this purpose.

So I would end up by saying that there is no contradiction between creative thinking and a strong sense of purpose.

The simplest illustration of this is the *designer*. The designer must have a very strong sense of purpose. Otherwise how is he or she ever going to tell if the design is successful?

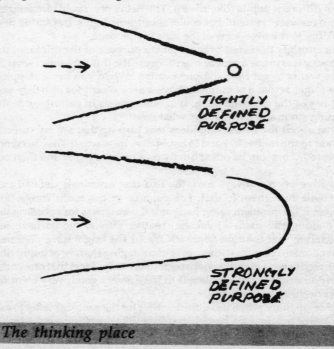

TIGHTLY
DEFINED
PURPOSE

STRONGLY
DEFINED
PURPOSE

The thinking place

A friend of mine (Gordon Barton, the Australian entrepreneur who built up IPEC and Sky-pak) remarked to me that if you wanted to get ahead you must 'put exams before education'. It is possible that this particular way of expressing the sentiment has been used before and that this is a second-hand quote. But it remains both pithy and true.

We have set up exams for very practical purposes. In professional areas we need the exams in order to test for professional know-how (doctors, lawyers, architects etc). In school exams are there because we need some way of motivating youngsters to work and also because we need an assessment system that is not so subjective as to be useless.

Nevertheless once such exams are set up then they become an end in themselves. The purpose of school now becomes to pass these exams because they are the gateways to future success. The emphasis is on those subjects that are tested by the exams. A number of youngsters in the UK still learn Latin because that subject is required by the Common Entrance examination of many public schools. Once an exam is in existence then pupils take it and teachers teach it. It is not easy suddenly to remove that examination. Yet other subjects may be much more important.

SELF-DEFEATING ACHIEVEMENTS

In Hungary, I believe, they teach 'systems theory' throughout education. This seems to me to be a very sensible idea. Understanding how systems work helps one understand how the world works. And it can be done in a very simple way. I would also like to see 'thinking skills' taught as a subject area since thinking is one of the most basic life skills. Until these became examination subjects it would be very difficult to teach them at high school level. And until they are taught it is unlikely that they could become examination subjects.

There must be many other situations where something that is set up for a particular purpose in the end thwarts that very purpose.

I want readers to think of just such examples and to let me know what they find. Another classic example is rent control and tenancy protection. This is designed to give some security to tenants. It ends up, however, by killing the rental market. This in turn makes it virtually impossible to find accommodation for rental. So what was set up to help tenants ends up depriving tenants. It is true that in this particular case it helps tenants in accommodation at the expense of future tenants. Even so existing tenants dare not move for fear of losing the benefits they enjoy. There are also very few places they could move to because of the lack of accommodation for rental.

The over-all concept is that of a self-defeating procedure.

25

Why banks are obsolete

The paradox is that banks – as we know them – are fast becoming obsolete and yet a new type of 'banking function' is becoming more important than ever. But the banks, as such, have no special hold on these banking functions.

For a long time now Sears Roebuck in the USA has probably done more 'banking' than any other bank in the world. This is in terms of the credit it extends to its customers. Recently Sears has launched its own credit card to emphasise its 'banking' role.

In January 1985 British Petroleum launched its own bank: BPFI (British Petroleum Finance International). The £10bn financial assets of BP would place this bank amongst the top 100 in the world. The Swiss based Dow Banking Corporation was set up in 1965 by Dow Chemical of the USA to handle accumulated overseas earnings. This bank has since taken off as a bank in its own right and behaves like any other bank. ICI Finance plc has existed as a bank since 1972. Volvo has recently announced decisions that would make it one of the largest financial institutions in Sweden, with the creation of an in-house bank.

It is obvious that large corporations have their own huge amounts of cash to handle, their own financing requirements and their own exposure to currency fluctuations. In their own special areas (like oil) they may indeed have more expertise than any outside bank. So the finance group gradually takes over more and more of the banking functions. Eventually that group wants to become a bank and a profit centre in its own right.

The fashion of investment in high tech. has somewhat passed as it has been seen to be spectacularly risky. In almost every country at the moment there is a rush to invest in 'financial services'. The capital investment, development time and risk are seen to be very low. Effort, new concept and the right people can quickly pay dividends. The right people can always be hired away from existing institutions with better job titles and more money. It would be impossible for existing institutions to resist people raids of this sort. The electronic ease of communication makes possible widespread functioning of a financial services group. Outside regulated areas there is nothing that a bank can do that cannot be done with – possibly – more flair and enthusiasm by a new and pushy financial services group. Such a group can establish a new identity and is not imprisoned by its past connections.

At one time the Bank of America was the star banking performer in the USA. The Bank of America was started to take care of the savings of Italian immigrants in California. In fact it was called the Bank of Italy for a while. This powerful base of depositors kept the profits of Bank of America very healthy in the good old days when banks took the deposits of the customers and then lent the money out at very nice 'spreads'. Today that is all gone. Depositors in the USA (and increasingly elsewhere) want interest on the money the bank holds for them. Banks compete for customers by offering more attractive interest rates. The NOW (negotiated order of withdrawal) and Super-NOW accounts put paid to interest-free loans from depositors. In other countries where the banks operate a tacit cartel on such matters the danger is not yet so great. But the day will come everywhere.

If banks have to buy expensive money in order to make loans, then their spread (difference between the interest they pay and what they charge) gets smaller and smaller. For the best customers there is more competition and the spreads get driven even lower.

In any case the best customers (the large multinationals) do not need banks any more. They are their own banks. They handle their own affairs and they issue their own certificates of deposit ($250bn US commercial paper market).

If the best customers no longer need banks then the banks are forced to deal with more risky matters. For a while lending to nations seemed to be the answer but the industrial recession and the fall in commodity prices, plus the high dollar made that very unsatisfactory. Paradoxically both the rise in oil prices and the fall in oil prices can be blamed for Third World debt trouble, which only goes to show how loan officers on a performance basis have to let greed exceed prudence (ie each officer is right in his own little sphere but not taken on aggregate).

As banks are driven to more and more risky lending (Continental Illinois and other US bank troubles) there must arise a point of absurdity when the banks come to realise that they are taking more and more risk on the behalf of their lenders and at spreads which get smaller and smaller.

So the emphasis shifts to the 'handling fees' which have always been the payment form of the investment banks. In all the rescheduling of debts for Third World countries the banks have done very well indeed out of such fees.

So the trend is for all banks to become bodies which charge service fees. These are fees for convenience, expertise and for communicating functions. Once the deposit and risk element is taken out of it then these are all functions that can be performed by anybody.

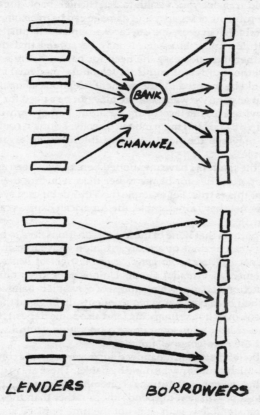

The Chemical bank in New York has a home computer system (called Pronto) with 37,000 subscribers paying about $12 a month. At any time of day or night a subscriber can dial a sixteen digit code number and get access to his or her accounts. He or she can then move funds around as desired. This is a concept of ultimate convenience and total flexibility. A consortium of four major corporations (including AT & T) is going to take this concept further.

Theoretically every person could keep his or her own bank in his pocket. The technology of 'smart cards' makes this possible. A smart card is like a plastic credit card but it has on board a number of chips. In a sense it is a micro-computer. You could insert your card into a terminal and transfer your wealth to a particular 'bank' for overnight use. If the problems of security and damage can be overcome (they are not insuperable) then everyone can carry around the requisite notation that constitutes financial assets. It may be argued that this would increase rather than decrease the need for banks. There would be a need for all these different points (or telephone modems) into which the card could be inserted. At the moment telephone companies allow us to call up anyone we want so there may not be a need for 'banks' as such to provide a higher level of organisation. Perhaps any individual could call up BP and lend them money directly. I think it could go both ways. We may see the need for more intermediate organisational levels or for less.

Many of the matters I have mentioned here may be seen as opening up new opportunities for banks rather than reducing their role. To some extent this is true. For example the VISA debit card system has a much wider net than, for example, the American Express card (which is a T&E card).

The key point is that none of these new functions *need* to be done by a bank. They can be done by any organisation with sufficient concepts and confidence. *There is no longer a divine right of banks.* In some countries (such as Canada) Credit Unions took over much of the lending function of banks when groups of consumers banded together to service their own borrowing requirements. In England the Building Societies took over house financing (and also some deposit functions). There is no reason why some new co-operative ventures could not take over these new 'channel' functions.

It is my belief that there are indeed some very specific concepts and functions which could only be done by banks. These are to do with the trend of what we may call the new economics which will, I believe, be based on the 'permission to spend' idiom rather than the old capital idiom of transferable wealth. It is not the time or place to go into the intricacies of these concepts here and I hope to do so eventually in the ampler space of a book.

I believe that banks do a great deal of conceptual thinking. But this is of the reactive kind. Small steps ahead and reactions to what someone else is doing. It is a game of catch up and move ahead in catching up. There is also the muscle game: do what someone else does and do it with more muscle. For a while such strategies are enough then suddenly they will go bad. This is exactly what happened with the US auto industry which relied for far too long on muscle.

When is a new idea a new idea?

For a long time a new idea may be a modification or an extension of an old idea. Then suddenly it floats free as a new idea.

The life-and-soul-of-the-party puts on a funny hat. It is still John with a funny hat on. Then he puts on some make-up and maybe a loose smock. All of a sudden it is a clown and 'John' has disappeared. That is supposed to be the difference between a film actor and a stage actor. On films it is always James Mason playing some character. On the stage there is the character in her own right – it just happens to be Glenda Jackson who provides the 'body' around which the character has been created.

In a previous *Letter* I have dealt at some length with the problem of the killer phrase: 'the same as . . .'. This danger arises when a new idea has some resemblance to an old idea and so the listener says, 'that is the same as we are doing already . . .'. I explained that this killer phrase is much more lethal than an outright rejection because a rejection can be argued against and a case made for the new idea. But when a new idea is dismissed as being 'old hat' then it really is dismissed and any discussion at all is a waste of time.

I am writing about something different here. I am writing about the budding off of a new idea. I am writing about the setting up of a new concept direction. The new idea has a life of its own. Once it has detached itself from the old idea it acquires its own identity. Perhaps we should regard it as a 'bud' which then separates and falls on the ground to grow roots and become its own plant.

The following is an imaginary conversation focused on the topic of football crowd violence.

We could have swivelling TV cameras so that we could take pictures of those using violence.

What about microphones hidden in the concrete of the terraces so that conversations could be picked up. Perhaps hidden loudspeakers could warn people when they start violence that they are being observed. "The fellow in the yellow hat – we know what you are up to."

Why do these things have to be hidden. I would like the TV cameras to be highly visible on posts. The crowds should see the cameras swivelling in their direction. It would be like a policeman turning to watch what you are doing. That is part of the deterrent effect.

People might then act up. They like being on TV. They might be incited to make a scene just to be on camera. In fact I can visualise two different groups at opposite ends of the area making a scene just to see which gets the camera's 'attention'.

What about a bank of lights facing the crowd rather than the pitch. When those lights are switched on it means that police with telephoto lenses are taking pictures of the crowd. You cannot actually see these cameras so you cannot play up to them. The whole section of the crowd will be illuminated. So that section knows that it is under close observation. Remember the Brussels picture on TV of the man firing the pistol. Cameras or film would have much better definition.

What about plain clothes people mingling with the crowd and somehow taking photos or even just mental notes of who causes the trouble.

If they were invisible they would have no deterrent effect..

You would not be able to spot them but you would know that they were there 'somewhere'.

What about visible deterrents: people who could be spotted?

They would become special targets for attack. They would actually exacerbate the violence.

Po we have a visible violence deterrent who would not be attacked.

Po it could be one of the violent ones.

Perhaps some sort of leader?

So we somehow make one of the leaders responsible for the behaviour of the group.

That becomes an interesting concept direction.

How do we get leaders to co-operate? How do we identify leaders? In what way could they co-operate?

Let's leave it as a concept direction for the moment.

In this short exchange we can see several different concepts. There is the concept of 'visibility'. This only makes sense in the context of the usual 'anonymity' of a crowd. There are suggested ways of making individuals stand out so there can no longer be 'anonymity'. If people know this is the case then it serves as a deterrent – or at least lessens the attraction of anonymity. So we get the concept of 'deterrence'. The concept of deterrence is then enlarged to include deterrence then and there. This can be achieved with the swivelling TV camera. Or it could be achieved with the bank of lights that switch on. Once we have the bank of lights then we move into another concept. This is the concept of 'staged' deterrence. In other words there are two stages to the deterrence: switch on the lights which means you are potentially under surveillance; then the possibility that you will figure in a tele-photo. This could lead to a whole concept direction of staged deterrence or levels of detection. Although there are a number of concepts and concept directions I would still include these within the general notion of removal of anonymity, fear of detection and deterrence.

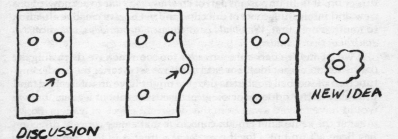

NEW IDEA

DISCUSSION

Then the conversation switches to human detectors and the possibility of making leaders somehow responsible for the behaviour of their 'followers'. Although this could still fall within the general direction of deterrence it becomes a new concept direction in its own right. We could now start to examine the role of leaders. We would not necessarily be examining the role of leaders in group behaviour or their responsibility in bringing about the violence. That would be a different concept direction. *The specific concept direction is the role of leaders in being 'in charge of' and accountable for the behaviour of their group on the terrace.* It may well be that there will not emerge any way of doing this (one idea might be to give such leaders free tickets for distribution and then to reduce or remove this privilege depending on behaviour).

When a new idea or concept direction emerges, do we want to follow it? If we hare off after each new concept then we may never spend enough time focused on a particular area. This is a serious danger and has contributed to the bad name which brainstorming has earned in some quarters. If each new idea is pursued then the purpose seems to be to distract oneself from staying with an idea for enough time. On the other hand, *the whole purpose of creative exploration and the idiom of 'movement' is to use ideas as stepping stones to new ideas.*

It is difficult to lay down hard and fast ground rules for this behaviour. It is more a matter of experience. When it seems that any one concept area has had reasonable attention (like the deterrence concept in the conversation) then it is possible to move off and follow the new direction. If this is not the case, then a note should be made of the new direction (the concept direction of using group leaders to deter and control behaviour) and then attention continues on the present concept area. Later attention can be switched to the noted area. The difficulty is always that the person who has suggested the new direction will constantly be trying to take the thinking into that direction. It is an important part of *creative discipline* to acknowledge a new and interesting concept direction and yet to give creative attention to another area first. *We should be stimulated by our ideas, but always in control of their handling.*

If we let an idea become a new idea too soon then we risk losing the contribution of that idea. For example if we set off after the 'leadership' function of football hooligans then we might have an interesting (and probably cliché ridden) sociological discussion about leaders, but we would have moved away from the 'deterrent effect' of leaders. So we must at the same time remain conscious that a new concept direction has been set up but – for the moment – treat it in the framework of the existing concept direction.

As readers of this publication will know, one of the ways of getting movement is to 'focus on the difference'. This means paying attention to the points of difference between the provocation and the usual idea. In a parallel manner we can focus on the difference between an emerging new idea and the idea from which it emerges. For example the suggestion that in a motor car there should be braking wheels that are separate from the driving wheels opens up a whole new concept direction of specific braking mechanisms. Such mechanisms could include special braking wheels, pads, or even retro-rockets. In the course of such a discussion there might arise the concept of having special 'unbraked' wheels so that if all the braked wheels locked these unbraked wheels could provide directional stability. These might be guidance only wheels which descended into position whenever the brakes were fiercely applied. Such an idea can now bud off on its own. It becomes a different way of treating skidding and loss of control (as distinct from the present intermittent braking systems).

Imagine that you are looking at fabric colours. You are shown a whole range of 'reds'. It soon becomes clear that something may be treated as a type of 'red' but that really it exists almost as a different colour: as a crimson or scarlet or maroon or wine. Whenever we are generating ideas we need to have the same sort of sensitivity.

The whole point behind noticing the budding off of a new idea is to be able to focus directly on it. The new idea then becomes the centre of attention and the 'suburbs' of other ideas radiate from it. In fact it is not unlike the emergence of a particular suburb as a town in its own right.

As I have so often written, one of the biggest problems with the usual report-back stage of any creative session is that the reporter tends to lump different ideas under the same heading – through laziness or a sense of logical tidiness. This is a bad mistake which severely curtails the value of the creative session. We can always put things under a broad heading – but you cannot get them out again with their original characteristics.

The thinking place

This *Letter* and most of my publications contain diagrams. Anyone who has seen me give a talk or lecture knows that I use the overhead projector at every moment to illustrate ideas or processes.

There are some people who like diagrams and some who are intensely irritated by them. Some people feel they add to the message of the text; others feel that they detract from it.

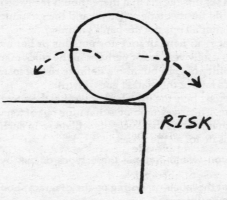

I certainly feel that in explaining an abstract subject like thinking, diagrams are very helpful. This is especially so if they are the dynamic diagrams which happen there and then with the help of the overhead projector. I am very conscious that static diagrams are not nearly as effective.

Diagrams have different roles. There are explanatory diagrams which can tend to be very complicated and rather confusing. In such diagrams the author attempts to put in all his or her meaning. The result can be confusion because the author knows how it goes in but this does not mean that the viewer will know how to get the information out again.

I prefer what I call 'perceptual' diagrams. This means that they illustrate or re-inforce the text by providing a visual image that parallels the message in the text. Often it is easier to show a process in a picture than in words. Words can then be used to describe a picture. In this way we can hold in our memory a simple picture instead of a string of words.

There are some cases where a diagram is particularly helpful.

1. In making contrasts betwen different effects.
2. In showing the development of a process in stages.
3. In showing complex relationships.

The thinking task I am going to set readers this time is to figure out a way of showing 'risk' in a visual form. The illustration shown here is very crude and does not show the most important aspects of risk. You may use this as a starting point or you may start off on a different tack.

I want you to consider – and illustrate – three types of risk:

1. Bankers' risk: this means that there should really be no risk at all. There should be adequate collateral and the guaranteed ability to pay back (after all it is not the bank's money).
2. Investment risk: here an investor puts his or her money at risk, perhaps in a new venture or perhaps in the stock market. There is the possibility of gain but also a definite risk of losing money (if the venture fails or the market goes down).
3. Broadway risk: here the investor knows that the situation is highly speculative. The investor knows that nine out of ten ventures will fail – but that the one that succeeds will do so in such a fashion as to compensate for all the losses.

See how you would contrast these types of risk by means of a diagram.

Note that the labels or writing on the diagram should be kept to the absolute minimum.

26

What do we really want?

I was shopping with my wife in Malta. We were looking for a table-cloth to cover a long table that was going to be used for an al fresco dinner party. We tried a number of shops. No one had a table-cloth of the right size. The only available table-cloths were small and very expensive. In one shop we saw what looked like a table-cloth but it turned out to be a bed sheet. Suddenly we realised that a bed sheet would do just as well. It turned out that the sheets were much cheaper and came two at a time. Everyone had bed sheets and there was a variety of patterns to choose from. The interesting question is: why it was so difficult to think of bed sheets in the first place? In hindsight it was obvious.

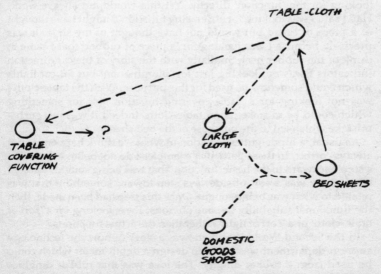

In my first book (*The Use of Lateral Thinking*) I tell of a dark lane leading to the cottage I had near Cambridge. It was necessary to reverse down that lane but there was no street lighting. In those days few cars had reversing lights. What surprised me was that no one thought of using their flashing direction indicators as illumination. They worked very well. But indicators were not mentally filed as 'lights'.

There is a well-known psychology experiment in which a number of people were asked to construct some simple electrical circuit. Most of them found that there was insufficient wire to complete the circuit. A few of them realised that the metal end of the screwdriver which had been supplied could be incorporated as part of the final circuit.

I was in New York and finalising some contracts. I had scribbled my comments in pencil in the margin. These points were then agreed to and so I had to erase the pencilled comments and to insert them in ink so that the contract could be signed. I did not have any eraser to hand, and the shops were shut since it was a Sunday. I suddenly realised that there was a rubber heel on the casual shoes which I happened to have in my luggage. The heel proved an excellent eraser and so the contracts were finalised.

It is easy to say that we normally look for 'things' in order to get some specific function from that thing – and that we should really be looking for the 'function' directly. Yet this would not always work. Had I said I was looking for an 'erasing function' I might have thought of a piece of bread but would not have thought of my shoe. It was precisely because I was looking for 'a piece of rubber' that I came to think of the rubber heel. Similarly with the story of the car direction indicators I was not looking just for 'illumination' but for car lights which could somehow be used for this purpose. With the table-cloth I was not looking for a 'table covering function' but for something which could be mistaken for a table-cloth. Indeed it was just such a mistake which led to the purchase of the bed sheets.

As usual, a hindsight explanation of what we think happens is not always correct. In these particular examples I do not believe there was a step backward to the basic 'function' that was being sought. Rather I think there was a sort of sideways step toward something that was related to what was being sought. Once this step had been made, then the functional suitability became obvious. I was looking for a 'sort of table-cloth' or a 'sort of light' rather than the actual functions.

In the Second World War there was a story of how the technology support department was asked to design a depth meter which could be used from a rubber dinghy. The idea was that rubber dinghies would be released from submarines near the Normandy coast so that the depth of the approach passages could be measured. The project had got quite far when someone pointed out that the tides were so high in that area that an aerial reconnaissance at very low tide would reveal the approach contours. This is what was done.

In this particular case the question: 'What are we really trying to do?' would have given this sort of answer.

I am not against the technique, or habit, of trying to go back to the basic need or desired function. In fact, I believe that to be a most useful process. Nevertheless, I believe that it can be useful to go back in stages:

I want a table-cloth
I want a sort of table-cloth
I want a table covering function
I want a surface covering function
I want a large piece of cloth
I want a large piece of any smart material

In spite of this I still have a feeling that the best approach might have been: 'What large pieces of material are used domestically?' This would have led very quickly to sheets, bedspreads, curtains and carpets. It should be remembered that I had been looking in shops that catered for domestic needs so these shops were readily to hand.

This choice of 'search frame' is extremely important in creative thinking. If it is too specific we shall be limited. If it is too broad we may have difficulty in getting started.

My car was parked at the airport and had become snowed up. The lock was frozen and I could not insert the key. You are supposed to heat the key with matches or a cigarette lighter. I did not have either of these, and in any case a high wind made it difficult to keep a flame going. I did, however, have some duty-free brandy with me. So I poured a little into the lock. This unfroze the lock and I was able to get into the car and start the engine. In that instance there was a basic function question: 'How do I unfreeze something?'

A large piece of apparatus was vibrating so heavily that it was impossible to contine the experiments. The engineers suggested embedding the legs of the table in concrete. In the end a simple bathroom sponge with a kilogram weight resting upon it killed the vibration by spoiling the resonance. Here the question was a simple means-to-an-end: 'How do I stop vibrations?'

It is always easy in hindsight to define the question we should have asked. I have always thought that that sort of analysis is spurious. The best we can do is to have a repertoire of questions we might ask. As I suggested earlier, these questions would span a spectrum ranging from a precise object need to a general function need. To my mind, going at once to the most basic underlying need is not always the best approach.

Joy of the negative

'I could stand on that table in order to change the light bulb.'
'That table will not hold your weight. In any case I do not think the fault is in the bulb, I think it is in the switch.'

There is room for plenty of disagreement in matters of opinion, guessing and forecasting the future.

'I think that this increase of violence amongst young people is simply due to boredom. They want some instant adventure, some instant adrenalin.'
'I do not agree. I think the violence is due to the frustrations of unemployment and the lack of hope.'

There is room for disagreement in hypothesising and in explaining things. That is why we have the scientific method and various forms of statistical proof. In the law courts there is one side which seeks to 'prove' a case and the other side which seeks to show that this is not proof at all.

IT IS SO
NO, IT IS NOT SO

In some other systems disagreement is on firmer ground. For instance 4 + 5 do not add up to 11. The word 'receive' is not spelled 'recieve'. Cars do not drive on the right-hand side of the road in England.

In such systems it is much easier to check whether something is wrong, because we have ourselves set things up in a certain way. In any case, we can check out the answers in many different ways. For example:

'This picture could not possibly be by Rafaello because those clothes only came into fashion one hundred years after his death.'
'This could not be salmonella poisoning from the food you ate in the place because that type of food poisoning takes very much longer to become manifest.'

Here disagreement is based on an appeal to factual evidence. There are people who have established facts about the history of costume and about the behaviour of different types of food poisoning.

Again we could have:

'There is some dirt on the surface of the glass table. Would you be so kind as to wash it off?'

'You have a streptococcal infection of the throat, and I am going to give you some penicillin which will clear it up very quickly.'

'We must expose this police corruption and so put a stop to it.'

Here we imply there is a fault. There is a defect. Things are not what they should be. We must remove the fault and put things right. We must correct errors.

Now consider the following statements:

'That design for a chair is very stark and boring. It looks like a schoolroom chair or even a prison chair. It is quite out of place in a drawing room.'

'That design for a chair is over-elaborate and fussy. It is pretentious and quite horrible. There is no simple elegance about it.'

In these cases the critic is comparing what is to what he, the critic, thinks things should be. The critic is free to change his comparison ideal from moment to moment. If the offered chair is simple, then the ideal is less simple. If the offered chair is elaborate then the ideal is more simple.

Clearly there is a wide span use of the negative. This ranges from the allowable use (difference of opinion) to the logical use (especially in constructed systems) and on to what is sometimes a dishonest use. What interests me here is not so much the philosophy of the negative but the behaviour involved in its use.

I once made a mistake in one of a series of problem-puzzles that I had prepared for *The Telegraph* week-end magazine. There was, I recall, a careless mistake in the wording. I had a great number of people writing to me to point out this mistake. This they did with great glee. In a way this is understandable. We do not expect this sort of mistake and are correspondingly delighted to find one. There is also the element that, if a person finds a mistake, then he must be superior to the person who has made the mistake.

There are people who will eagerly scan every point in an argument in an effort to find a point of error. It is not so much a point of disagreement as an actual point of error. If there is no actual error then it is pointed out that something is merely an assumption and cannot be used as the basis for anything. Discussing matters with such people is very tedious. In sharp contrast to such people are those who listen carefully to what is being said and then wait to see what conclusion is reached. If the conclusion seems to be based on an earlier error or assumption, then this is now pointed out. Quite often the conclusion still makes sense even through one of the supports for it is actually faulty.

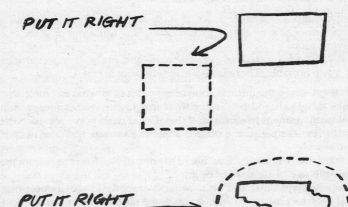

There are indeed those who feel acutely distressed by what they perceive to be an error. I do not think this is just to do with the faulty logic of an error. The response is much too emotional for that. There is something in the brain mechanics which makes an error distinctly uncomfortable. In some classic experiments Jerome Bruner showed that when a black eight of 'hearts' was inserted into a pack of cards some people felt physically nauseated when they came across this anomalous card.

We do need error detection. We do need those who are continually asking for proof of matters. But this only one aspect of thinking. We need to go beyond critical thinking to develop skills of creative and constructive thinking.

There is a notion of development which holds that if you just put right the faults then things will get better and better. I do not quite see how this works. It seems to suggest that there is some innate nature in affairs that is good unless it is contaminated by error. All we need to do is to correct the error. The model is that of the glass table with the smudge of dirt or the person with a sore throat. If we stop pollution the world will be a better place. If we remove poverty then people will be happier. If we overcome famine then people will not starve. If we conquer disease then people will live longer and better lives. If we get rid of incompetent and dishonest politicians, then the country will be run in a better way. It is not difficult to see how persuasive the argument can become. Yet it is a very limited line of thinking. If a particular country has a bad government then we condemn that government in order to remove this fault or error. The present government may fall and be replaced by one which is even worse. That is not our business. In time we shall also condemn the new government. If we constantly strive to remove error then surely things must be right in the end?

The validity of this argument is emphasised by the impossibility of the opposite argument. Should we condone and support dishonesty, incompetence and brutality? Even if we know that things will only get worse we cannot therefore refrain from attacking what is bad.
'This is wrong. We ask you to put it right.' In a way that is a vote of confidence in the perpetrators of the error. We believe that they can remove the error and put things right. If I tell you that your house is dirty, then surely you can clean it up? Why should I clean it up for you? My role is only to point out the dirt.

Condemnation is easy to simplify and to put into a slogan. The slogan is self-justifying: if something is wrong it must be condemned. There can be no argument.

I do not particularly want to get into considerations as to how much condemnation taps the energies of hate, aggression and anger. Perhaps we do like to have something to hate because it makes us feel righteous and instantly compensates us for perceived personal shortcomings. I am sure there is a lot of truth in that particular approach to negativity. What I am more interested in is the intellectual aspect of negativity.

Do we really believe that constructive thinking is someone else's business? Do we really believe that systems are intrinsically good, and that removing the faults will let flower this goodness? Do we really believe that the correction of faults is the major pressure that improves design? I fear that we must believe much or even all of this.

What I find so strange is the high esteem we give to negativity and to the argument mode of thinking. I can see that argument does sometimes force exploration of a matter. But if exploration is what we are seeking then there are far more effective 'scanning' methods of exploration. Perhaps we like the security of a line of argument from which all error has been expunged. Yet we know that logic can never be any better than the perceptions, values and context of the situation allow.

Perhaps it is simply that the whole emphasis of education is on the avoidance of error. Outside a very few areas (such as English essays) the avoidance of error is a sufficient strategy. Yet there remains with me a certain puzzlement over the manifest 'joy' of negativity.

The thinking place

Euclid's geometry seems to contain eternal logic. It was a surprisingly long time before someone pointed out that Euclid's geometry only applied to the particular 'universe' of a plane surface. For example, on a spherical surface the angles of a triangle certainly add up to more than 180 degrees. Imagine a globe representing the earth. Any selection of two lines of longitude (except those exactly opposite each other) will form a triangle with the apex at the North Pole and the base at the equator. Since each line cuts the equator at a right angle, then the sum of the base angles is already 180 degrees – not yet counting the apex angle.

To illustrate the importance of different 'universes' I sometimes use the following sequence:

12	6
8	4
4	7

I then ask the audience to explain the logic of this sequence. They first think in terms of mathematics. Then they think in terms of the spelling of the numbers. In fact the sequence can only really be solved in Italy. There are six letters in the word for 12 (dodici); four letters in the word for 8 (otto) and seven letters in the word for four (quattro). No amount of thinking in the 'English' universe will solve this problem. The point

I want to make is that if we are thinking in the wrong universe, then we may be unable to understand something that is logical and even obvious in the right universe.

Another example I use is that of the three men, each of whom is holding a block of wood in his hand. Each man releases this block. In the first case the block falls downward. In the second case it rises upwards. In the third case it remains in exactly the same place. The first case is easy to understand. But the second and third cases seem bizarre and incredible. Yet when I explain the particular universe in each case what had been bizarre becomes logical and obvious.

In the first case the man is standing on the surface of the earth so the block falls downwards.

In the second case the man is standing under water so the wooden block floats upwards.

In the third case the man is in an orbiting spacecraft with zero gravity. So the block remains where it is.

A change in universe is more than just a change in circumstance. A change in universe means a different set of behaviour rules whereas a change in circumstance may still occur without a change in the basic rules.

The specific challenge and thinking task is to invent ways of illustrating what is meant by a change in universe.

27

Open letter to Reagan and Gorbachev
Subject: Summit November 1985

Gentlemen,

When you meet in Geneva on 19 November, you will both be served by teams of brilliant and experienced people who will direct the logic of their analyses to the objectives and values of each of your positions – and the meeting itself. Yet there will be a serious thinking deficiency. Perhaps for the first time in history we can show why logical analysis can never be enough to generate the new concepts and perceptions that are so badly needed.

Would you follow a navigator who had an incomplete understanding of the methods of navigation? Would you employ a chauffeur who could not use the reverse shift?

It took two thousand years for mathematicians to realise that the beautiful logic of Euclid's geometry only applied to the 'universe' of a plane surface. When you are within a particular universe the sufficiency and completeness of the rules make it almost impossible to conceive of their limitation to that particular universe.

The time has come when we may have to accept that our traditional logic (both verbal and mathematical) is not more than a particular form of 'object-logic' based on 'passive' information universes. All the information systems we use in ordinary life or in computers are passive. You make a mark on paper or a computer disc and both the surface and mark remain passive. We have to bring along a thinker or processor to manipulate those marks according to some rules. This is the object-logic that gives rise to symbols and language; judgement, categories and identities; and the law of contradiction. It is the logic that has served us so very well in the technical world because that is where we deal with objects. In human affairs we can continue to ascribe our failure to the immutable basics of human nature (greed and aggression) – or we can examine the failure of our thinking. A failure to realise that human perception operates in an 'active' information universe which is totally different from the passive universe of object-logic.

We know that in 'active' information universes the information and the recording surfaces interact to give gradients, circularities, patterns and asymmetries. This is the very basis of perception (and also why a finger shapes itself into a finger). Perceptual-logic is sharply different from object-logic: instead of category there is flow and context; instead of judgement there is movement; the law of contradiction does not apply etc. Humour is an excellent model of perceptual logic and its neglect by traditional philosophers and logicians only confirms their restriction to the object logic of passive information universes.

The problems and conflicts of the world have not yielded to logical analysis; we need new concepts, new perceptions and new approaches. For these we need new types of thinking based on perceptual-logic. A concrete example of the effectiveness of such thinking was provided by the amazing success of the 1984 Olympic Games. In an interview (*Washington Post*, 30 September 1984) the organiser told how he had used the techniques of lateral thinking (concept generating techniques based on perceptual-logic, that I designed some years ago) in order to generate the new approaches and concepts that made the Games so successful. Am I suggesting that a creative conceptual approach might do the same for international affairs? Yes. Certainly, logical analysis by itself will not.

We come here to the deadly creativity dilemma. All valuable creative ideas will always be logical in hindsight – otherwise we could never recognise their value. So we insist that such ideas must be accessible to better logic. Hence in a passive information system creativity is indeed a luxury. But in an active information system this view is demonstrable rubbish. The asymmetry of patterns means that an idea may only be logically obvious after it has been thought.

For politicians it has always been a sufficient thinking strategy to defend the ideas they hold. The generation of new concepts has never been a priority. That is why the summit teams will make no provision for this.

It is bad enough that our traditional logic systems are inadequate to solve the problems, but in many cases the polarisations of object-logic have helped to create the problem in the first place.

There is a second level on which the summit meeting will be deficient. The clash of both argument and negotiation sterilises perception. For example, opposing parties can never accept the 'negative cash-flow' of a position that ultimately leads to an outcome satisfactory to both parties. Negotiation is based on object-logic: design makes use of perceptual logic. That is why there has to be a formal third party role if the design mode is to replace the conflict mode.

What I am saying here is that the reliance on logical analysis and argument is necessarily inadequate and as a result the summit is doomed to relative failure. I am aware that the true purpose of the summit is the gesture that it is taking place at all (and the theatrics which will arise from this). I know that there is no real need for any serious constructive thinking to take place in Geneva. What I have written here applies, however, not only to the Summit but to the future relationship between the super-powers and the future of the world. Let us never again be confined to the arrogance of our limited logic which declares that there cannot be alternatives beyond those we can see at this moment.

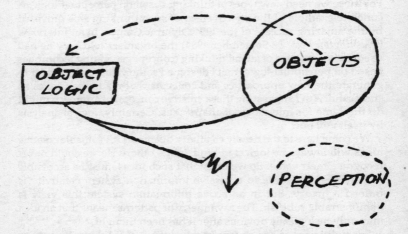

As a constructive suggestion I would suggest a permanent USA/USSA Council that would consist of three functional sub-councils. These should be an adversarial, antagonistic and negotiating council (much as we now have). A constructive council would provide for joint work on agreed matters of mutual interest (which also happens now in different ways). A specifically creative council would design new concepts and approaches in order to transfer matters from the adversarial council to the constructive one.

This year the USA will spend $246 billion on defence. The world will spend over $1,000 billion on armaments. Against this background – and the vulnerability of the mutal deterrent policy to 'creep' strategies – it must make sense to look more closely at the very nature of our thinking and not just at what we think about. There is nothing to lose except our mistaken arrogance. New concepts will eventually be valued with our existing currency.

Quite simply our traditional methods of logic are demonstrably inadequate on their own – no matter how expertly they are applied.

Lessons from a story

Those who have been to a seminar of mine will recognise the story I am about to relate. I use it frequently because it summarises in such a neat manner the essence of lateral thinking. On one occasion I was even accused of stealing my own story. Jim Slater had used the story in his book *Return to Go* and had attributed it to me. Someone at the seminar had read the story, forgot the attribution and accused me of claiming the story as my own.

The story is about the tennis championships at Wimbledon. Some 131 players have entered for the men's singles. Unfortunately it rains all the first week so the organiser has to try to fit all the matches into the second week. Naturally he wants to find the minimum number of matches that need to be played. What is this minimum number? There may be byes in the first round or even in the second round.

That is the story, puzzle or problem. We start off by visualising the structure of a normal elimination tournament. Two players play and the winner goes on to play another winner and so on until there is a final champion. We might have a go at guessing how many matches there would have to be in the first round and then working forward. Or we could work backwards by saying that there will be two players in the last match, four in the semi-finals, eight in the quarter finals, then 16, 32, 64 and 128. Or we could do it by games instead of players: one game, two games, four games . . . Then we just add up the games. But what about the extra three players? How do they enter the system?

Up to this point there are two lessons to be learned. The first is that visualising the structure of the situation appears to help. It gives us something to go on. The second lesson is that the idea of working 'backwards' from the winner, instead of 'forwards' from the players, seems promising. At this point we might even be congratulating ourselves on having found a clever approach. I suspect that many people in a lateral thinking seminar reckon that the trick is to switch to working backwards from working forwards. The approach does seem promising.

This raises an interesting point. When we have switched from one approach to a new one how hard do we try to make this work before switching to yet another approach? I suspect it depends on how well the new approach seems to work at first glance. If it seems at all promising then I think there is considerable danger of our becoming stuck in this new approach. In fact we may end up much worse off than if we had not thought of this approach in the first place. In such matters the mind is insufficiently fickle.

In fact at this point the problem is not really difficult. We seem to have three extra players (131 minus 128) so we have to eliminate them. We can only do this via a tennis match. So three out of the 128 have to be involved in eliminating the extra three. So six players play round one (three games) and all the rest have a bye into round two. The three winners join the 125 with byes and this gives the 128 ready to play each other in round two. We now add up all the games: $3 + 64 + 32 \ldots$ etc.

That is not too difficult. But, of course, there is a far easier way of doing it. This is where lateral thinking comes in.

It is obvious that the purpose of a tennis tournament is to produce a winner. So a tournament is a winner-producing machine. So it is quite natural to go through the stages of producing a winner. This is what we do when we visualise the playing chart and proceed to work with it as I have done here.

The lateral thinking approach is to escape from the great importance of the winner. Instead we shift attention to the losers. I want to emphasise that this is totally arbitrary. *We do it because we want to*. Indeed this is one of the main reasons I use this story. This shift of attention is capricious. It is a sort of provocation. We cannot justify it. The only possible justification would be that we had tried other approaches and they had failed (which they would not).

It is the essence of a provocation that there need not be a reason for doing something until after it has been done. I do want to dwell on this point. In our traditional logical structures each step must somehow be derived from the preceding step. The step must make sense. If such a step did not make sense, then it would open up the possibility of totally random behaviour. The answer is that there is logic even in random behaviour – once we are in a patterning system. The logic of a patterning system is very different from our normal logic. So could the thinker break off to go and pick daisies (as random behaviour)?

The answer is that he probably could – provided he was trying to relate daisy picking to the problem.

So we shift attention to the losers. Perhaps a tournament is a machine for producing losers? Certainly a lot of losers are produced. How many? That is easy enough because there is only one winner. So we have 130 losers.

Now we look more closely to see how each loser is produced. We can state that 'a loser is produced by a loser-producing game'. That is such a tautology it is hardly worth saying. But in thinking tautologies are *very much worth saying*. This is a very important point and one of the main reasons for writing this piece.

In thinking we need to place a marker and then look around from this new position. A statement serves as a marker. Without such a marker we would have gone on past the point at which a new track becomes visible. So having said the unnecessary thing (losers are produced by loser-producing games) we reach the conclusion that there must be 130 loser-producing games. This might not seem to have got us very far. But it has. We now set out to add the other games to these 130 loser-producing games. We stop to consider the other sort of games. There are none. Each and every game is a loser-producing game (no draw in tennis). So suddenly we find we have the answer. The minimum number of games is 130.

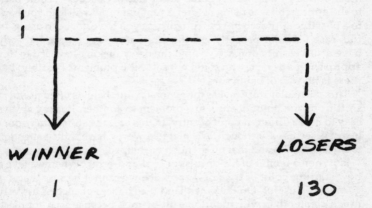

Rather surprisingly this answer upsets many people and they set about proving it wrong. Many many years ago I included this problem in a piece I did for the IBM magazine *Think*. I got quite a lot of letters saying I must be wrong. There was one very fierce letter from a senior US Navy officer – there was even a covering letter from the editor to the effect that the editor thought the correspondent had a good point. Alas, I do not think this can be so.

How might we prove that this simple approach does give the right answer? We could use the traditional logic method of reductio ad absurdum. If you were to lose in the first round of the tournament, is it conceivable that the organiser would ask you to play again 'in order to make the numbers right'. This would be very nice but everyone knows it can never happen. We can try another approach. Can you imagine reading a newspaper headline which says: 'Becker wins Wimbledon final after having lost to Connors in the second round'. That is equally absurd. Each loser is out and for every loser there is a game which threw him out. Nor can there be any games which did not throw out a loser. So the number of losers must equal the number of games.

All this seems very simple in hindsight. Excellent solutions are always obvious in hindsight: that is the essence of the creative dilemma which I have described previously.

What about the fellow who went to pick daisies. His line of thinking might be as follows. Daisies are picked one by one. The more I pick the fewer there are left. Players are plucked out of the tournament one by one. At the end only one is left. Some 130 have been removed so there must be 130 games. This is rather unsatisfactory because I come back to the approach I was using before. A random input will lead you back to a possible approach but can turn up one you have not been using. In this case I cannot properly use the random input because I already have a successful approach. Would the daisy picking have led to this approach in a person who could not solve the problem? Possibly, but there is no way of being sure.

This particular story makes the general point that it is often useful to shift from one point of entry to a problem to another. It is not always easy to find a different point of entry. In this case the shift from winner to losers seems easy enough. We might, however, have shifted attention to the spectators and that might not have helped.

Is it then a matter of hit-or-miss or trial-and-error? When we take a new starting point or try a new approach we cannot be sure that it is going to be useful. On the other hand the chances of success are very much greater than with traditional hit-or-miss because each approach does in fact become a logical approach. In hindsight we cannot see why it is more logical to start with the winner than with the losers. We tend to forget that our traditional starting point is usually arbitrary in itself (winners are more important than losers).

Can we draw any further lessons from this simple story? Well, the quick answer (via the losers) will not tell us how many games have to take place at each round and will not give us the structure of the byes. This could be bonus information or it could have really been part of the original requirement. So it is important to know exactly what you are looking for. You could actually use the over-all figure of 130 games to work backwards. You would find that in the 'first' round you had only used up 127 games. That would mean that you needed three more games. So there would need to be a preceding round with three games in.

The history of science is full of 'arbitrary' or unjustified steps which people took. This is not surprising because the logical steps within any particular framework are taken quite quickly. It may take ages before the unjustified step is taken – because no one feels justified in taking it.

Our perception is so patterned that only unjustified steps are likely to open up new patterns.

The thinking place

There is a tendency in the USA to turn nouns into verbs. An air hostess might say: 'In a few minutes I shall beverage you all'. Some people find that very ugly and sloppy. But is it? It is certainly much neater than saying: 'In a few minutes I will offer you all something to drink'.

Does the verb 'strand' come directly from the noun 'strand' (shore) so that to strand someone means to leave them behind on the beach as you return to your ship?

I have not yet heard the expression 'I will keyboard that' but it would seem to be a mildly convenient meaning that I will enter that via the keyboard. We talk about 'parking' a car rather than putting the car into a 'park'. We say 'I will finance that deal' rather than 'I will provide finance for that deal'. We 'paper' a wall when we put paper on to the wall.

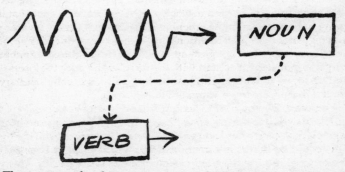

The process of making nouns into verbs has such an obvious convenience that it has been happening quietly all the time.

There is an interesting process when a verb becomes a noun and then the noun comes back as a new verb. For example this can happen with an airline where the booking clerk might say: 'I will flight you via Chicago on American Airlines'. Obviously this means: 'I will arrange a flight for you via Chicago on American Airlines'. The clerk could have said: 'I will fly you . . .' but this is much less exact than 'flight you'. So 'flight' is the noun from 'fly' and then 'flight' becomes the verb from 'flight'.

I must confess that I am in favour of the evolution of language provided this happens smoothly. Why should we imagine that the words we had before there were airlines will still suffice. They will suffice on a descriptive level (just as an iron road describes a railway) but new words can be much more convenient.

There is another convenient language device emerging in the USA. This is the use of the word 'absent'. You might say: 'This deal will go through absent any interference from the SEC'. This simply means 'in the absence of'. The single word is neater and once established can spread its meaning. For example you might say: 'This deal will go through absent your falling ill'. This does begin to get a little ugly but it allows the single word absent to be used to cover a wide range of situations which would not otherwise be covered by 'in the absence of'. For all I know there may be the symmetrical use of 'present'. This would mean 'in the presence of these conditions'. So you say: 'This deal will go through present a guarantee from your bankers'.

28

Introducing creativity to an organisation

Participants at my seminars often ask me how they should set about introducing creative/lateral thinking to their organisations. They come to the seminar with expectations and an interest in the subject. At the end of the seminar they see the importance of lateral thinking as one of the key modes of thinking and they want to introduce it into their organisations. What can they do?

There are ideal answers to that question as well as practical answers.

Ideally there should be interest, enthusiasm and leadership from the highest levels – indeed from the chief executive himself. In my experience the best results have always been obtained when the chief executive has personally taken a lead. Outstandingly this has happened with Ciba-Geigy, with General Foods and with Pharmacia (Sweden). In these, and other cases, the chief executive has seen that some understanding of the idiom and principles of lateral thinking was essential as part of the corporate culture. The expectation was not that everyone should go away and use the lateral thinking techniques deliberately in order to generate powerful new ideas. The expectation was that executives should understand the nature of lateral thinking and its importance as part of their thinking equipment. It was hoped that their attitude towards change, innovation and the willingness to find new and better ways of doing things would all be motivated by some exposure to lateral thinking.

The introduction of an organisation to lateral thinking would then normally take the form of an in-house seminar on lateral thinking. This would typically be of a day's duration. There would be no limit on the number of people present. Typically the number present would range from 70 to 150. What is important is that all the top people should be there. I was once asked to give such an in-house seminar to all the top management at KLM. All of them were there including the three (troika system) chief executives. The purpose of such a seminar would be simultaneously to give everybody a common language and a common idiom which could then become part of the culture. This would then be followed up by other one-day seminars for different departments: research, marketing, finance, production etc. Very often there would also be a seminar for overseas senior personnel – perhaps attached to an annual meeting.

I have always insisted that lateral thinking is not some magical or exotic skill but a normal and necessary part of thinking. It is indeed different from – and in some aspects quite contrary to – ordinary thinking but it is a skill that can be learned. For the perceptual part of thinking lateral thinking is essential if we are going to escape from patterns and cut across them. Lateral thinking is not a luxury. That is why some exposure to it is essential for all senior management (ideally for everyone).

Sometimes the exposure is much more thorough. For example Seafirst bank in Seattle organised three two-day courses for all their senior people in the operations side. In this case I worked more thoroughly with smaller groups.

Unfortunately senior management is often not interested in lateral thinking. There are senior executives who still firmly believe that efficiency and problem solving are all that an organisation requires. Creative thinking to them seems a luxury and something less than solid. This old-fashioned 'maintenance' view of management can work when there is market domination or where the particular business segment is still growing. Where, however, there is competition then this complacent attitude can only lead to disaster.

In my experience I have found a strange paradox. Those organisations that most need some creative thinking are the least interested. I am referring here to organisations in deep trouble. It seems that the executives in such organisations have to blame all the trouble on outside forces such as change in market, subsidies to the competition, exchange rates, government interference, labour intransigence etc. Once they admit that some improvement in their thinking could make a difference, then they would be in trouble. Because now they would have to shoulder some of the blame. In contrast, the most successful companies (like IBM) have always been interested in lateral thinking. Successful companies believe that they are where they are because they are continually developing new skills and keeping on their toes.

So this first introductory seminar would be a way of introducing the idiom of lateral thinking to a corporation. What sort of structure should follow?

I am convinced that in the future every corporation is going to have to treat concepts in a very serious manner. As I have said on many occasions there is a need for a concept R & D department that would be treated just as seriously as our existing technical R & D departments.

Nor should we ever make the mistake of assuming that concept R & D is already being done in the technical research department. It is not – the style of thinking and orientation is quite different.

The notion that concepts just turn up out of the air or that it is enough to borrow ideas or jump in with a me-too is obviously inadequate. We would never handle any other part of corporate needs in this haphazard way.

In addition to this concept R & D structure I would like to see a 'concept manager'. This is someone who would have focusing, organising and liaison responsibility for this area of concept review and concept change. This would be the person who then became responsible for introducing lateral thinking and developing skills in its use. Lateral thinking is, of course, a key tool in the development of concepts.

I am aware that it is going to be some time before corporations understand the importance of concept R & D. So this avenue of introduction of lateral thinking is not very practical at the moment. Let me therefore shift to the opposite extreme and look at some simple and practical ways of introducing lateral thinking.

There are training departments that are introducing elements of lateral thinking into their regular management development courses. There are training departments that are beginning to offer specific training in lateral thinking. Once a year in Brussels I run (with Management Centre Europe) a formal course for corporate trainers so that they can go back into their own organisations and train people in lateral thinking.

Nevertheless this training approach is slow. One of the major dilemmas for lateral thinking is that, in order to see its logic and value, you first have to be exposed to it in a seminar. Unfortunately only those who are already interested make the effort to come to seminars. Those who most need it never get the chance to see how much they need it. This is a serious dilemma. I always find myself talking to the wrong people.

There has to be some way of showing the need for lateral thinking before much will happen. I am now going to discuss a very simple way of doing this.

The focus list

If you ask an executive to write down ten problems he or she will probably do so with ease. In fact the executive is likely to go on to list twenty problems. Executives are aware of problems because problems hit them. Problems are an ache and a pain. You are aware of that ache or pain and try to get rid of it.

But ask an executive to write down some 'opportunity areas' (areas that might benefit from new thinking or better ideas) and most executives will have a hard time putting down anything at all. Yet it is obvious that everything is not done in the best possible way. It is obvious that new ideas may make a dramatic difference at certain points. Yet there is nothing in an executive's training, experience, or job specification which requires that executive to look for such opportunity areas.

I believe that every executive and every corporation should have a well known 'focus list' of specific areas which need better ideas. Such a list can be circulated and changed and up-dated. Once this focus list is in existence then there is a clear need for lateral thinking. How else are we going to get better ideas?

So the first step is to find a constructive and cooperative department. You work with that department to come up with their 'focus list'. You then send a copy of this focus list to the next cooperative department. You then send copies of both lists to the next and so on. In the end you tackle the most resistant areas. But now you show them that other departments have been able to come up with focus lists – why not them?

When you have assembled these focus lists you might set out to make a simpler master list for the whole organisation.

Now that you have the focus lists you ask the simple question: where are the new ideas going to come from? Clearly the focus list areas are ones which have not yielded to conventional thinking.

It is now necessary to feed these focus lists to creative individuals or idea-generating groups. But such groups will need training in lateral thinking techniques. In fact everyone needs such training.

In this way the need for lateral thinking is demonstrated first and then training in the method follows. The focus list approach is both solid and practical. It demonstrates to an organisation that there are areas which need better ideas.

Focus areas

The simplest things are always the hardest to teach. Everyone assumes that because something is simple, he or she must already know it or do it. The teacher can do little more than explain the matter and cannot dwell upon it as is possible with something more complex. Students get bored and irritated if the teacher does hammer on at a simple matter. That is why it is so hard to teach simple things.

In lateral thinking the focus area is very important indeed. The focus area is the link between our thinking skill and the real world. The focus area determines exactly where we apply our thinking skill and techniques.

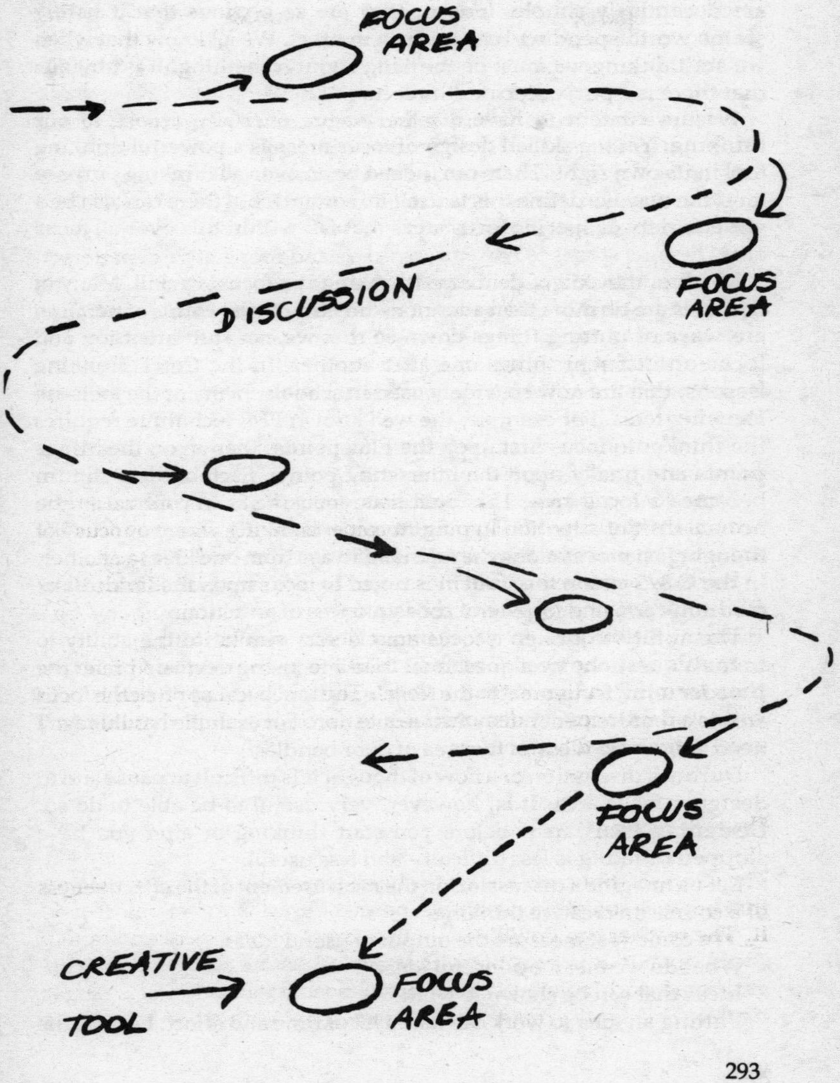

FOCUS AREA

FOCUS AREA

DISCUSSION

FOCUS AREA

CREATIVE TOOL →

FOCUS AREA

My experience has shown me that the skilful designation of focus areas is by far the weakest part of creative thinking. Ineffective harvesting come next. Now these are not the exotic parts of lateral thinking (like PO, movement, random input etc.). Focus and harvesting are deceptively simple. Indeed, they are so obvious that it hardly seems worth spending time on such matters. We all know that when we are thinking we must be thinking about something. It is obvious that there is a purpose to our thinking.

We are content to have a rather vague over-all purpose to our thinking. Yet the skilled design of focus areas is a powerful thinking tool in its own right. There can indeed be an over-all thinking purpose (and the way we define this is itself important). But there can also be a wide variety of specific focus areas that fall within this over-all focus area.

Much of the skill of deliberate thinking is a focusing skill. Many of the tools are no more than attention-directing tools. Forms of notation are ways of putting things down so that we can shift attention and focus on different things one after another. In the CoRT Thinking lessons, that are now so widely used in schools, many of the tools are focusing tools. For example, the well known PMI technique requires the thinker to focus first upon the Plus points, then upon the Minus points and finally upon the Interesting points. Each of these in turn becomes a focus area. This deliberate focusing is in contrast to the normal drift of attention in point to point thinking where our flow of thought just moves along the main highways from one idea to another. In the C & S lesson the student is urged to focus upon the immediate, medium-term and long-term consequences of an action.

The ability to design a focus area is very similar to the ability to frame a question, for a question is also a focusing device. I prefer the broader term 'focus area' to the term 'question' because often the focus area is a requirement rather than a question. For example I could say: 'I need some new ideas in the area of door handles'.

During a discussion or a flow of thought it is difficult to pause and to design a focus area. It is, however, very useful to be able to do so. Designing focus areas before you start thinking or after you have stopped thinking is less difficult – and less useful.

Let us imagine a discussion on the measurement of the effectiveness of a course on creative thinking.

'We could just measure the output of useful ideas.

What do we mean by "useful ideas".

Ideas that can be shown to work.

Putting an idea to work can take a lot of time and effort. Besides the idea may be good, but no one may want to try it out.

(define a new focus area as: "ways of testing the value of an idea short of trying it out")

Perhaps we could measure the increase in alternatives or options. We could count the number of fresh approaches that had been turned up.

Number may not mean much. Some approaches might be frivolous or worthless. Removing criteria of practicality is not the same as creativity.

(define a new focus area: "ways of distinguishing between ideas which are generated but never put forward (suppressed) and ideas which were never generated")

Perhaps we could measure people's behaviour. Their reaction to new ideas. Their willingness to consider the possibility of further alternatives.

(new focus area: "ways to measure a thinker's feeling that there may or may not be further alternatives")

What is most important, the willingness to use a creative effort or the result of that effort?

Results may only occur occasionally but the use of the effort may be present on every occasion. Without that effort there may be no results.

(new focus area: "need for some indicator that shows that a person is making a genuine creative effort")

Actual results must come in somewhere.

Over time but not necessarily at any moment in time.

There should be evidence of "creative ideas".

The ability to look creatively at a situation may allow a thinker to come up with a perfectly logical idea. The perception may be creative and the idea quite logical. Ideally we should like to compare this performance with that of someone else in exactly the same situation.

(new focus area: "could we design some sort of duplicate system as in duplicate bridge where two teams play identical hands")

If people feel that they have become more creative is that enough? Probably not.

(new focus area: "a way of seeing whether the feeling of being creative actually relates to creative performance. What is it that makes a person feel creative?")

Let's look at how we measure other things.'

In this short conversation we see the designation of six new focus areas. Each one of these focus areas can then be tackled deliberately with a lateral thinking tool.

Let us choose the focus area: 'an indicator that shows that a person is making a genuine creative effort'.

We use the stepping stone technique: 'Po a person goes red in the face when making a genuine creative effort.'

Immediately we think of some possible physiological response. A lie detector is supposed to tell when we are lying. Perhaps the same instrument could give a characteristic response for a creative effort.. Perhaps there would be a characteristic hesitancy or spacing of words as a person tried to think further even when speaking. Perhaps the excitement of possible creativity would give a galvanic skin response. It is claimed that a person's eyes shift to the left if he or she is using the right hemisphere (or is it the other way around?).

Red in the face suggests blushing. Blushing is embarrassment (most fear is about something about to happen next). What natural state would creative effort relate to? Does curiosity or anticipation have a visible effect?

Red in the face suggests anger and characteristic tensing of the neck muscles. Does creative effort give a characteristic neck posture?

This exercise sets up many more questions. Each of these questions can in turn become a new focus area. For example: 'a way of measuring neck posture in people being creative'.

Designating a focus area is like zooming in one part of the scene with a telephoto lens. For the moment you forget about the rest of the scene or even how that area fits in with the rest. You just treat the area in its own right.

As creative practice it is most useful just to have a normal conversation about a subject and then to designate a required number of focus areas. Take one of those and repeat the exercise.

The thinking place

Have you ever given thought to the more obvious limitations in our thinking habits? One of my favourites is what I call the 'salt curve' and I may indeed have mentioned it in previous issues of this *Letter*.

No salt on food is awful. Some salt is good. Some people may like a bit more salt. More salt is terrible.

The 'Laffer curve' from Reagonomics indicates the same thing. As you go on increasing taxes you may actually get a diminishing yield. The same thing happened with cinema prices. As attendances fell so prices were increased to maintain revenue but the increased prices reduced attendance so the total revenue starts to fall.

The basic difficulty is that in our simple category system we have boxes, but such boxes are a very poor way of dealing with quantities. In a commonsense way we can handle this when we are dealing with matters within our own experience. For example it is not difficult to believe that whilst ice-cream is good a great deal of ice-cream might make you sick. We have a simple code that says excess of anything (perhaps even honesty) is bad. But this rule of thumb does not cover matters outside our direct experience and it does not cover matters where the change from good to bad is well below 'excess' levels.

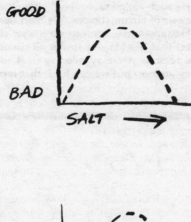

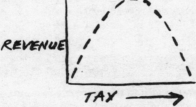

The same thing happens in reverse. If something is bad at one level then we assume it must always be bad. For example most people believe that excess memorising in schools prevents thinking and learning. So memorising is a 'bad thing'. Yet there are certain matters, like the multiplication tables, which need to be memorised.

We do use phrases like 'within limits' or 'up to a point'. But even as we use them we are aware of how weak they are. 'Police firmness is a good thing – up to a point'. But where is that point?

Very few arguments are based on logical inconsistencies. More usually they are based on different perceptions, different data bases, different value systems and looking at different aspects of the same thing. This trouble with the 'salt curve' is a classic basis for an argument. One party is arguing before the inflection in the curve and the other party after the inflection.

This happens to be my favourite instance of the inadequacies of our normal 'box-based' thinking system. You may have your own favourites or even your own examples of this particular limitation.

Perhaps the simplest solution to this particular difficulty might be to eschew blanket labels such as 'good' or 'bad' altogether and to deal only with particular sets of circumstances. We then need to be more careful in defining circumstances. We can no longer slap a label on something and expect that label to stay under all circumstances. For practical and ethical reasons, we may need to treat some things as absolute (even if they are not) but we can limit that type of thinking behaviour.

29

What do you expect creativity to do for you?

I have asked this question at the beginning of seminars on creative thinking. Below I give a sample of the answers – and some comments.

I should say at once that with these particular seminars the people were required to attend. If it was a matter of free choice then those coming might have had a higher motivation or a different understanding of creativity.

'Let me look at my job in a new light – in other words, to get out of the rut of doing my job in a certain way merely because it is comfortable and currently works.'

'I would like creativity to free me from the constraints of my current job. I would hope that it could assist me to interject new enthusiasm for my work.'

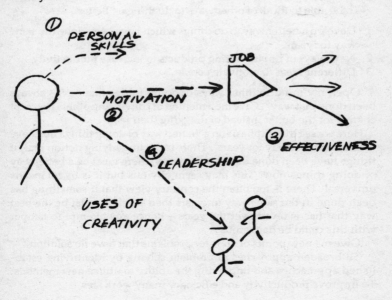

'I would like to learn the skills of creative thinking so that I can be more innovative on the job – and teach my staff how to use the skills to enrich their jobs.'

'1. Make the job we have to do easier.
2. Find things to do which are more exciting and motivating.'

The interesting aspect of these particular comments is the 'motivating' use of creativity. The suggestion is that creative skills may re-new interest in a job because there would now be some hope of improving it or doing things differently. Whether or not this hope was realised it would still have value as an hope. In my experience, this important aspect of creativity thinking is usually overlooked. Managers look for solutions to problems and are less concerned with the motivating effects of this sort of thinking. This is surprising because one of the main benefits of Quality Circles is that it gets the workers interested in what they are doing – quite apart from the actual changes that may come about through the work of the Circles.

'To help me look beyond what we "have always done" – not necessarily to improve productivity etc. as we are continually requested to do, but to identify other options that would work just as well. Broaden my options.'

'To be able to think of other ways to do things. "Better" '

'1. Develop a better way to do things which have been done the same way for years.
2. New ways of implementing products to increase productivity.
3. Different ideas to motivate people.'

'Open my mind to other ways of doing things that have "always been done that way". Give me a method of convincing others to accept change for the better instead of dragging their feet.'

Here we see the emphasis on a 'better' way of doing things that have 'been done that way for years'. There is the underlying notion that, if things have been done that way for years, there must be a better way of doing things now. This may seem obvious but it is by no means universal. There is too often the contrary view that if something has been done in the same way for years then surely it must be the best way that has evolved over the years – hence any attempt to tamper with this could be dangerous.

'Give me new points of view for problems that have no solution.'

'To broaden approaches to problem solving by identifying established approaches and improving the ability to utilize new methods. To improve productivity and efficiency in my work area.'

'I would like creative thinking to enable me to evaluate problems and determine the best possible solutions: to put things together in the most optimum ways.'

'Expand my global perspective to enable a complete viewing of the problem set. This will allow for a more precise (accurate) solution set to be developed.'

'Free my mind from all past experience. See problems as they are and not as they compare to prior similar problems. From there adapt solutions that address real problems and not the symptoms.'

Here is the traditional emphasis on problem-solving. There is a difficulty with the word 'problem'. Far too often the word 'problem' is used to denote any type of thinking activity that has a desired end point. This covers all purposeful thinking. Yet the word 'problem' then ends up being used in the narrow sense of a deviation from the norm, an ache or pain, a difficulty to be removed. One of the big difficulties with management thinking is that it is so problem oriented. This type of thinking makes it very difficult to think in terms of opportunities. Indeed, areas which are not seen as problems tend to get no thinking at all. The result may be a steady drift away from what is potentially possible. So it is important to emphasise that the purpose of creative thinking is not just 'problem-solving'. We need firmly to establish some other types of thinking in people's minds, for example 'opportunity thinking' or 'design thinking'.

'Unleash the mental energy that I know exists in me so that I can organize my people to be more efficient and effective.'

'Improve management of personnel and projects.'

'I would like to be more creative so that my staff and I could be more productive (increase corporate profitability) and also have more time to enjoy the quality of life.'

'Improve an ability to work with people to address key issues – realistically.

Save time and effort in addressing critical concerns.

Improve quality of individuals.'

'Creative thinking in the motivation of my staff.'

Here the emphasis is on creative thinking as an aid to leadership skills. It does not seem that the emphasis is on the leader being more creative than anyone else but that the leader develop creative ways of dealing with people. There is also the use of creativity to motivate people (as mentioned earlier). It may be enough that the leader shows an interest in creativity and encourages it. There may not be a need for the leader to be especially good at it.

'Provide me with the tools to increase productivity in my department.'

'I would like creativity to make me a more productive person.'

This emphasis on 'productivity' reflects a drive for productivity in a particular service organisation. As a general term 'productivity' is safe enough since it seems to embrace most of the things that are required of an executive. It is certainly a legitimate use for creative thinking. Nevertheless it is somewhat weak as a desired use of creativity. It is somewhat similar to saying you want creativity to 'make you a better person'.

'Re-evaluate my career path. I have already learned some lateral thinking from my kids who aren't tainted by experience.'

'I would like creativity to increase my earning power by at least triple in two years without requiring more than 12 hours/day of work.'

'Means to accomplish any personal, career or financial objectives and achieve more satisfaction to boot.'

Here we have the emphasis on personal development and personal objectives. Creativity is seen as a life skill that could make a difference to one's own life and not just the profitability of the corporation for which you work. This raises a most interesting point. Is creative thinking simply a corporate tool that is used for specific corporate needs? Or, should skill in creative thinking be acquired first as a 'personal skill' and then used on corporate matters? Is creative thinking a set of techniques that can be used like any other office techniques for a practical purpose or is it a change in a thinker himself or herself? I see it as both. I like to emphasise that the tools of lateral thinking can be used in a direct and deliberate manner. Nevertheless the actual use of the tools carries with it certain attitudes, and creative behaviour then follows. This is the reverse of the usual assumption which is that, if you become a creative person, you will be able to do creative thinking. My view is that if you learn to do creative (lateral) thinking you will indeed become a creative person.

'I would like creativity to unconstrain my normal thinking processes that currently tend to stress why things can't be done in a new way – I'd like to be an unconstrained thinker.'

Suggestion boxes

Many corporations have had suggestion boxes and suggestion schemes for a long time. Sometimes they work and sometimes they do not. When a suggested idea proves useful and saves money then it is normal to reward the person putting forward the idea. Typically that person may get 10 per cent of the first year's savings.

Quite often the suggestion scheme becomes a channel for complaint. The complaints may be disguised as suggestions ('why don't we have more coffee machines' is clearly a disguised complaint that there are not enough). The availability of the suggestion scheme and the availability of complaints make it natural that the two should go together. If we could all generate ideas as easily as we generate complaints then the world would indeed be a creative place. In many suggestion schemes there is an obligation on management to respond to the suggestion quickly. This very much suits the complainer who likes to know that the complaint has been received and may even be acted upon.

The fact that suggestion schemes are so often used for complaints may suggest that the normal channel for complaints is not functioning as well as it should. So one approach might be to install a better complaints system. There could even be a red-telephone hot-line system where the complainer picks up the phone and deposits a message on a recording machine.

Yet I see no problem in the suggestion system being used for complaints. Clearly there would be a problem if it was only used for complaints.

One of the major weaknesses of suggestion schemes is the idea that they are there for major ideas which will save the company money and reap reward for the originator of the idea. Most ordinary people never believe that they are going to have this sort of great idea, so the suggestion box is not for them.

We need to escape from this notion of the 'great and useful idea'. We need to escape from the notion that the suggestion box is only for one type of idea.

In letter boxes there is often a separate opening for first class and then other mail; or domestic and overseas. So let us imagine a suggestion box which has several openings.

Each opening is for a different type of idea. There could be entirely different, differently coloured boxes. There could be one box for different coloured slips of paper. There need be no differentiation, but the depositor of the idea states at the top which type of idea (from a given selection) he is depositing.

What might this range of ideas be?
Complaints: there could indeed be complaints, and these would be cleary acknowledged as complaints. Obviously there is a spectrum that runs between legitimate complaints and finicky grumbles. It is difficult to see how this discrimination could be made in advance.

Except perhaps by putting a price on the complaints or by asking that it be signed by more than one person (becoming a sort of mini-petition). There could even be a simple division between major complaints and minor complaints. The complainer would be forced to decide whether the complaint was major or minor. This might even discourage too many minor complaints.

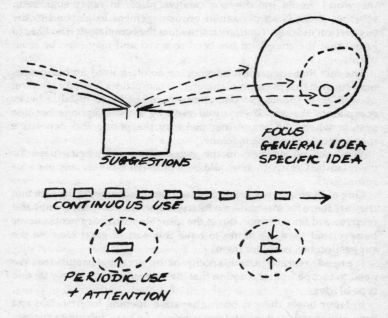

SUGGESTIONS

FOCUS
GENERAL IDEA
SPECIFIC IDEA

CONTINUOUS USE

PERIODIC USE
+ ATTENTION

Focus areas: I see this as a very important possibility. Most people are not very good at having ideas. Few people are capable of having really worthwhile ideas. Yet most people are able to spot problem areas (just as they are able to complain). So there should be a way in which a suggested 'focus area' could be deposited in the suggestion box. In effect this would mean: 'this is a problem area and we really need to do something about it'. It could also mean: 'this is an area in which a better way of doing things could really make a difference'. It could simply mean: 'this area would benefit from more attention than it is getting'. There is no attempt to give a solution or an improvement idea. The contribution is to call attention to areas – to list them as focus areas. I see this as a very important part of the thinking process. We need to know where to focus our thinking. Very often senior management cannot tell which the important focus areas might be. It has to be someone working at that level who identifies the area. Once the focus areas have been identified then they can be listed and put out as a 'focus list'. This in turn can be used in several ways. It can be used to encourage individuals to come up with suggestions in these specific areas. The list can also be fed to Quality Circles. The list can be fed to specially trained lateral thinking groups. It can even be circulated by means of Creative Task Sheets. This focusing could be a most useful contribution.

General ideas: these are vague ideas. There is not a specific suggestion that can be put to work. The general ideas can be concept directions or broad approaches.

'Could we perhaps keep these pieces somewhere else.'

'Somehow I would like some way of gluing these pieces together.'

'I have a vague idea that this operation is not really necessary.'

'I would like something to colour the pieces before we assemble them.'

'Some way in which different people can all work at their own rate.'

Too often we shy away from vague ideas because we know that vague ideas cannot be put into action. But in the creative process vague ideas have a very useful function. They get the mind moving in a certain direction. It may even be that the person putting in the idea is incapable of taking it further but someone else, receiving the idea, knows exactly how it might be done. Therefore the advantage of permitting vague ideas is that it allows people to put forward suggestions, even if they do not have the technical knowledge for the implementation of those ideas.

Specific ideas: these are the traditional ideas that can be put to use. A specific idea may require further development, but it is concrete enough to be developed and acted upon.

I believe that widening the scope of the suggestion scheme to cover all these types of input will prove motivating and workers will feel more involved. The suggestion box will be seen as a more integral part of the workplace instead of something reserved only for the very bright. It may be argued that many of these functions are now being carried out by Quality Circles. This may be so, but I believe the special personal character of the suggestion box gives it a unique value. We need to build on this value.

Timing and attention

If the suggestion box is there the whole time then it tends to fade into the background. In order to give it more attention, it might be better to have the box available only for short defined periods. This allows the box to be heavily promoted during these short bursts – in a way that is not possible if the box is there the whole time.

Another way of doing it is to have the box available the whole time but to devote certain periods of time to specific themes – just as hotels have Mexican weeks or Provencal weeks in their restaurants. So for one week the theme might be: cost saving ideas. Later on – after a suitable gap – the theme might be: time saving ideas. A further theme might be: ideas to make the workplace more attractive. There are any number of themes that can be used. Each theme would have its own publicity campaign. Indeed, for each theme the could be a campaign manager who is an employee. A certain budget would be provided for the theme and the campaign manager and his or her team would use this as he or she wishes.

Rewards

This is always the weakest part of any suggestion scheme. For the great ideas that ultimately save the corporation a lot of money, the rewards might be quite good. But few people feel that they are ever going to come up with this sort of idea. So they do not even try to think creatively about matters. Because they are not even trying, creative ideas do not emerge. Far better to have everyone motivated to think creatively. Useful ideas are then far more likely to emerge – some big ideas and some small ideas.

The reward also has to be immediate. It should not be a matter of waiting months for this first selection committee to vet the idea and then the second selection committee and then the implementation years later. We know well from psychology that, if behaviour is to be encouraged, then the reward must come quickly. Yet the reward need not be substantial. Very often creative people want no more reward than recognition and the knowledge that someone is actually considering their idea.

A simple scheme would be to call together for a drink – once a month or less often – all those who had bothered to put an idea into the suggestion box. It would not matter whether the idea was any good or not. Another way would be to publish in the house journal a list of all the names of those who had contributed ideas. This sort of simple recognition reward can make a big difference to motivation. Yet it costs very little and does not interfere with other reward systems.

As I have said so often, it is important that there be a reward for creative effort, not just for creative success. If the effort is there then the success will eventually follow.

I also believe that there should be thought given to enlarging the reward so that it does not only go to the originator of the idea. For example, part of the reward should go to the workmates of the idea originator. This is not just because these workmates may have contributed to the idea but because of the motivating effect.

In any working group the 'ideas person' is usually easily recognised by the people around. They know who to go to for suggestions or new ideas. They know who will listen to new ideas. They know who is always trying out new ideas. In a study in the General Electric laboratories the sociometric diagrams would all point to the same person as the 'ideas person' in the group. So if the working group were also going to benefit from the successful idea they would be motivated to encourage the 'ideas person' to work on ideas. Indeed they would push that person to come up with ideas.

In a similar way the people involved in implementing the idea should also share in the reward. After all theirs is also a crucial role. If the implementers knew they were going to share in the reward, they might make more effort to see that the idea worked and might be more inclined to try out new ideas. Without such encouragement the trying out of any new idea is a hassle and a risk.

It should never be felt that these extended reward ideas would mean that a lot of money would be wasted on suggestion schemes. The actual amount of money would be very small. But the effect on work motivation and the general creative attitude could be very large. Just as Quality Circles are there as motivators as much as they are there to make actual changes, so suggestion schemes should also be seen as motivators.

The thinking place

I was talking to someone who was about give a party to bring together a group of people who did not know each other. I asked whether she was going to give each guest a thumbnail sketch of the other guests so that they had some sort of starting basis. In the course of the conversation we talked about 'labels'.

Obviously there are labels which people give to other people, but there are also the labels which we give ourselves – or hope that other people give to us.

Suppose that at this party each person could pick a label for himself or herself, what might that label be? Should there be a free choice so that a guest could select any label, or should there be a very limited choice so that the guest was forced into a few defined categories.

With the open-choice system there might need to be a few 'for instances . . .' in order to indicate what was required. Otherwise some guests might write mini-essays whilst others might just give their social security number.

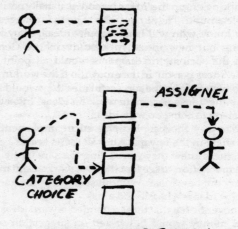

RANDOM DISTRIBUTION

Let us look at defined categories. Suppose there were only a very few defined categories, what might those categories be? This is something to which each reader could give some thought. If there were to be but four categories, what should these be? On that particular occasion the four categories that emerged were as follows:

'I am a talker': this might imply someone who was looking for an audience. It might imply someone who did not want to spend time competing with another talker. It might just imply someone who enjoyed talking. Would anyone actually choose this label?

'I am a listener': possibly this would be the most popular because it seems the most socially acceptable, implying as it does some humility. Listening is also a lazy occupation and there is no need to make an obvious effort (though good listening is actually very active). But once you put the label on, then you impose a certain restraint on yourself. What happens if two 'listeners' find themselves talking to each other?

'There is more to me than meets the eye' (or a simpler version of that sentiment). Most people probably believe this about themselves. They believe that they could be fascinating people if only those around took the trouble to dig deep enough. Yet there would be a certain presumption in wearing the label. A presumption that there were indeed treasures at the end of the search. Perhaps the hostess should allot the badges instead of leaving the guests to choose their own.

The obvious badges stopped at this point. There is a need for a fourth one. The one suggested was intended as an opposite for the last one. It would read:

'I just look good': the idea is that there is actually less than meets the eye. In a way it is a strange category because on the one hand it implies the humility of acknowledging that there are no treasures, yet at the same time it claims that the surface experience is good.

It is an interesting exercise to speculate how these badges might work: first if the guests choose their own; second if the hostess gives out the badges. A third possibility is if the hostess gives out the badges randomly. How will people try to live up to them?

Another exercise is to design your own set of badges.

30

Discipline, structure and control

The format of the CoRT Thinking Lessons that I designed for use in schools (and now used with several million schoolchildren every day) allows only 3-4 minutes thinking time on each practice item. The original reason for this is that I wanted the students to use the thinking tool that was the subject of that particular lesson, on as many practice items as possible. In this way the tool would stay constant and the practice items would change. This is what I call the 'Tools' method. Skill is built up in the use of the tool, which can then be used directly in other situations. This is contrasted with the discussion method in which there is a discussion about some subject, and it is hoped that the thinking used in that discussion will somehow carry over to new situations. Unfortunately, the transfer effect is small since the thinker's attention is not on the thinking processes but on the content of the discussion.

So in the CoRT Lessons, the thinking time on each item had to be short in order to fit several items into one lesson. At first the teachers hated it. They could not see how any useful thinking could be done in just a few minutes. They were used to lengthy discussions during which the teacher put questions and tried to elicit the 'correct answer' from the students. The students, themselves, disliked the short time because if the subject was interesting they found they had a great deal to say and they resented being cut off after the prescribed few minutes. It must be remembered that in all these lessons the students were working in groups. Whilst 3-4 minutes might be quite long for individual thinking it is certainly not long in a group where each person has to tell the others about his or her ideas.

The students adjusted very quickly. They found that they could think and say a great amount in just a few minutes. Once they knew they had a short time they just concentrated on putting forward the ideas they had thought up. They did not waste time in discussion or argument. Each idea was put forward in parallel with the other ideas. So the idea field was enriched and the 'perceptual map' was built up. There was no need to argue, since no point was being made. It was understood that some ideas were more realistic and more valuable than others, but that sort of assessment could come later. The first task was to think of the ideas and to put them forward. When one reads the transcripts from these sessions, it is astonishing how much thinking can take place in such a short time.

CONSTRAINED

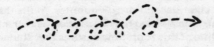

FREE

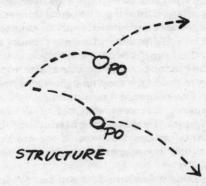

STRUCTURE

Adults find that they can do as well. As soon as they drop the discursive mode and switch into the 'output' mode then their thinking speeds up.

So what started out as a mere practical convenience has become a key part of the teaching method. If students have a short time, then they focus much more directly on what they are supposed to be doing. If they have a longer time they waffle around and have conversations, and not much actual thinking takes place. When I am teaching lateral thinking to adults I use the same method. Those adults who are used to the loose behaviour of brainstorming sessions find this strange and awkward. They want to mess around in the hope that an idea might strike them.

In contrast to brainstorming lateral thinking is very structured. There are specific tools that can be applied. Within each tool there are specific steps to be taken. Each step is taken deliberately. The tool is applied deliberately. For example when using the 'escape' technique, some aspect of the subject matter is spelled out. There is then an attempt to escape from this (drop it or change it). This creates the provocation. The thinker then uses the provocation for its movement value. In seeking to get movement from this provocation, the thinker can go through four formal ways of getting movement: extract a principle; focus on the difference; moment to moment; positive aspects. The next stage is to consolidate an idea. The final stage is to take the idea and find a better way of implementing it. All this is supposed to take place in 4 to 5 minutes. With the random word technique, the time allowed may be as short as two minutes.

The discipline of this short time ensures that students stick to what they are being asked to do. There simply is not time to drift. This ability to stick to what you are trying to do is itself an important part of the 'discipline' of lateral thinking. The lateral thinker should be able to direct his mind towards any subject, apply any tool and get an output. This should all be as deliberate and as under control as aiming a gun.

At first sight this horrifies people who believe that the very basis of creative thinking is to be unconstrained. The rigid structure and discipline of the tools and the short time allowed seem directly contrary to the notion of unconstrained 'free' thinking.

There is this notion that we are all bubbling with creative talent and that this is suppressed by the training of education, by our need to fit in and our fear of making mistakes. If we can but remove these inhibitions – so the theory goes – then we shall all be wonderfully creative.

I am not sure this theory works. If you succeed in removing most inhibitions, you will get freer behaviour and also a superficial sort of creativity inasmuch as the fear of being different will have gone. But I do not believe this is enough to produce good creative ideas. It may produce slightly crazy 'gee-whiz' ideas, but not those powerful ideas which seem totally logical in hindsight.

I quite agree that we need to be freed of our inhibitions. That we need to overcome the fear of making mistakes. That we need to break out of the patterns of experience. But instead of the loose and general notion of 'freedom' I prefer some tougher tools. The concept of PO and provocation not only allows us to escape from the usual tracks but allows us deliberately to create concepts that have never existed in our experience (and often never could exist). The concept of 'movement' as contrasted with 'judgement' gives us the means to treat ideas and provocations in a way that is entirely different from the usual way. These are the powerful tools that get us our freedom. Without tools, freedom is just a wish – there are times when we need powerful wire-cutters in order to cut through the wire and to escape. Attitudes alone are much too weak.

The well-known provocation 'Po cars should have square wheels' forces us to develop new concepts. The general notion that we do not have to be constrained by the usual round shape of the wheels is very much weaker.

Now if we have these tools they have to be used effectively. They have to be used in a deliberate and disciplined manner. That is why it is necessary to have structure and discipline. An escape from prison is usually a very disciplined and tightly timed procedure. It is not just a matter of messing around crying out 'freedom'.

I know that this all sounds very paradoxical and almost like painting by numbers. Yet, once a thinker becomes familiar with the techniques, then there is a tremendous sense of freedom. A thinker who has grasped the concept of provocation and the concept of movement knows that he or she can set up or receive any provocation whatever and work from that towards a useful idea. There are no longer any boundaries of reasonableness or experience when carrying out the thought experiments that are used in lateral thinking. At first it takes a great deal of courage to use PO properly. Eventually this courage is replaced by confidence.

Consider the reversal type provocation: 'Po the best salesman should be punished'. This is so directly contrary to normal experience and normal good sense that we feel uncomfortable even saying it. Yet the confident lateral thinker would immediately set about using this provocation for its movement value. Who would the salesman be punished by? Perhaps by his colleagues who were jealous of his success or jealous of the standards which he was setting. This leads to the notion of some group consideration. Perhaps the group should seek to restrain the super salesman. Perhaps they should seek to catch up with him. We might now develop an idea in which each salesman rewarded the leading salesman depending on the difference in performance between the leading salesman and the trailing salesman. There might now be a stronger motivation to catch up. An alternative idea might be that the leading salesman would only get his reward if the average performance had also increased. This might motivate that salesman to train and help his or her colleagues. The confident lateral thinker knows that in the end the ideas will start to make sense.

There is then the discipline of the focus area. There is a need to be precise about the focus of the thinking and the purpose of the thinking. Even the simple generation of alternatives becomes a powerful tool when there is a tight definition of the 'third point'. When we know exactly where we are going to look for alternatives and exactly the function of the alternatives, then we can generate new ideas. Messing around with only a vague notion of what we are trying to do has little generative power.

As usual we make the 'opposites' mistake. If rigidity makes us unimaginative then freedom must make us imaginative. If bad logic makes for bad thinking then good logic must make for good thinking. In neither case is this simple opposite true. If being rich makes someone miserable does being poor make that person happy?

I know many people who are by nature highly creative. They have also become very skilled at using the methods and attitudes of lateral thinking. Yet these people assure me that they still get the best results when they set out to use the lateral thinking techniques in a deliberate and disciplined manner. I find the same myself. The new ideas that really surprise me are the ones that come about in this way.

Free thinking?

Is there such a thing as free thinking?

There are many in the education world who believe that all thinking is very heavily dependent on the particular field or 'domain'. So there is history thinking and there is physics thinking and there is business thinking. Such people believe that we can never learn 'thinking skills' as such, but only the skilled use of the thinking idiom that has developed within a particular field.

It must be obvious to anyone who knows my work that I do not believe in this domain-specific thinking. I believe there are thinking skills that can be learned as such and then used in any domain. That is why I have been involved in the direct teaching of thinking in schools as part of the curriculum. This has now been taken up in many countries. Schoolchildren actually sit down to a lesson on 'thinking' as such.

It seems clear to me that thinking skills such as the use of provocation and movement in lateral thinking can be applied to any field, just as mathematics is also field free. There is not a different sort of addition if you are dealing with history. I believe that there are many more general skills than we suppose. In this area of the development of thinking skills I feel we have only just scratched the surface. There is a great deal more to be done.

So do I believe that thinking is free?

The answer is that I do not. I believe that thinking is restricted in a number of ways.

Circumstance and role

The particular role a person is playing, or the circumstance in which that person is to be found, can severely restrict thinking (or at least the thinking that can be made visible). There are things a politician simply cannot say, no matter how true they are. For example, Sir Keith Joseph, a much respected politician, is believed to have irretrievably damaged his career when he made a speech in which he seemed to imply that the wrong people were breeding. He seemed to say that the better educated professional and more highly educated people were having fewer and fewer children (possibly because of the high cost of education or a preference for material goods) whereas the less able people continued to have large families. The statistics did indeed show that the AB birthrate was considerably lower than the DE birthrate. There was immediate outrage, and this was seen as blatant elitism. For a politician, truth is never a good enough excuse. A politician has always to be looking at the press, at current value-moods, at potential voters and especially at those encapsulated tags which can haunt a politician for ever more. For example, Mrs. Thatcher could never escape from the 'milk snatcher' tag which she acquired when, as Minister of Education, she stopped free milk for schools. That was the origin of the harsh uncaring image.

In the USA, a politician has to be extremely careful as to what he or she says with regard to the Middle East or Ireland. There are powerful sectors of Jewish and Irish voters. This is not just a matter of numbers but also of power – the power of organisation, the power of campaign contributions, the power of media control.

None of this is a fault of politicians, or indeed any weakness on the part of politicians. They are put into a game, and they must play that game as the rules are written. There are serious limits to democracy and this is one of them. On the whole, we believe that the virtues outweigh the limitations. Nor can we devise a better system since clearly tyranny is far worse.

So politicians are locked in by their political sensitivities and vulnerabilities.

They are also locked in by time scales. In the USA, there is about one and a half years of true Presidential office. It take one year to recover from the election and to sort things out. One and a half years before the next election the campaigning starts again. This means attention to campain matters. It means postponing or avoiding issues that might be an election liability. It means a certain amount of pork-barrel politics to give aid to those states or population segments where more support is needed. We live in a real world and these are the realities. If it means postponing a super power summit until after the mid-term elections, then that postponement is necessary even though there is an urgency for such a meeting (from a disarmament point of view).

It was for exactly these reasons that I have set up the SITO organisation. The name SITO stands for Supranational Independent Thinking Organisation. The idea is that this organisation would be able to carry out neutral, objective and creative thinking, free from the political constraints that affect political thinking at both national and international level. Sometimes SITO would come up with original ideas and additional options that had not so far been considered. SITO would be in a better position to do this because there would be a deliberate use of lateral thinking and other thinking skills, rather than the swapping of argument and experience. But, even if SITO never came up with an original idea, there would still be a need for such an organisation. SITO could serve as a channel to put forward ideas which were already known but which could not be put forward because of the political risks for any politician who put forward the idea.

Even if an idea was known and could be put forward, there might be a greater value in channelling the idea through SITO. For example any US proposal would be seen by the USSR as a strategic or propaganda move (and vice versa). So it would be rejected. In any case acceptance of the idea would be seen as weakness. But if the same idea were to be put forward by SITO then it could be judged on the actual merits of the idea.

So at all three levels there is an urgent need for something like SITO because politicians are simply not free to have the ideas that may be needed for the future survival of the world.

Repertoire of idioms

No thinker can ever go beyond his or her existing repertoire of idioms and possibilities.

Consider those feats in which thousands of dominoes are placed in such a position that, when the first domino falls over then each domino in turn knocks over the next one and so on until the whole lot have fallen over. This seems simple enough, but the idiom is an interesting one. It applies directly to the way the nerves in the human body carry messages. This is quite different from the way a water pipe or an electric cable carries energy. In a water pipe pressure at one end forces water through the pipe. At the other end there is an output of flow or even just pressure (as in an hydraulic system). With electricity the potential difference (voltage) across the system determines the energy transfer. Nothing of the sort happens with nerves. Each little section has its own energy source. Activity in the preceding section triggers release of that energy so that section becomes active. This in turn triggers the energy release of the next section and so on. This is exactly what happens with the dominoes. Each domino delivers energy in falling. This in turn upsets the balance (triggers activity) of the next domino which has its own energy of falling. It is a triggering or de-stabilising effect that is passed along rather than actual energy.

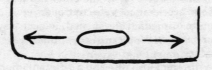

CONSTRAINED

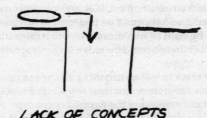

LACK OF CONCEPTS

It is precisely this difference in idiom that has made it very difficult for computer people to understand the human brain and to design thinking computers. At long last such people are beginning to look at the behaviour of self-organising systems. I had written up this behaviour as long ago as 1969 in my book *The Mechanism of Mind* (published by Penguin books as a Pelican).

If a person's background is in logic, linguistics, mathematics, computers or information science then it would be very difficult for that person to have developed the concepts of lateral thinking. This is because the notion of information in such systems is totally different. We generally hold that communication or a transfer of information has taken place if the receiving system records what the transmitting system has sent out or intended. If you want to write your name on a piece of paper you would be very frustrated if the paper consistently showed a different name as the result of your efforts.

Yet in the biological world 'information' has a different meaning. With the exception of the gene system there is little transfer of information as such. Instead there is triggering. One system has an 'effect' on another. The result of that effect depends on a lot of things. On the energy state of the affected system, on its remote history, on its immediate past history and on all the other influences acting at the moment (blockers, accelerators, gate controllers etc.). So the received effect may be quite unpredictable. Indeed, in such a system you may try to write your name on the piece of paper but always what you have written reads 'Mary'.

In short it is a different universe and a different idiom. It is not only my background in medicine and biological systems that enabled me to develop the concepts of lateral thinking but also my lack of background in computers and logic. You cannot easily escape from your basic idioms but always try to interpret new phenomena in terms of these established idioms.

For example the whole of our logic system with language, categories, is/is not, the law of contradiction etc. is actually based on one particular information idiom. It so happens that this system has been remarkably successful in dealing with technical matters, but it is less than successful in dealing with human matters where we have unstable systems and complex feed-back loops.

The point that I want to make with this particular example is that the idioms of our fields severely restrict our thinking. Sometimes it is that we do not have in our repertoire the necessary concept. At other times the concepts that are already firmly established make it impossible for us to use different concepts.

Is this just a way of saying that we cannot think beyond our experience? In part it is that but it is more than that. Few of us have been to the moon, and yet we can accept on second-hand evidence what the moon surface is like. So we can supplement our limited experience by listening to others and accepting what is said – even if we may be doubtful about some of it. But if we do not have in our repertoire certain organising idioms then we cannot understand, and can never accept experience that depends on such idioms. If you do not know that the puzzle 12/6, 8/4, 4/7 is set in Italy, then you can never solve the linkage between each of the figures in the pair. If you are in the wrong universe you will simply never understand what can only be understood in a different universe.

So the conclusion is that we may be free to think, but are by no means free in our thinking.

The thinking place

I often get very frustrated by the limitations of language. It is clear that different languages handle things differently. For example, one language may not make a distinction and another language does. Spanish has two useful ways of saying 'is'. There is a permanent way which could refer to your name, nationality, character and other things which will always be with you. This is the identity type of 'is'. Then there is a completely different word for the sort of 'is' that just

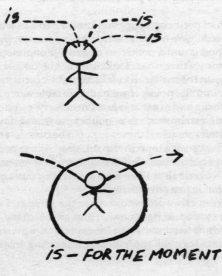

IS – FOR THE MOMENT

describes a temporary positioning in space or time. 'He is in the restaurant' is clearly very temporary. 'He is a big man' is much more permanent. English makes no distinction. The nearest equivalent in English is the pidgin expression (Papua New Guinea) or 'bilong' which can imply belonging to a particular scene. But that is not a close equivalent.

The French term 'informatique' has a neatness which is not obtained by the English expression 'information technology' nor does it mean quite the same thing.

In English we badly need a new word to cover the expression 'the way we look at things'. 'Perception' is the nearest word, but it has overtones of visual perception and psychological overtones.

Sometimes it is difficult to think about things unless there is a particular word which encapsulates a situation.

We badly need a simple term to cover the concept of 'this thing is working well according to its nature'. The behaviour may not be what we want, but we cannot blame the thing for working according to its nature. Nor should we hold out much hope of change. We have phrases like 'children will be children' or 'true to type'. But these are not strong enough. In other words, we need to distinguish whether behaviour is derived directly from the nature of the system or is but one option and therefore alterable. For example, it is hard to blame a politician for behaving as a politician or a banker for behaving as a banker.

The mention of politicians suggests another area in which we badly need a new word. We need a word for 'necessary public noises'. Something happens and a politician makes a pronouncement. Everyone listening knows that what is said may not be closely related to the actual thinking on the matter. It is said for public consumption. It is in fact a necessary public noise. If we had a suitable name for this, then we could just shrug and say that is just a necessary-public-noise. Once this had become established, then politicians would have to be more careful about their remarks if these are not to be dismissed in this way.

We do have just such a term in 'advertising'. We expect advertising to make outrageous claims. But we still read advertising and even respond to it. Nevertheless if we read something outrageous, we just dismiss it as 'that is just advertising'.

Another convenient word would cover the phrase: 'I would like to establish where we are at right now'. This can, of course, be conveyed with such words as 'summarise' or 're-cap' but the meaning I have in mind is broader. It could apply before a meeting instead of in the course of the meeting: 'Where are we at' or 'Where are we both coming from?'

There may be other situations which seem to you to require encapsulation in a more specific way.

Index

This index includes the main headings for the articles in each of the thirty letters, plus the Introduction and the initial article 'A new concept for Democracy'. It does not number 'The thinking place', which is the heading repeated at the end of each letter.

FOR THE BEST IN PAPERBACKS, LOOK FOR THE 🐧

In every corner of the world, on every subject under the sun, Penguin represents quality and variety – the very best in publishing today.

For complete information about books available from Penguin – including Pelicans, Puffins, Peregrines and Penguin Classics – and how to order them, write to us at the appropriate address below. Please note that for copyright reasons the selection of books varies from country to country.

In the United Kingdom: For a complete list of books available from Penguin in the U.K., please write to *Dept E.P., Penguin Books Ltd, Harmondsworth, Middlesex, UB7 0DA*

In the United States: For a complete list of books available from Penguin in the U.S., please write to *Dept BA, Penguin, 299 Murray Hill Parkway, East Rutherford, New Jersey 07073*

In Canada: For a complete list of books available from Penguin in Canada, please write to *Penguin Books Canada Ltd, 2801 John Street, Markham, Ontario L3R 1B4*

In Australia: For a complete list of books available from Penguin in Australia, please write to the *Marketing Department, Penguin Books Australia Ltd, P.O. Box 257, Ringwood, Victoria 3134*

In New Zealand: For a complete list of books available from Penguin in New Zealand, please write to the *Marketing Department, Penguin Books (NZ) Ltd, Private Bag, Takapuna, Auckland 9*

In India: For a complete list of books available from Penguin, please write to *Penguin Overseas Ltd, 706 Eros Apartments, 56 Nehru Place, New Delhi, 110019*

In Holland: For a complete list of books available from Penguin in Holland, please write to *Penguin Books Nederland B.V., Postbus 195, NL–1380AD Weesp, Netherlands*

In Germany: For a complete list of books available from Penguin, please write to *Penguin Books Ltd, Friedrichstrasse 10 – 12, D–6000 Frankfurt Main 1, Federal Republic of Germany*

In Spain: For a complete list of books available from Penguin in Spain, please write to *Longman Penguin España, Calle San Nicolas 15, E–28013 Madrid, Spain*

FOR THE BEST IN PAPERBACKS, LOOK FOR THE 🐧

A CHOICE OF PENGUINS AND PELICANS

Adieux Simone de Beauvoir

This 'farewell to Sartre' by his life-long companion is a 'true labour of love' (the *Listener*) and 'an extraordinary achievement' (*New Statesman*).

British Society 1914–45 John Stevenson

A major contribution to the Pelican Social History of Britain, which 'will undoubtedly be the standard work for students of modern Britain for many years to come' – *The Times Educational Supplement*

The Pelican History of Greek Literature Peter Levi

A remarkable survey covering all the major writers from Homer to Plutarch, with brilliant translations by the author, one of the leading poets of today.

Art and Literature Sigmund Freud

Volume 14 of the Pelican Freud Library contains Freud's major essays on Leonardo, Michelangelo and Dostoevsky, plus shorter pieces on Shakespeare, the nature of creativity and much more.

A History of the Crusades Sir Steven Runciman

This three-volume history of the events which transferred world power to Western Europe – and founded Modern History – has been universally acclaimed as a masterpiece.

A Night to Remember Walter Lord

The classic account of the sinking of the *Titanic*. 'A stunning book, incomparably the best on its subject and one of the most exciting books of this or any year' – *The New York Times*

A CHOICE OF PENGUINS AND PELICANS

The Informed Heart   Bruno Bettelheim

Bettelheim draws on his experience in concentration camps to illuminate the dangers inherent in all mass societies in this profound and moving masterpiece.

God and the New Physics   Paul Davies

Can science, now come of age, offer a surer path to God than religion? This 'very interesting' (*New Scientist*) book suggests it can.

Modernism   Malcolm Bradbury and James McFarlane (eds.)

A brilliant collection of essays dealing with all aspects of literature and culture for the period 1890–1930 – from Apollinaire and Brecht to Yeats and Zola.

Rise to Globalism   Stephen E. Ambrose

A clear, up-to-date and well-researched history of American foreign policy since 1938, Volume 8 of the Pelican History of the United States.

The Waning of the Middle Ages   Johan Huizinga

A magnificent study of life, thought and art in 14th and 15th century France and the Netherlands, long established as a classic.

The Penguin Dictionary of Psychology   Arthur S. Reber

Over 17,000 terms from psychology, psychiatry and related fields are given clear, concise and modern definitions.

The Literature of the United States   Marcus Cunliffe

The fourth edition of a masterly one-volume survey, described by D. W. Brogan in the *Guardian* as 'a very good book indeed'.

The Sceptical Feminist   Janet Radcliffe Richards

A rigorously argued but sympathetic consideration of feminist claims. 'A triumph' – *Sunday Times*

The Enlightenment   Norman Hampson

A classic survey of the age of Diderot and Voltaire, Goethe and Hume, which forms part of the Pelican History of European Thought.

Defoe to the Victorians   David Skilton

'Learned and stimulating' (*The Times Educational Supplement*). A fascinating survey of two centuries of the English novel.

Reformation to Industrial Revolution   Christopher Hill

This 'formidable little book' (Peter Laslett in the *Guardian*) by one of our leading historians is Volume 2 of the Pelican Economic History of Britain.

The New Pelican Guide to English Literature   Boris Ford (ed.)
Volume 8: The Present

This book brings a major series up to date with important essays on Ted Hughes and Nadine Gordimer, Philip Larkin and V. S. Naipaul, and all the other leading writers of today.

A CHOICE OF PENGUINS

An African Winter   Preston King   With an Introduction by Richard Leakey

This powerful and impassioned book offers a unique assessment of the interlocking factors which result in the famines of Africa and argues that there *are* solutions and we *can* learn from the mistakes of the past.

Jean Rhys: Letters 1931–66
Edited by Francis Wyndham and Diana Melly

'Eloquent and invaluable . . . her life emerges, and with it a portrait of an unexpectedly indomitable figure' – Marina Warner in the *Sunday Times*

Among the Russians   Colin Thubron

One man's solitary journey by car across Russia provides an enthralling and revealing account of the habits and idiosyncrasies of a fascinating people. 'He sees things with the freshness of an innocent and the erudition of a scholar' – *Daily Telegraph*

The Amateur Naturalist   Gerald Durrell with Lee Durrell

'Delight . . . on every page . . . packed with authoritative writing, learning without pomposity . . . it represents a real bargain' – *The Times Educational Supplement*. 'What treats are in store for the average British household' – *Books and Bookmen*

The Democratic Economy   Geoff Hodgson

Today, the political arena is divided as seldom before. In this exciting and original study, Geoff Hodgson carefully examines the claims of the rival doctrines and exposes some crucial flaws.

They Went to Portugal   Rose Macaulay

An exotic and entertaining account of travellers to Portugal from the pirate-crusaders, through poets, aesthetes and ambassadors, to the new wave of romantic travellers. A wonderful mixture of literature, history and adventure, by one of our most stylish and seductive writers.

A CHOICE OF PENGUINS

A Fortunate Grandchild 'Miss Read'

Grandma Read in Lewisham and Grandma Shafe in Walton on the Naze were totally different in appearance and outlook, but united in their affection for their grand-daughter – who grew up to become the much-loved and popular novelist.

The Ultimate Trivia Quiz Game Book Maureen and Alan Hiron

If you are immersed in trivia, addicted to quiz games, endlessly nosey, then this is the book for you: over 10,000 pieces of utterly dispensable information!

The Diary of Virginia Woolf
Five volumes, edited by Quentin Bell and Anne Olivier Bell

'As an account of the intellectual and cultural life of our century, Virginia Woolf's diaries are invaluable; as the record of one bruised and unquiet mind, they are unique'– Peter Ackroyd in the *Sunday Times*

Voices of the Old Sea Norman Lewis

'I will wager that *Voices of the Old Sea* will be a classic in the literature about Spain' – *Mail on Sunday*. 'Limpidly and lovingly Norman Lewis has caught the helpless, unwitting, often foolish, but always hopeful village in its dying summers, and saved the tragedy with sublime comedy' – *Observer*

The First World War A J P Taylor

In this superb illustrated history, A. J. P. Taylor 'manages to say almost everything that is important for an understanding and, indeed, intellectual digestion of that vast event . . . A special text . . . a remarkable collection of photographs' – *Observer*

Ninety-Two Days Evelyn Waugh

With characteristic honesty, Evelyn Waugh here debunks the romantic notions attached to rough travelling: his journey in Guiana and Brazil is difficult, dangerous and extremely uncomfortable, and his account of it is witty and unquestionably compelling.

Edward de Bono

Opportunities
A Handbook of Business Opportunity Search

'An opportunity is as real an ingredient in business as raw material, labour or finance – but it only exists when you can see it'

Everybody assumes that he or she is opportunity-conscious – but is frequently only conscious of the *need* to be opportunity-conscious. For often what looks like an opportunity isn't one after all.

Opportunities is a handbook which offers a total, systematic approach to opportunity-seeking at both corporate and executive levels. It is Edward de Bono's most significant contribution to business since he developed lateral thinking – and it should have just as much impact. Remember:

'Just before it comes into existence every business is an opportunity that someone has seen'

The Happiness Purpose

The proposed religion is based on the belief that the legitimate purpose of life is happiness and the best foundation for happiness is self-importance.

The happiness purpose is to be achieved through the use of thinking and humour and dignity. The ideal of love is to be replaced by the more reliable practice of respect.

The new religion may be used as a framework or as a philosophy. It may be used as a way of living or a way of looking at things. The new religion may be used on its own or in conjunction with any other religion.

Lucid, entertaining and provocative as always, Edward de Bono presents his blueprint for the disciplined pursuit of happiness which, in his opinion, is the legitimate purpose of life.

and

Six Thinking Hats

Edward de Bono

Future Positive

Change by drift, change by protest, change by compromise; these are the moods of the sad seventies.

Edward de Bono writes here of the energetic eighties, of the positive future we can have if we want it. Societies, like organisms, develop certain characteristics that make further evolution impossible. At that point hallowed institutions and sacred ways of thinking have to be replaced with more positive ways. Our ancient negativity has to go.

Throughout the book Edward de Bono is not afraid to be provocative, for as he says, 'provocation is as important for creativity as analysis is for truth.' Some ideas he suggests are meant to be taken seriously but others are meant only as provocations. He has no time for the CYA attitude – which suggests that you are unable to do anything positive because you forever hold your hands in such a position as to minimize the effect of a kick in the pants.

Lateral Thinking

'Thinking,' says Edward de Bono, 'is a skill, and like a skill it can be developed and improved if one knows how.' This book is a textbook of creativity. It shows how the habit of lateral thinking can be encouraged, how new ideas can be generated. The author has worked out special techniques for doing this, in groups or alone, and the result is a triumph of entertaining education.

Practical Thinking
4 ways to be right; 5 ways to be wrong; 5 ways to understand

How is it that in an argument both sides are always right? How is it that no one ever makes a mistake on purpose but that mistakes get made? These are some of the questions that Edward de Bono answers in this book. His theme is everyday thinking, how the mind actually works – not how philosophers think it should work.

and

Teaching Thinking

Edward de Bono

Wordpower

Could you make an *educated guess* at the *downside-risk* of a *marketing strategy*? Are you in the right *ball-game*, and faced with a crisis could you find an *ad hoc* solution?

These are just a few of the 265 specialized words – or 'thinking chunks' – that Dr de Bono defines here in terms of their usage to help the reader use them as tools of expression. So the next time an economic adviser talks about cash-cows, or the local councillor starts a campaign about ecology, you know what to do. Reach for *Wordpower* and add a 'thinking chunk' to your vocabulary.

The Mechanism of Mind

Patterns made by drops of water on different surfaces or by electric bulbs in advertising displays help Dr de Bono, in this fascinating and provocative book, to build up a picture of a 'special memory-surface', which might resemble the brain in its selection, processing and rejection of information. With simple analogies he illustrates the mind's tendency to create and consolidate rigid patterns, to build myths, to polarize and divide, and then relates these mechanisms to the various modes of thinking – natural, logical, mathematical and lateral.

Po: Beyond Yes and No

NO is the basic tool of the logic system.
YES is the basic tool of the belief system.
PO is the basic tool of the creative system.

Po: Beyond Yes and No is the basic primer of a revolutionary new way of thinking. Edward de Bono maintains that most of us are trapped within the rigid confines of traditional ways of thinking, limited by concepts which have developed simply for the purpose of arriving at the 'right' answer. While humanity has advanced technologically, in the realm of ideas and thought process we are, he says, still using the restricted and restricting concepts that have always been used.

Edward de Bono

The Use of Lateral Thinking

This is Edward de Bono's original portrayal of a mental process which he in no way claims to have invented. In it he deliberately uses the lateral approach (with intriguing visual examples in one chapter) to sketch in the nature of lateral thinking.

There emerges the concept of an imaginative, free-wheeling, opportunist (but low-probability) mode of thought in which fresh ideas, which may well be simple, sound and effective, are often thrown up. Lateral thinking is thus contrasted with the orthodox, logical, unimaginative (but high-probability) process of vertical thinking, from which it differs as a bus differs from a tram. In a changing world both modes are required.

The Five-Day Course in Thinking

Edward de Bono, originator of 'Lateral Thinking', believes that thinking is an enjoyable skill.

This book offers a series of simple but intriguing problems in thinking that require no special knowledge and no mathematics. The problems are designed to let the reader find out about his own personal style of thinking, its weaknesses and strengths, and the methods, latent in himself, that he never uses. Being right is not always important – an error can lead to the right decision.

A copy of the famous L game is inserted in each book for use in the section on strategy. This classic game was designed by de Bono as a basically simple game that can be played with a high degree of skill – and in the process can promote stratetic thinking.

Also published in Penguins:

Children Solve Problems
Lateral Thinking for Management